JORDAN
HIGHLIGHTS
PETRA • WADI RUM • DEAD SEA • AQABA

PAUL DOYLE

www.brad

Bradt Gui
The Globe Pequot Press Inc, USA

Bradt GUIDES
TRAVEL TAKEN SERIOUSLY

This is
Jordan

Jordan, officially the Hashemite Kingdom of Jordan, is a remarkable destination enduringly celebrated for the city of Petra. On her travels around the Middle East in the early 20th century, British explorer Gertrude Bell described Petra as "like a fairy tale city, all pink and wonderful". Yet there is so much more to see and experience than just this awe-inspiring ancient Nabataean city. There are the architectural and cultural footprints left by the Romans, Crusaders, Mamluks and Ottomans, not to mention some of the most important biblical sites of early Christianity.

Beyond these historical treasures, the cosmopolitan capital of Amman is a friendly, liberal and hybrid city of old and new, where centuries-old ruins sit comfortably with modern cafés, hotels, a thriving arts and cultural scene and a slew of excellent museums. The capital also makes an excellent base for day trips to explore the Roman city of Jerash and the Dead Sea, the lowest point on earth.

This compact country is also a land of incredible natural beauty. The clear waters of the Red Sea, teeming with colourful and exquisite marine life, offers some of the world's best diving at the seaside town of Aqaba. Equally impressive is the undulating, dramatic, red-hued desert wilderness of Wadi Rum, one of the Middle East's most spectacular desert landscapes, which has always attracted hikers, trekkers and climbers. Jordan's flagship Dana Biosphere Reserve, meanwhile, is packed with diverse flora and fauna throughout its breathtakingly varied environment.

Jordan is also home to Bedouin communities, many of whom continue to eke out a traditional lifestyle in the desert and whose legendary hospitality is found throughout Jordanian society. Located in a volatile region, Jordan stands almost alone as a beacon of peace and stability, where visitors are welcomed with open arms, and where tradition and modernity coalesce in a country which has so much more to offer than just Petra.

Paul Doyle

Best of
Jordan

❶ Amman

Jordan's capital is a vibrantly go-getting and surprisingly modern addition to the country's ancient treasures. Take in the impressive exhibits at the Jordan Museum, look out over the cityscape from Jebel al-Qala'at, then café-hop down Rainbow Street to soak up Amman's youthful buzz. Page 24.

❷ Jerash

Sit atop the highest tier of Jerash's south theatre and allow the ancient world to come alive. This is Jordan's best-preserved classical-era ruin, with extensive Greco-Roman temples and Byzantine churches to explore, all linked by the long column-lined cardo maximus where Roman life played out. Page 46.

❸ Dead Sea

Act up for the camera in the sea where you can't sink. The Dead Sea's unique buoyancy makes big kids out of everyone who takes a dip. For a more luxurious approach, make a beeline for the many spas where the Dead Sea's mineral-enriched mud is put to good use. Page 64.

❹ King's Highway

This winding road, along the spine of the Great Rift Valley, is Jordan's best road trip. The route is scattered with ruins, Byzantine churches and Crusader castles to explore, while the views – tumbling down to the Dead Sea – are spectacular. Page 78.

❺ Madaba

Kick back in the mosaic city, home of St George's Church and the famed Madaba map. The distinctly relaxed vibe and streets scattered with remnants of Byzantine might make Madaba a great base for day trips to Mount Nebo and down to the Dead Sea. Page 79.

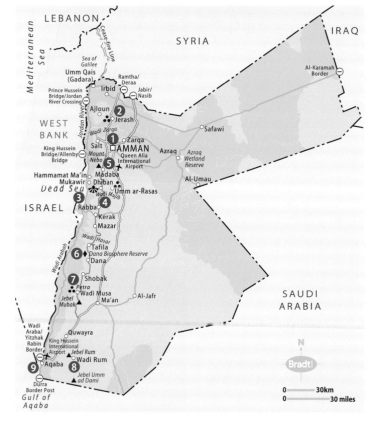

❻ Dana Biosphere Reserve

Pull on your walking boots and hit the trails of Dana Biosphere Reserve, where the scenery swoops from forest to the barren sands of the Wadi Araba on a day hike. Afterwards, reward yourself for all the exertion by chilling out at one of the reserve's ecolodges. Page 98.

❼ Petra

Walk through the Siq at dawn to catch shards of sunlight lighting up the rock. Huff your way up to the monastery to be dwarfed by its soaring façade and go one better than Indiana Jones by hiking Jebel al-Khubtha to view the treasury from above. Page 106.

❽ Wadi Rum

This epic landscape of red sands framed by massive sandstone cliffs enchants all who visit. Spend a night under the stars here to witness the sunrise shimmer across the rock outcrops and you'll understand why T E Lawrence fell under Wadi Rum's spell. Page 132.

❾ Aqaba

Wash off the desert sand and relax on the beach or sit by the pool in Jordan's year-round and only coastal resort town. Go scuba diving or snorkelling in the Red Sea and be amazed by the spectacular coral reef gardens and eclectic technicolour marine life. Page 144.

Route planner

This compact little country is packed with sights. The world-famous monuments of **Petra** and **Jerash** are obviously not to be missed, but there are plenty of other ruins and historical monuments scattered around the nation that are just as impressive in their own right.

However, Jordan's historical treasures are just the tip of the iceberg. It's the stunning landscapes here that will really take your breath away. This nation's natural beauty is incredibly diverse, ranging from the grand desert vistas of **Wadi Rum** and the vast Rift Valley cliffs that tumble down to the **Dead Sea**, to the beautiful coral reefs of the Red Sea.

For most people, the real beauty of Jordan is that you can combine all these things in one visit. The nation's small size means that even the shortest trip allows for all the major highlights of the country to be covered, and those with more time up their sleeve can fully explore the variety that Jordan offers.

> **Tip...**
> To save money on your Jordan trip, buy a **Jordan Pass** (www.jordanpass.jo) before travelling. The pass allows entry into over 40 tourist sites, including Petra and Jerash, plus waives the tourist entry visa fee. See page 172 for further details.

Suggested one-week itinerary

For most people a trip to Jordan begins in **Amman** (two days). However, if you're not a city person, nearby **Madaba** is a more laid-back alternative. Head out on a day trip to **Jerash** the next day, comfortably visited from either town.

Spend the next day on the **King's Highway**. This mountainous road boasts a whole array of sights. **Mount Nebo** and **Kerak** are two of the many highlights, and you can take a precipitous route down to the **Dead Sea** for a float before ending in **Petra** (two days).

After a full day exploring this colossal remnant of the Nabataean kingdom head to **Wadi Rum** (one day) and spend the night under a million stars in a Bedouin camp amid the sands. It's the perfect ending before driving back to **Amman** (one day) for your flight home.

BACKGROUND

With a territory extending over some 89,342 sq km, the Hashemite Kingdom of Jordan is around three-quarters the size of the US state of Pennsylvania, slightly smaller than the US state of Indiana and over a third the size of the UK. Situated at latitude 31° 00′ N and longitude 36° 00′ E, Jordan borders Syria in the north, Iraq in the northeast and Saudi Arabia to the east and south, and shares the longest land border of any Arab nation with Israel and the West Bank (307km and 148km respectively) in the west. Jordan's 26 km (16 mile) slither of coastline in the southwest of the country at the Gulf of Aqaba (Red Sea) prevents the country from being totally landlocked and contains the nation's only port, Aqaba.

A compact country displaying great topographical variety, Jordan's landmass has three distinct geographical regions. The dominant feature of the country's western flank is the **Jordan Rift Valley**, which extends the length of the country. The valley is part of the more extensive Great Rift Valley that extends from Syria all the way down to Mozambique in east Africa; the result of geological forces dating from pre-history that saw the separation of the Arabian and African tectonic plates which gave birth to the Red Sea. Breathtakingly beautiful and diverse in equal measure, the northern valley region is marked by its fertility, with numerous streams irrigating the landscape, while further south are the salty waters of the landlocked Dead Sea (the world's second saltiest body of water after Lake Assal in the east African state of Djibouti) fed by the Jordan River and, at -431 m below sea level, the lowest natural point on the earth's surface. South of the Dead Sea the valley continues as the arid Wadi Araba gorge, terminating at the coastline of the Gulf of Aqaba, the location for Jordan's must-see colourful marine life and coral reef ecosystem.

East of the Jordan Rift Valley and running parallel to it are the Jordanian highlands, the **Mountain Heights Plateau**, a rugged mountainous region varying from c600-1,500 m (2000-5000 ft) in altitude. It stretches from Umm Qais in the far north to Ras al-Naqab in the south, with a sharp decrease in elevation towards Aqaba and the Red Sea. Thanks to its generous rainfall, this fertile agricultural area has throughout history been the centre of Jordan's 11,174,024 population, and areas of interest to visitors include the capital Amman, Jordan's second city of Irbid, Kerak, Jerash, Madaba, Petra and Zarqa.

Covering over three-quarters of Jordan's surface area is the eastern and southern **desert** or **Badia** region, an extension of the deserts in Syria and the Arabian Peninsula. Given the aridity and harsh desert conditions, with only a smattering of oases, this region is home to a meagre 5% or so of Jordan's population. Its northern section is composed of volcanic basalt while further south it gives way to sandstone and granite as the predominate rock forms. This region is the location for one of the Middle East's most spectacular desert landscapes at Wadi Rum, much feted in the writings of T E Lawrence (Lawrence of Arabia) and where the Bedouin continue to live out their traditional way of life. South of Wadi Rum, close to the Saudi Arabian border, is Jebel Umm ad Dami, Jordan's highest peak at 1,854 m (6,082 ft), offering superlative views over Saudi Arabia and the Red Sea.

When
to go

… and when not to

Climate

Roughly speaking, the best times to visit Jordan are during the spring (March-May) or autumn (September-November), when the climate is at its most pleasant. Even during these seasons, daytime temperatures at Petra and Jerash can reach over 30°C in the sun, although it does at least cool off from late afternoon through to early/mid-morning.

During the summer (June-August) it is scorching hot throughout most of the country, with temperatures often heading over the 40°C mark. Along the Red Sea coast, down at the Dead Sea and through the Jordan Valley the humidity at this time can be unbearable.

Winter (December-February) can be quite severe with the majority of the region's rain falling during this period and temperatures dropping below 0°C at night. In Petra, snow is not uncommon during December and January. Winter daytime temperatures in Wadi Rum average 15-20°C, ideal for walking and climbing, though it gets bitterly cold at night.

Festivals

During **Ramadan** (the Muslim month of fasting), all of Jordan's tourist sites and facilities geared towards tourists still open as normal and travelling during this time is generally not a problem. However, many smaller restaurants (particularly the budget ones) will close during daylight hours, and some may be closed for the entire month. Non-Muslims are not expected to join the fasting but you should refrain from eating, drinking and smoking on the street out of respect.

Jordan's top annual event is the **Jerash Festival of Culture and Arts** (www.jerashfestival.jo). This fortnight of cultural celebration, held in July and August, hosts theatre, dance and music performances from local and international artists both within the Greco-Roman ruins of Jerash and at venues in Amman (see pages 42 and 61). See also Public holidays, page 175.

What to do

from excavating ruins to rock climbing

Archaeology

There is a wealth of archaeological sites in Jordan. Some of them have been undergoing excavation for decades and still have far more work left to be done on them. Others have yet to be explored. Each season, armies of archaeologists descend on new and existing sites to carry out excavations. Some of the digs have taken to recruiting amateur help by organizing 'working holidays' where you actually pay to join the dig.

Much of the work is very tedious and even if you're not particularly skilled, it is often possible to get involved. Note, however, that it is not possible to simply turn up at a dig and join in; official permits and authorizations have to be applied for well in advance and invariably take a long time to process. If you're interested in joining a dig, you need to plan ahead. The following list of contacts is a good starting point:

American Center of Research (ACOR) (ACOR) (www.acorjordan.org). As well as being a good resource for all things archaeological in Jordan, it also has a list of links to archaeological dig websites across the country.

Archaeological Institute of America (AIA) (www.archaeological.org). Excellent source of information on everything archaeological and lists fieldwork opportunities.

Biblical Archaeology Society (www.biblicalarchaeology.org). Advertises a host of volunteer opportunities on digs and runs archaeological-based tours.

University of Jordan (www.ju.edu.jo). A good starting point for information regarding archaeological work in Jordan.

Near Eastern Archaeology Foundation (www.neaf.sydney.edu.au) Part of the University of Sydney, NEAF organises volunteer programmes to Jordan.

Climbing

The spectacular landscape of **Wadi Rum** has been attracting rock climbers to Jordan ever since the Ministry of Tourism commissioned a British climber, Tony Howard, to explore the area and map the possibilities. His resulting book, *Treks and Climbs in Wadi Rum*, gives details on nearly 300 climbing routes in the region. There are a few local Bedouins who are now qualified to lead Western-style ascents, but you will usually need to bring all your own equipment. For more details, see Wadi Rum, page 143.

Desert safaris

Wadi Rum is the main centre for desert safari activities. The visitor centre here has a list of official rates posted for both camel and 4WD trips, lasting from 30 minutes to a couple of days. If you want to go for longer, you'll have to negotiate a price. Be sure to establish exactly what is included in terms of food and camping arrangements. A number of tour operators based in Rum village, Aqaba and Wadi Musa can arrange longer camel/trekking/4WD/horse-riding tours from Wadi Rum to Wadi Musa or Wadi Rum to Aqaba. For more details, see Wadi Rum, page 142.

Skydiving and ballooning

The **Royal Aero Sports Club** of Jordan (see Facebook), based at King Hussein International Airport in Aqaba, organizes hot air ballooning and microlight flights over **Wadi Rum** and tandem skydiving over the Dead Sea (though flights were temporarily suspended at the time of research). These activities should be booked well in advance when flights resume. **Skydive Jordan** (see Facebook) organizes tandem skydiving over the **Dead Sea**.

Hiking and trekking

Due to extensive efforts by Jordan's **Royal Society for the Conservation of Nature (RSCN)** (www.rscn.org.jo), a whole network of trails has been opened up to hikers and trekkers within their nature reserves.

Dana Biosphere Reserve, situated to the west of the King's Highway between Tafila and Shobak, has accommodation available at Dana village as well as within the reserve itself, and a number of hiking trails to choose from. For travellers on a budget this is the easiest RSCN reserve to access as the **Wadi Dana Trail** is able to be hiked without a guide and there is excellent budget accommodation available in the village.

Mujib Biosphere Reserve, on the Dead Sea Highway, provides ample opportunities for dramatic canyon-hiking and is rich in flora and fauna. The hikes here range from medium to hard so aren't suitable for those who are just out for a stroll.

Tip...

Travellers looking for longer trekking opportunities in Jordan should check out the **Jordan Trail** (www.jordantrail.org), which weaves 675 km from the Roman ruins of Umm Qais in the very north of the country down to the Red Sea near Aqaba, and the **Abraham Path** (www.abrahampath.org), which is part of a long-distance walking trail across the entire Middle East and utilizes the same route as the Jordan Trail. Both organizations have excellent websites packed full of information on walking the trail.

Shopping tips

The best items to shop for in Jordan tend to be Bedouin handicrafts. Handwoven woollen rugs, embroidered textiles, pottery, silverware, jewellery, finely decorated daggers and swords, and items of traditional Bedouin dress (such as the ubiquitous and distinctive head cloth or *keffiyeh* and the black cord or *aqal* used to tie it), all make excellent souvenirs. Amman and Madaba have the best selection of handicrafts with Madaba also leading a local revival in traditional mosaic art.

Also worth checking out are the products sold through the RSCN's shops (outlets in the Wild Jordan Center in Amman and at all of the RSCN's visitor centres within their reserves). The handicrafts and jewellery here use traditional techniques but have usually been given a contemporary twist. They also sell a range of dried herbs, jams, olive oil and various 'natural' products. All of their products are made by local projects set up to produce an income for rural communities living within or near the reserves.

All guided treks should be booked in advance through the **RSCN** (see opposite). Their **Wild Jordan Center** in Amman (see page 43) is a mine of information on the reserves and can help with all bookings.

Petra and **Wadi Rum** are also brilliant places for hiking and trekking, with a huge number of trails to choose from. Most of Petra's hiking can be done unguided but in Wadi Rum it is wise to take a local guide (from the visitor centre) who knows the area.

Although currently out of print, but still available from Amazon et al, an excellent reference work for Jordan's walks is Di Taylor and Tony Howard's *Jordan: Walks, Treks, Caves, Climbs and Canyons* (Cicerone Press Ltd, 2008).

Where
to stay

from five-star luxury to Bedouin camps

Hotels

Most luxury hotels in Jordan are part of the big-name hotel chains, though boutique hotels are starting to pop up around the country. At the top end, a government tax of 16% and sometimes a service tax of 10% is added to your room rate. Luxury hotels and resorts are concentrated in Amman, Wadi Musa, Aqaba and the Dead Sea; the latter two offering luxury spa facilities.

Mid-range hotels vary hugely in style and atmosphere and range from charming family-run guesthouses to decent business hotels. Budget places are generally small and standards of cleanliness are variable. There are some extremely good budget hotels offering dormitory accommodation and basic private rooms in Amman, Wadi Musa and Madaba, but away from the main tourist centres they can be real dives.

Bedouin camps

One unique accommodation option that no visitor to Jordan should miss is a night spent under the stars in Wadi Rum. The local Bedouin-run camps usually comprise of basic accommodation in goat-hair tents with a shared bathroom block (most offering Western-style toilets). The incredible hospitality of your Bedouin hosts, plus the delicious food, more than make up for a night without

Price codes

Where to stay

$$$$ over US$150
$$$ US$66-150
$$ US$30-65
$ under US$30

Price of a double room in high season, including taxes.

Restaurants

$$$ over US$12
$$ US$7-12
$ US$6 and under

Price for a two-course meal for one person, excluding drinks or service charge.

life's normal luxuries. Taking your mattress outside the tent to fall asleep on the sand while watching the night sky is an experience that no five-star resort can ever live up to.

Nature lodges

A few special places to look out for are the accommodation offered by the **Royal Society for the Conservation of Nature** (RSCN) (www.rscn.org.jo) inside their nature reserves. Although the facilities at many of these places are actually quite basic, they're perfect sites to relax and admire Jordan's incredible natural environment. The **Rummana Campsite** (see page 101) and the privately run **Feynan Ecolodge** (see page 101) are particularly wonderful places to get away from it all.

Useful Arabic words and phrases

Learning just a few basic words and phrases of Arabic is not at all difficult and will make an enormous difference to your travelling experience.

hello (informal; 'hi')	*marhaba*	how far?	*kam kilometre?*
hello ('welcome')	*ahlan wa sahlan*	let's go	*yallah*
	or just *ahlan*	I understand	*ana afham*
hello	*asalaam alaikum*	I don't understand	*la afham*
(peace be upon you)		how much?	*bikam/adesh?*
hello (response)	*wa alaikum as-salaam*	expensive	*ghaali*
goodbye	*ma'a salaama*	cheap	*rakhees*
how are you?	*kif halak/halik?*		
	or *kifak/kifik?* (m/f)	**Numbers**	
fine, good, well	*qwayees*	1	*wahad*
what is your name?	*shoo ismak/ismik?*	2	*itneen*
	(m/f)	3	*talaata*
my name is...	*ismi...*	4	*arba'a*
please	*min fadlak/fadlik* (m/f)	5	*khamsa*
thank you	*shukran*	6	*sitta*
sorry	*aassif*	7	*sabba*
no problem	*mush mushkilay*	8	*tamanya*
yes	*naam/aiwa*	9	*tissa*
no	*laa*	10	*ashra*
where is...?	*wain...?*		

Food
& drink

from *falafel* and *mannoushi* to *mansaf*

Food

Two typical Jordanian dishes you should try while in the country are *mansaf* and a *zarb*. *Mansaf* is a combination of chunks of tender lamb (on the bone) served on a bed of rice with a spiced yoghurt sauce. It's usually eaten from a communal bowl and, as any Jordanian will inform you, it tastes even better eaten with your fingers (though restaurants will always provide cutlery). A *zarb* is a Bedouin-style barbecue cooked underground using hot coals and usually consisting of chicken, baked potatoes and whole baked onions. If you're spending the night at Wadi Rum, this is typically cooked for your dinner.

Tip...

Known in Arabic as *khubz* or *eish* (literally 'life'), bread is the mainstay of the Jordanian diet. It is baked unleavened (without yeast) in flat round discs and accompanies just about every meal or snack. Often it serves as an eating implement, or is rolled up with a filling inside to make a 'sandwich' snack.

Jordanian main courses are largely variations of the ubiquitous kebab. Although vegetarians are not specifically catered for, the varied options provided by a mezze spread or non-meat snacks, such as falafel sandwiches, *fuul* and hummus, as well as a range of salads, mean that you can still eat well.

Drink

Bottled water is available everywhere. Most towns have numerous traditional-style cafés where you can go for a cup of Arabic tea or coffee. If you're craving Western-style coffee, the upmarket cafés in the wealthier districts of Amman can do cappuccinos and lattes as good as anywhere in the world. Soft drinks (Pepsi, Coca Cola, 7-Up and various local varieties) and fresh seasonal juices are widely available throughout the country.

Local beer brands include the excellent Carakale (from Jordan's first microbrewery), the light lager Philadelphia and the darker and more hoppy Petra, which comes in either 8% or 10% and has been the cause of many a traveller's morning headache. Common imported brands include Amstel and Carlsberg, which are usually more expensive. To sample Jordanian-produced wines, look out for the St George and Mount Nebo labels. If you like spirits, there's plenty of locally made *arak* (similar to Greek *ouzo*), but imported spirits are hugely expensive and best avoided if you're on a budget.

Outside of Amman actual bars are less common, but many restaurants and hotels serve alcohol. You can also buy it directly (and far more cheaply) from liquor stores in most towns. Note that while alcohol is easy to obtain, it is forbidden to drink it in public (except of course in a licensed bar/restaurant); if you buy alcohol from a liquor store, you should drink it in the privacy of your hotel room (with the permission of the manager).

Eating out

Amman has a vast range of eating options, including lots of upmarket restaurants serving excellent Arabic cuisine, or else specializing in the cuisine of just about every other region/country of the world. Unfortunately in Petra, except at the luxury hotels, the selection is very limited and the quality not very good.

Cheap diners can be found just about everywhere in the country and are generally excellent value, although the level of hygiene at these varies greatly. Always choose a busy place as a high turnover of food ensures freshness and the simple fact that it is busy means that the locals think it is good enough to eat in. In terms of cheap snacks, hummus, *fuul*, *fatteh*, falafel or *shawarma* sandwiches, kebabs and roast chicken (whole or half portions) are the staples.

Mezze dishes

Perhaps the most attractive feature of Arabic cuisine is the mezze. When done properly, this consists of a spread of numerous small dips, salads and nibbles of fresh raw vegetables, olives, etc, which are served as an extended starter course though it's perfectly acceptable to do away with the main courses and just concentrate on the mezze.

Baba ganoush (moutabbal) Chargrilled eggplant (aubergine), tahini, olive oil, lemon juice and garlic blended into a smooth paste and served as a dip.

Falafel Small deep-fried balls of ground, spiced chickpeas.

Fattoush Salad of toasted croutons, cucumbers, tomatoes, onion and mint.

Hummus Purée of chickpeas, tahini, lemon and garlic, served as a dip with bread.

Kibbeh Ground lamb and bulghur (cracked wheat) meatballs stuffed with olives and pine nuts and fried or baked.

Kibbeh nayeh Raw *kibbeh*, eaten like steak tartare.

Loubieh (fasulya) Cooked French beans with tomatoes onion and garlic, served hot as a stew or cold as a kind of salad.

Mouhammara Mixture of ground nuts, olive oil, cumin and chillis, eaten with bread.

Tabouleh Finely chopped salad of bulghur wheat, tomatoes, onions, mint and parsley.

Warak enab (warak dawali) Vine leaves stuffed with rice and vegetables.

Main dishes

Bamia Baby okra and lamb in a tomato stew.

Bukhari rice Lamb and rice stir-fried with onion, lemon, carrot and tomato.

Fatteh *Fuul* and *laban* mixed together with small pieces of bread and topped with pine nuts and melted butter. Also sometimes served with fried minced meat mixed in.

Kebab If you ask for 'kebab', you will most likely be offered *kofte kebab*, though strictly speaking *kebab* is just chunks of meat chargrilled on a skewer.

Kofte kebab Minced meat and finely chopped onions, herbs and spices pressed onto a skewer and chargrilled. You often order by weight.

Kouzi Whole lamb baked over rice so that it soaks up the juice of the meat.

Mansaf A traditional Bedouin dish, consisting of lamb cooked with herbs in a yoghurt sauce and served on a bed of rice with pine nuts. Regarded as Jordan's national dish.

Saleek Lamb and rice dish cooked in milk.

Sayyadiya Delicately spiced fish (usually red mullet or bass) served with rice.

Street food

Falafel Several falafel balls are crushed on an open piece of Arabic bread, garnished with salad and pickled vegetables (usually tomatoes, beetroot, onion and lettuce), topped by a yoghurt and tahini sauce and then rolled up into a 'sandwich'.

Fatayer Triangular pastry pockets filled with spinach, meat or cheese.

Fuul Slow-cooked mash of fava beans and red lentils, dressed with lemon, olive oil

Shish taouk Fillets of chicken breast chargrilled on a skewer. Extremely popular and on offer in practically every restaurant.

and cumin, and sometimes a little yoghurt and tahini sauce.

Mannoushi Thin, crusty 'pizzas' topped with a thin layer of meat (*lahmeh*), cheese (*jebneh*) or *zaatar*, a seasoning with thyme and sumac.

Shawarma Layers of lamb or chicken roasted on a vertical spit are sliced off into small flat breads and rolled up with salad, pickled vegetables and a garlic sauce into a sandwich.

Sweets

Asabeeh Rolled filo pastry filled with pistachios, pine nuts and cashews and honey.

Baklawa Layered pastry filled with nuts and steeped in honey syrup.

Basboosa Semolina tart soaked in syrup.

Borma Crushed pine nuts or pistachios wrapped in shredded pastry and sliced into segments.

Halwa A sweet made from sesame paste, usually studded with fruit and nuts and made in a slab.

Kunafi Pastry stuffed with sweet white cheese, nuts and syrup.

Muhalabiyyeh Fine, smooth-textured semolina and milk pudding, sometimes with pistachios, pine nuts and almonds, served cold.

Umm Ali Literally 'Ali's mother', a pastry pudding with raisin and coconut, steeped in milk.

Amman
& Jerash

Amman

Handpicked to become the capital of the newly independent nation of Jordan in 1946, Amman has mushroomed into a sprawling and confusing metropolis that rambles over 22 hills. At first sight, it can look unappealing; its blocky architecture of white-stone buildings, marching across the hillslopes, lacks the historic charm of other Middle Eastern cities. But despite its façade of modernity there are significant archaeological remains here, attesting to Amman's long history and former glory as the Decapolis city of Philadelphia.

Away from its ancient remnants, Amman is also as cosmopolitan as Jordan gets and provides a glimpse into contemporary Jordanian life. It's a city of vibrant café culture and excellent restaurants; a place where you're as likely to see stiletto heels and skinny jeans as the more traditional *galabeyya* and *hijab*.

Many travellers only pay this city lip-service, passing through Amman in the bat of an eyelid. But if you're curious as to how a modern city in the Middle East functions then Amman deserves some time. There's no other place in the country with such a fusion of culture and modern buzz. Once you get under this city's skin you'll discover an energetic and vivacious capital, disarmingly friendly to outsiders (not counting road crossings) and openly willing to embrace change.

Standing at the centre of the modern city, just to the north of the Downtown area, is an L-shaped hill known as Jebel al-Qala'at (literally 'Citadel Hill'), which contains some of Amman's most important, and impressive, ancient remains. At 837 m above sea level the citadel is one of the highest points in Amman. There are excellent views from here out across the city and down onto the Roman theatre below. The citadel served as a stronghold from the Middle Bronze Age onwards, and is surrounded by a massive defensive wall. In its present form, this dates primarily from the Roman period, with evidence of repairs and additional fortifications dating from the Islamic era.

Visiting the citadel
The entrance and ticket office are on Qala'at Street. The site is open daily 0800-1600 Nov-Apr, 0800-1730 Apr-May, 0800-1830 Jun-Oct, 0900-1700 during Ramadan. Tickets cost 3JD, including entry to the Jordan Archaeological Museum (see page 28). Multilingual guides hang out at the entrance gate, just after the ticket office, and cost around 15JD per hour.

Roman Temple of Hercules
On the south side of the citadel mound are the remains of what is popularly referred to as the Roman Temple of Hercules (or Heracles). Although it has never been conclusively identified as such, the discovery here of an elbow and hand from a larger-than-life statue of Hercules makes this identification seem very likely. A dedicatory inscription firmly dates the temple to 161-166 CE, during the term of the Roman governor Geminius Marcianus (the period of joint reign of the emperors Marcus Aurelius and Lucius Versus). When first discovered, the remains comprised a large part of the temple podium (44 m by 28 m), the bases of three columns, plus a large fallen column. The columns have subsequently been rebuilt and a section of the decorative architrave restored to its original position. The re-erected columns, together with the various fragments scattered around on the ground, give a good idea of the huge scale of this temple (each column section, or 'drum', weighs up to 11 tonnes).

Excavations have also revealed the remains of what appears to be a sixth- to seventh-century BCE Iron Age temple, and it seems likely that the Temple of Hercules was built over the ruins of the Ammonite Temple of Milkon which was destroyed by King David (11 Samuel 12; 26-31). The Roman temple originally stood within a large rectangular *temenos* (or temple enclosure) surrounded by a colonnade,

Tip...
A series of staircases connect the citadel with the Roman theatre in Downtown but it's a bit of an uphill slog on a hot day. It's much easier to grab a taxi here and then walk down. To head Downtown from the citadel, turn right from the exit and follow Qala'at Street around as it shoulders the fortifications, until it veers off to the left. About 5 m after taking this left turn, you'll see a staircase on your right. Take these stairs down to Salamah Bin al-Akwa Street where there's a lookout platform with views over the Roman theatre. Just before the viewing platform another staircase heads straight down to Hashemi Street, depositing you directly in front of the Roman theatre.

Finding your feet

Amman sprawls over many *jebels* (hills) and isn't the easiest city in which to orientate yourself. It's much easier to think of it as a series of separate neighbourhoods, each with its own distinctive atmosphere.

Downtown is the bustling, grubby heart of the city where you'll find budget hotels, plenty of street food, shopping, souqs and some of the city's important historical sites including the Roman theatre.

Rising steeply above Downtown to the north is **Jebel al-Qala'at** (also called Citadel Hill), the oldest section of Amman. The hilltop, with its sweeping views over the city, is crowned by a jumble of impressive ruins dating from the Roman era through to the Umayyad period.

West of Downtown, is **Jebel Amman** with the excellent Jordan Museum at its southern end, many of the city's luxury hotels based around 3rd Circle to the west, and the café and restaurant hub of Rainbow Street running east from 1st Circle.

The leafy and quiet residential neighbourhood of **Jebel al-Weibdeh** sits just northwest of Downtown and the winding hilly streets hide the arty treats of the National Gallery and Darat al-Funun as well as good mid-range hotel options.

Walking in Amman

Generally Amman's topography means that a walk of any length will involve steep climbs. Walking can, however, be an option for getting around within specific districts. The Downtown area is relatively compact, flat and easily explored on foot. Jebel Amman and Jebel al-Weibdeh are also great districts for walking as long as you're reasonably fit and don't mind some uphill slogs.

Running from Downtown to Shmeisani and bordering Jebel al-Weibdeh to its west, grimy, run-down **Abdali** isn't much to look at but it's worth popping into the district to visit the King Abdullah Mosque. The JETT bus station is also based here.

Northwest of Abdali is the modern commercial district of **Shmeisani**; a see-and-be-seen area with luxury hotels, and plenty of shopping opportunities as well as trendy cafés and restaurants. It also lays claim to a decent swath of greenery, with the parks of Sports City lying to its north.

South of Shmeisani is swanky **Abdoun** where the pristine streets are lined with huge walled-off villas and embassies. Its centre is Abdoun Circle, surrounded by a glut of foreign chain restaurants.

Weather Amman

January	February	March	April	May	June
13°C 4°C 58mm	13°C 4°C 37mm	17°C 7°C 49mm	23°C 11°C 16mm	28°C 15°C 16mm	31°C 18°C 0mm

July	August	September	October	November	December
32°C 20°C 2mm	33°C 20°C 18mm	31°C 18°C 8mm	27°C 15°C 20mm	20°C 10°C 38mm	15°C 6°C 35mm

West from here brings you to the upmarket residential neighbourhoods of **Swafiyeh** and **Umm Uthayna** where you'll find modern shopping malls and luxury hotels.

Getting around

For the new arrival, getting around Amman can be confusing and frustrating. The busy main roads and complicated intersections are anything but pedestrian-friendly while new initiates are also usually confounded by the seemingly mysterious routes of the public transport system. Once you get the hang of using the city's service taxis though, getting around becomes infinitely easier.

White **service taxis** (shared taxis, known as 'serveece') run along fixed routes for a fixed fare (the majority cost around 40 piastres), carrying up to five or six passengers at a time. Almost all begin from various points around Downtown, shuttling to surrounding districts and back, and can be waved down anywhere along their route. They are a cheap and convenient means of getting around. See page 45, for route details.

The **local bus** system is very confusing and, with a couple of exceptions, is best left to the locals. However, taking a **bus tour**

Best places to stay

Art Hotel, see page 39
Hisham, see page 39
Caravan, see page 39

Best places to eat

Sufra, see page 40
Hashem, see page 41
Beit Sitti cooking school, see page 42

of some of the main sites in the city with Amman City Tour (www.ammancitytour. com, Wed-Mon 0900) can be a good way to get your bearings. The approximately three-hour tour of the capital takes in the main sites and the 45JD cost (online payment only) includes lunch, site entry fees where applicable and an English-speaking guide.

Yellow **private taxis** are the simplest method of getting from A to B in the city and are affordable. You'll have no problem finding one, even when you don't want one. See Transport, page 43.

When to go

March to May and September to October have the pleasantest weather for city sightseeing. July and August are hot but the midsummer months also bring a series of concerts and performances to Amman's Roman theatre. November to February can be rainy and cold. Snow isn't unheard of in January.

Time required

One day to explore the sights of Downtown, Jebel al-Qala'at and Jebel al-Weibdeh. Add another day to soak up modern Amman's buzz in Jebel Amman and go café-hopping on Rainbow Street.

though nothing of this remains. A stairway would have led from the civic area of the city below up to the temple, passing through a monumental gateway in the southwestern corner of the temple's *temenos*. Nothing survives of this either, but the views from this point out over to Downtown are excellent.

Jordan Archaeological Museum

Heading clockwise around the citadel area (past an early Bronze Age cave), you next come to this small well-presented museum packed with exhibits presented in chronological order from the Neolithic era right up to the early Arab empires. This was Jordan's first museum, opened in 1951, and there's a wealth of small finds on display here; much of it excavated from this site.

In particular there is an extensive collection of Roman ceramic lamps and glassware, some exquisite pieces of Abbasid-era pottery and three anthropoid coffins that date from between the 13th and seventh centuries BCE.

Amman overview

To Tabarbour Bus Station & Jerash

Wafsi al-Tal (Gardens) St

Sports City Interchange

Sport City

Ash Shari (Nasir bin Jamil)

Queen Alia

SHMEISANI

Jamal 'Abd an Nasir Interchange

Abdullah Ghosbeh St

Al Madina al Munawwara

Bike Rush

Mecca St

King Abdullah Gardens

UMM UTHAYNA

Wadi Saqra Circle

Queen Noor

JETT

7th Circle

6th Circle

5th Circle

Ibn Sina

King Abdullah Mosque

8th Circle

Al-Kulliyah al-Islamiyah (Zahran) St

Amman City Tour

4th Circle

Arar

3rd Circle

To Wadi Seer

SWAFIYEH

ZAHRAN

2nd Circle

Visa Extensions

To Queen Alia Airport & King's Highway

Princess Basma

Muhajireen

ABDOUN

➡ **Amman maps**

2 Downtown, page 34

3 Abdali, Jebel Amman & Al-Wiebdeh, page 36

N

Bradt

0 ——— 800m
0 ——— 800yds

Umayyad Palace complex, 'Great Square' and congregational mosque

Walking behind and to the north of the museum brings you to the remains of the hill's Umayyad settlement, and the main focus of the citadel area. Almost certainly the site of another Ammonite and later Roman temple, what survives today is the extensive eighth-century Umayyad settlement, consisting of a 'great square', a large congregational mosque and a lavish palace complex.

Standing as a testimony to the new Umayyad ascendancy, both the architecture and the overall layout of these buildings are, in part, the result of Sassanid and Byzantine influences; they also bear a close resemblance to Umayyad projects in Andalucía such as the Alhambra Palace of Granada. Unfortunately, the Umayyads had barely finished their building work before the earthquake of 749 CE razed much of it to the ground.

The palace complex was the subject of an ambitious restoration project by a joint Spanish-Jordanian team who excavated and restored the great square and the congregational mosque, adding greatly to the overall understanding of the settlement. For visitors, the most visually striking aspect of the restoration work is the reconstruction of the dome over the audience hall.

The Great Square The 'Great Square' lies at the heart of the Umayyad settlement, providing a link between the palace complex and mosque to the north and south. As well as serving as an important meeting place, the square was also a focus for commerce, with rows of small shops running along its east and west sides. In addition to the street leading into it from the Byzantine church to the southeast, two further streets appear to have converged here.

Umayyad Mosque Wide steps lead up from the south side of the square into the Umayyad mosque, which occupied a raised platform measuring just over 33 sq m. The cobblestone floor of the mosque has been restored, along with the numerous column bases which would have supported the roof, and the mihrab in the southern wall, oriented towards Mecca. In the centre of the mosque was a small open courtyard.

Umayyad Palace The large palace complex to the north of the square was almost certainly built as the residence and administrative base of the *emir* (governor). It comprises three main parts. At the south end is the domed monumental gateway, a baths complex and open square. The central section is the main residential block, comprising nine residential buildings (of which four have been extensively excavated). The northern section was the palace proper, housing a throne room and the residence of the *emir*.

The monumental **gateway** provides a suitably grand introduction to the palace complex. It was built over the remains of an earlier Byzantine building and follows the same cruciform plan as its predecessor, the lowest course of stonework actually being of Byzantine origin. The lead-covered domed roof has drawn mixed responses in terms of aesthetics, but on a practical level is at least providing some protection against the elements and is removable if necessary. The whole of the front façade has also been extensively restored, complete with the decorative miniature pilasters and arches running in a band along the top. Inside, the wooden ribs and lattice of the new dome complement the further decorative bands of stonework in the walls, also extensively restored.

To the east of the gateway stands the restored royal **baths complex**, modelled on the Greco-Roman style. The present remains include what may have been an audience chamber and the *frigidarium* (cold room), though the *tepidarium* (warm room) and *caldarium* (hot room) have not survived. An interesting feature of these baths is that they could be entered from both inside and outside the palace complex, suggesting that they were used by the general public as well as the palace elite. The baths would have been fed by water from the deep circular **cistern** just to the east. You can see some of the original plaster lining inside the cistern, which could hold some 1368 cu m of water, along with part of a column in the centre which acted as a depth gauge. Both the cistern and the system of clay pipes and stone drains which channelled water from the area around the audience hall into it have been restored. Rain provided the sole source of water on the citadel, and the Umayyads made careful use of the extensive water collection system which had been developed over the centuries, modifying it to suit their needs.

From the gateway you pass into an open **plaza** (probably formerly a Roman courtyard) immediately to the north. A gateway in the north wall of the plaza leads via a **colonnaded street** to the governor's residence. You can see an exposed section of the sewage system that ran under part of the street. On either side of the open plaza and colonnaded street are a series of residential buildings, labelled by the excavators as buildings **A-I**. Four of the nine buildings have been fully excavated, though all follow roughly the same plan of an inner courtyard surrounded by porticoes with a series of rooms leading off it. The site's excavators draw particular attention to '**building F**', suggesting that its superior architectural features and proximity to the audience hall indicate its use for some form of official functions.

The northern section of the complex, or **palace** proper, is entered via the colonnaded street (as it would have been in the eighth century), which leads into a small porticoed court. The room that opens onto the court's north side probably served as an audience chamber, or *iwan*, while the cruciform room to its north may well have been the throne room. Beyond is a further small court. At the northernmost tip of the palace complex there is another large cistern, this one bell-shaped and hewn into the bedrock.

BACKGROUND

Amman

Rabbath-Ammon Excavations on and around the citadel area have provided evidence of settlement in the Neolithic period (5500-4500 BCE), though it is in the biblical accounts of the city that the first real interest lies. There can be little doubt that modern Amman occupies the site of the Old Testament Rabbath-Ammon which flourished as the capital of an independent Ammonite Kingdom until the sixth century BCE.

Philadelphia Around 259 BCE, the city fell under the influence of the Ptolemids, subsequently being renamed Philadelphia by Ptolemy II Philadelphus (285-246 BCE). Nabataean influence over Philadelphia grew in the second half of the second century BCE until 63 BCE, when Pompey subdued the city and attached it to the Roman Provincia Syria. Under Roman influence Philadelphia thrived, taking its place with pride as one of the cities of the Decapolis.

The Byzantines and the Arab conquest Philadelphia remained an important centre during the Byzantine period (324-635 CE), being the seat of a bishopric. Though the city was referred to by the name of Amman during the Byzantine period, it was only after the Arab conquest of 635 CE that this name gained general usage.

Amman appears to have undergone a gradual decline under subsequent Arab dynasties and was probably abandoned completely by the 16th century. The process of rejuvenation began in 1876 when a group of Circassians (refugees from the Caucasus region) resettled the site, though by the turn of the century Amman's population was still little over 2000.

The modern capital The new set of political realities that accompanied the conclusion of the First World War saw Amman established as the headquarters of King Abdullah, effectively as the capital of the internally autonomous Emirate of Transjordan. Following independence from Britain in 1946, it officially became the capital of the Hashemite Kingdom of Jordan.

Byzantine churches

Doubling back through the monumental gateway, and heading towards the entrance ticket booth, you pass by the remains of a Byzantine church dating from the sixth century CE. Trapezoidal in shape, the church features a central nave divided from the side-aisles by two rows of seven columns. Some of the columns have been re-erected, with decorative capitals placed on the top. The nave originally featured a geometric mosaic floor while the two aisles were paved with plain stone slabs. Nearby, traces of a smaller and older church have been uncovered. The discovery here of a coin from the reign of the Byzantine Emperor Constantius, dated to 348 CE, has led to the tentative dating of this church to the fourth century CE, which would make it one of the earliest known churches in Jordan.

Jordan Museum

Ali Bin Abi Taleb St, www.jordanmuseum.jo, Wed-Thu and Sat-Mon 0900-1700, Fri 1400-1800, 5JD, visitors with disabilities free.

This highly impressive museum is packed with well-curated exhibits that weave together the story of Jordan from the prehistoric age up to the Byzantine period. The star attraction is the **Dead Sea Scrolls**, found in the Qumran caves in 1947 by a Bedouin shepherd, but there's plenty more here for anyone interested in Jordan's vast history.

The Paleolithic and Neolithic halls are particularly interesting and contain the eerily beautiful Ayn Ghazal statues (the oldest human statues in the world). Other museum highlights include the preserved fragments of The Procession (a wall-painting dating from the late Chalcolithic era), a copy of the famed Mesha Stele (see page 156), and the Petra Papyri, found during excavation of Petra's Byzantine church.

All the exhibits are labelled in English and there are plenty of information boards scattered throughout the halls which do an excellent job of explaining and guiding you through Jordan's history.

Roman theatre

Al-Hashimi St, daily 0800-1900 summer, 0800-1600 winter, 2JD including entry to the odeon and both museums (closed Tue) inside the theatre complex.

While parts of the upper city of Roman Philadelphia are preserved on the citadel mound, most of the lower city has been submerged beneath modern Amman. A few relics remain, however, most notably in the form of the impressive Roman theatre (just to the east of the main Downtown area, and south of the citadel mound). The theatre partially fills a natural depression in the ground, with three tiers of seating cut out of the hillside. It was built between 169 CE and 177 CE, during the reign of Emperor Marcus Aurelius. At its peak the theatre would have had a capacity of around 6000, though it should be noted that unlike other contemporary Roman theatres the seats themselves were not actually cut out of the rock but were stone built. In recent years the *scaena* and *scaenae frons* (stage and backdrop) have been partially rebuilt.

Roman theatre museums Two small museums flank the Roman theatre, housed within the vaulted rooms either side of the stage area. On the east side (to your left as you enter the theatre) is the excellent **Museum of Popular Traditions**, which features a small but fascinating collection of beautifully displayed traditional Bedouin costumes, textiles and jewellery, as well as a room displaying various pieces of mosaic work from the churches of Madaba and Jerash. On the west side (to your right as you enter the theatre) is the **Folklore Museum** featuring displays of weaponry, musical instruments, jewellery, glassware, looms, woven rugs and embroidered fabrics, as well as reconstructions of traditional Bedouin households and an example of a traditional camel-mounted *howdah*.

Odeon After you've exited the Roman theatre don't forget to visit the odeon, which is just to the east of the theatre, across the small colonnaded plaza, now identified as Roman Philadelphia's *agora* (forum, marketplace, or place of assembly). The odeon was probably built a little before the main theatre and had a capacity of just 500, most likely being primarily used for council meetings and other official gatherings.

Nymphaeum
Quraysh St.

Another reminder of Amman's previous incarnation as Roman Philadelphia is provided by the nymphaeum, built in 191 CE and undergoing long-term restoration at the time of writing. Most public areas in Roman cities were marked by some sort of monumental structure – usually a fountain – though given the way that Amman's modern buildings have crowded and dwarfed this nymphaeum, it is hard to envisage this fine example dominating a large open area. It is located to the southwest of the Roman theatre, on Quraysh (Saqfa al-Seel) Street which almost exactly follows the course of the Roman decumanus maximus, or main street.

King Hussein Mosque
Hashemi St, not usually open to non-Muslims.

Although this mosque is not normally open to non-Muslims it could be worth asking at the entrance for a peek inside, but in any event it is still possible to admire the attractive façade. Built in 1924 by the present king's grandfather (reputedly on the site of the seventh-century CE mosque built by the caliph Umar), it was substantially refurbished in 1987 by the late King Hussein.

Duke's Diwan
Next to the Arab Bank, King Faisal St, entrance up yellow staircase from the street, daily daylight hours, free entry.

Once home to the central post office and, later, the Haifa Hotel, the Duke's Diwan is a well-preserved example of early-20th-century Ammani architecture. Rescued from decay by Mamdouh Bisharat (who holds the honorific title of Duke of Mukheibeh, bestowed upon him by King Hussein), the rooms have been somewhat restored and opened to the public allowing you to view the interior of a townhouse from this period. Various literary events and art exhibitions are also held here.

Jebel al-Weibdeh
leafy neighbourhood with an arty flavour

King Abdullah Mosque
Suleiman al-Nabulsi St, Sat-Thu 0800-1600 (but closed during prayer hours), 2JD, all visitors should wear modest dress to enter and take off their shoes before entering the prayer hall, women (and men wearing shorts) will be given an abeyya *(a long hooded cloak) to wear.*

While the King Hussein Mosque was built by the grandfather but named after the grandson, the King Abdullah Mosque reverses the compliment. Located just behind the Parliament House, the mosque's huge dome, decorated with pale blue and black geometric designs, serves as one of Amman's principal landmarks. Built in 1990, the brightness of the exterior is matched only by the simplicity of the interior. Tourists can go inside the huge octagonal dome-topped prayer hall of the mosque.

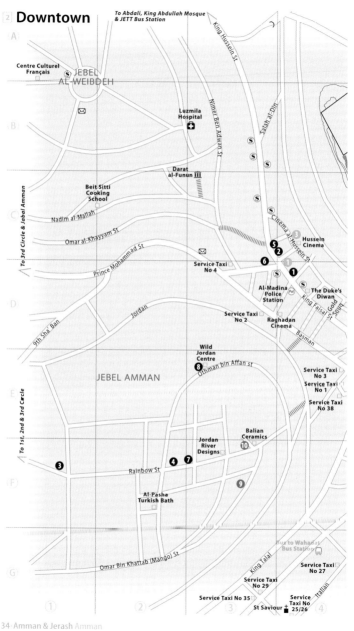

To Abdali, King Abdullah Mosque & JETT Bus Station

King Hussein St

A

Centre Culturel Français

JEBEL AL-WEIBDEH

Nimer Ben Adwan St

Salah al-Din

B

Luzmila Hospital

Darat al-Funun

Beit Sitti Cooking School

Cinema al-Hussein St

C

Nadim al-Mallah

Omar al-Khayyam St

Hussein Cinema

To 3rd Circle & Jabal Amman

Prince Mohammad St

5

2

6

1

Service Taxi No 4

Al-Madina Police Station

The Duke's Diwan

D

Jordan

9th Sha'Ban

King Faisal St Gold Souq

Service Taxi No 2

Raghadan Cinema

Basman

Wild Jordan Centre

JEBEL AMMAN

Othman bin Affan st

8

Service Taxi No 3

Service Taxi No 1

To 1st, 2nd & 3rd Circle

Service Taxi No 38

Balian Ceramics

10

Jordan River Designs

3

4 7

Rainbow St

9

E

Al-Pasha Turkish Bath

Bus to Wahadat Bus Station

Omar Bin Khattab (Mango) St

King Talal

Service Taxi No 27

F

Service Taxi No 29

Service Taxi No 35

St Saviour

Service Taxi No 25/26

G

Italian

1   2   3   4

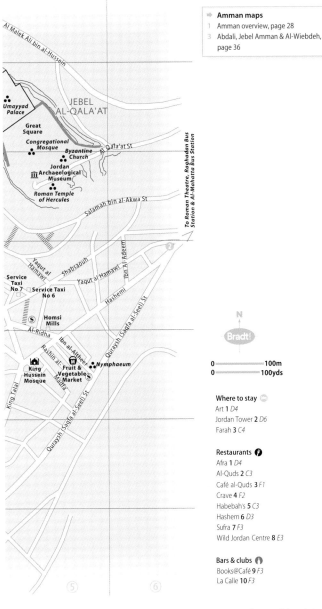

➡ **Amman maps**
1 Amman overview, page 28
3 Abdali, Jebel Amman & Al-Wiebdeh, page 36

Al Malek Ali bin al-Hussein

Umayyad Palace

JEBEL AL-QALA'AT

Great Square

Congregational Mosque

Byzantine Church

Jordan Archaeological Museum

Roman Temple of Hercules

Al-Qala'at St

Salamah bin al-Akwa St

To Roman Theatre, Raghadan Bus Station & Al-Mahatta Bus Station

Yaqut al Hamawi

Shabsaouh

Yaqut al'Hamawi

Ibn Al-Adeem

Hashemi

Service Taxi No 7

Service Taxi No 6

Homsi Mills

Al-Ridha

Ibn al-Aitheer

Rashin al-Madra

King Hussein Mosque

Fruit & Vegetable Market

Nymphaeum

Quraysh (Saqfa al-Seel) St

King Talal

Quraysh (Saqfa al-Seel) St

N

Bradt!

0 ———— 100m
0 ———— 100yds

Where to stay 🛏
Art **1** *D4*
Jordan Tower **2** *D6*
Farah **3** *C4*

Restaurants 🍴
Afra **1** *D4*
Al-Quds **2** *C3*
Café al-Quds **3** *F1*
Crave **4** *F2*
Habebah's **5** *C3*
Hashem **6** *D3*
Sufra **7** *F3*
Wild Jordan Centre **8** *E3*

Bars & clubs 🍸
Books@Café **9** *F3*
La Calle **10** *F3*

Abdali, Jebel Amman & Jebel al-Weibdeh

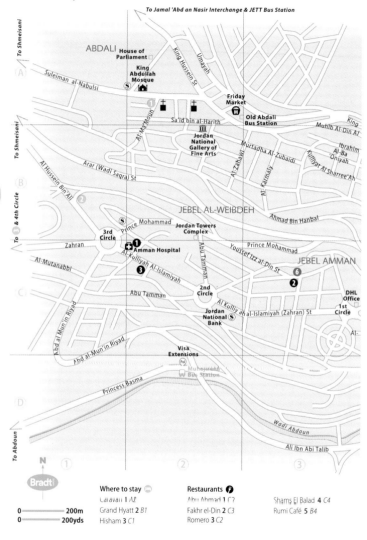

To Jamal 'Abd an Nasir Interchange & JETT Bus Station

ABDALI House of Parliament

King Abdullah Mosque

Suleiman al-Nabulsi

To Shmeisani

To Shmeisani

King Hussein St

Umayah

Friday Market

Sa'id bin al-Harith

Old Abdali Bus Station

Muhib Al-Din Al

King

Al-Ma'mun

Jordan National Gallery of Fine Arts

Murtadha Al-Zubaidi

Ibrahim Al-Ba 'Oniyah

Kuniyat Al Sharree'Ah

Arar (Wadi Saqra) St

Al-Zahawi

Al-Karmaly

Al Hussein bin Ali

To 3rd & 4th Circle

JEBEL AL-WEIBDEH

Ahmad Bin Hanbal

Prince Mohammad

Jordan Towers Complex

3rd Circle

Zahran

Amman Hospital

Al-Mutanabbi

Al Kulliyah Al-Islamiyah

Abu Tamman

Prince Mohammad

Youssef Izz al-Din St

JEBEL AMMAN

DHL Office

2nd Circle

Al Kulliyah al-Islamiyah (Zahran) St

1st Circle

Al-

Abu Tamman

Abd al-Mun'in Riyad

Abd al-Mun'in Riyad

Jordan National Bank

Visa Extensions

Muheyraat Bus Station

Princess Basma

To Abdoun

Wadi Abdoun

Ali Ibn Abi Talib

N

1

2

3

Bradt

0 ——— 200m
0 ——— 200yds

Where to stay
Caravan 1 A2
Grand Hyatt 2 B1
Hisham 3 C1

Restaurants
Abu Ahmad 1 C2
Fakhr el-Din 2 C3
Romero 3 C2

Shams El Balad 4 C4
Rumi Café 5 B4

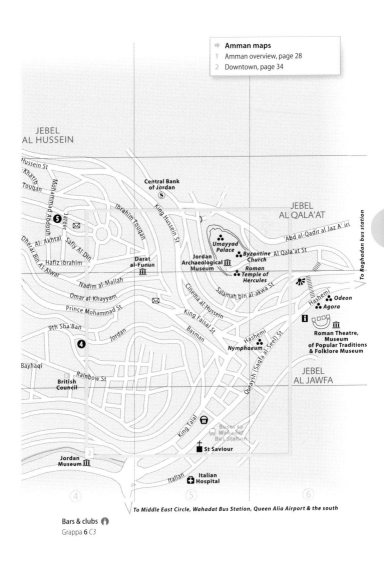

→ **Amman maps**
1 Amman overview, page 28
2 Downtown, page 34

JEBEL AL HUSSEIN

Hussein St

Khatib Touqan

Mohammad Abdoun

Jafeer

Dher Al-Akhtal

Safiy Al-Din

Hafiz Ibrahim

Dher Bin Al-Alwar

Nadim al-Mallah

Omar al-Khayyam

Prince Mohammad St

9th Sha'Ban

Jordan

Bayhaqi

Rainbow St

British Council

Jordan Museum

Italian

Italian Hospital

St Saviour

King Talal

Ibrahim Touqan

King Hussein St

Central Bank of Jordan

Darat al-Funun

Cinema al-Hussein

King Faisal St

Basman

Umayyad Palace

Jordan Archaeological Museum

Byzantine Church

Roman Temple of Hercules

Salamah bin al-akwa St

'Abd al-Qadir al Jaz A'iri

Al Qala'at St

JEBEL AL QALA'AT

To Raghadan bus station

Hashemi (Saqfa al-Seel) St

Hashem

Odeon

Agora

Roman Theatre, Museum of Popular Traditions & Folklore Museum

Nymphaeum

Quraysh (Saqfa al-Seel) St

JEBEL AL JAWFA

Bus to Wahadat Bus Station

④ ⑤ ⑥

↓ To Middle East Circle, Wahadat Bus Station, Queen Alia Airport & the south

Bars & clubs 🍸
Grappa **6** C3

There is a small **Islamic Museum** in the grounds of the mosque, with various Qur'ans, photographs and bits of Islamic pottery.

Jordan National Gallery of Fine Arts

Husni Fareez St, www.nationalgallery.org, Sat-Thu 0900-1900 summer, Sat-Thu 0900-1700 winter, closed public holidays, 7JD.

Founded in 1980, the Jordan National Gallery of Fine Arts houses an important permanent collection of more than 3000 contemporary artworks from the developing world, with a focus on artists from the Middle East and Africa. It's an excellent gallery space, very slick and modern, and there are good views over the city from the upstairs gallery/café. There is a second building, across the road on the other side of the sculpture park, with another three gallery floors and a small gift shop.

Darat al-Funun

Nadim al-Mallah St, www.daratalfunun.org, Sat-Thu 1000-1900, closed Aug & public holidays; free entry. To head here on foot from Downtown (a 10-min walk), head up Omar Khayyam St, turn right at the 1st hairpin bend and where the road forks turn left onto Nadim al-Mallah St for 20 m until you see the signed entry gate that leads into the lower section of the grounds.

Situated in an elegant turn-of-the-20th-century residence on the slopes of Jebel al-Weibdeh (a short, steep walk from Downtown), the Darat al-Funun houses an attractive art gallery, as well as the ruins of an interesting Byzantine church in the grounds. First built by the wealthy Hmoud family, it became the home of Lieutenant Colonel F G Peake ('Peake Pasha'), the founder and first leader of the Arab Legion, from 1920-1939. T E Lawrence was one of the many guests to stay here during this period.

In its present form, the Darat al-Funun (literally 'House of the Arts') was established by the Khalid Shoman Foundation, dedicated to "promoting the fine arts and fostering knowledge and cultural dialogue" in the Arab world. This quiet haven in the middle of the city is a wonderful place for art lovers to while away an hour or so.

St George's Church From the entrance off Nadim al-Mallah Street, you come to the excavated remains of St George's Church. Dated to the late sixth century or early seventh century CE, an inscription mentioning a "humble priest of St George" found near the altar forms the basis of its presumed dedication. The outline of the church is clearly visible, with the foundations of the apse to the east, and a number of re-erected columns, a couple topped by ornate Corinthian capitals, separating the central nave from the side-aisles. Traces of mosaic floors and some marble tilework can also be seen.

Cut into the rock of the steep hillside on the north side of the church is a small **cave**, with four niches in the walls, one of which appears to have contained a sarcophagus. The cave was clearly incorporated into the plan of the church and, along with a rectangular room opposite it (on the south side of the church), would have given it cruciform shape.

Gallery buildings From the excavations, stairs lead you through the gardens, dotted with contemporary art sculptures, to the main art gallery inside the restored former residence of Peake Pasha. The gallery houses a rotating schedule of art exhibits. Upstairs from the main gallery building, is another smaller gallery space and a secluded café terrace.

Tourist information

Amman Visitor Centre

Near to the Roman theatre in Downtown Amman, T06-464 6264. Summer Sat-Thu 0900-1900 (winter 0900-1800), Fri 1000-1600.
You can get a free map of the city and a whole range of pamphlets and brochures here but not much else.

Tourist Police

T06-569 0384.
There are usually a couple of members of the tourist police on duty at the visitor centre. You can also use the unified emergency telephone number 911 for ambulance, fire and police.

Where to stay

$$$$ Grand Hyatt

Hussein bin Ali St, 3rd Circle, Jebel Amman, T06-465 1234, www.hyatt.com.
Unlike most generic chain hotels, Amman's Grand Hyatt has injected a little personality and style into its rooms with chic interiors complemented by Eastern ornaments and modern art. The friendly service here is second to none and with a gym, swimming pool, spa and 2 excellent restaurants, this hotel is a sophisticated and smart choice.

$$$ Art Hotel

30 King Faisal St, T06-463 8906.
Downtown's first boutique hotel; the welcoming Art Hotel has 40 minimalist-styled spacious rooms decked out with lashings of white, seriously comfortable beds, and adorned with eye-catching artworks and murals. With doubles from 42JD, this place is great value for Amman. The top-floor terrace has expansive views over the bustling Downtown streets and the excellent top-floor restaurant serves a wide-ranging international menu. Breakfast, Wi-Fi included. Highly recommended.

$$$ Hisham

Behind the French Embassy, between 3rd and 4th Circle, western Amman, T06-464 7540, www.hishamhotel.com.jo.
In a quiet leafy backstreet the charming Hisham is an intimate and upscale boutique-style hotel. Everything here is immaculately presented, from the David Roberts prints that line the walls, the smart rooms (a/c, satellite TV, fridge) decorated with a touch of panache and the fabulous old-style oak bar, to the serene little courtyard where you can relax in the sun. Breakfast, Wi-Fi included.

$$ Caravan

Al Ma'moun St, Jebel al-Weibdeh, T06-566 1195, see Facebook.
A favourite with overland groups, the 27-room Caravan has a homely atmosphere with staff always happy to help with queries, and decent-sized rooms (fan, satellite TV) on a quiet street, a step removed from the Downtown hustle. If you need to get up early, don't fret – the early-morning call to prayer from the King Abdullah Mosque is the best alarm clock you could ever wish for. Breakfast, Wi-Fi included.

$$-$ Farah

Cinema al-Hussein St, Downtown, T06-465 1443, www.farahhotel.info.
This excellent backpacker establishment with 24 rooms knows how to pull the punters in. With a comfy lounge where you can kick back and watch movies and welcoming, clued-up staff who are a mine of knowledge on the city. There's a wide variety of clean, basic rooms ranging from dorms (7JD) to private rooms with/without bath (double 18JD with shared bathroom)

– some with the oldest TVs you've probably seen in a while. Breakfast extra 2JD, Wi-fi included. Good-value single rooms.

$$-$ Jordan Tower Hotel

48 Hashemi St, Downtown, T06-461 4161, www.jordantowerhotel.com.
In prime position, opposite the Roman theatre, the Jordan Tower is a highly popular choice for budget travellers with dorms (13JD) as well as tidy private rooms with piping hot showers, satellite TV and a/c. Staff are generally more than happy to negotiate on private room rack-rates (particularly outside of peak season). Breakfast and Wi-fi (in lounge and some rooms) included.

Restaurants

For cheap eats head Downtown, where there are numerous falafel and *shawarma* joints lined up in the alleyways off King Faisal St. For sweets head to **Habebah's** (King Faisal St), which is where the locals come to get their dose of *knafah* – an unlikely mix of filo pastry, *nablisi* cheese, syrup and vermicelli, which you'll soon become addicted to.

$$$ Fakhr El-Din

Taha Hussein St, 2nd Circle, Jebel Amman, T07-954 30055. Open daily 1300-2400.
Set in a grand Ammani villa that was once home to an ex-prime minister, this restaurant is at the centre of the city's social life. Try the *shanklish* (sheep's cheese spiced with onion, tomato and thyme), or the *mudardara* (lentils and rice topped with fried onions), and order the *noukha'a* (poached lamb brains), if you dare. During summer the seating spreads outside into the garden. Bookings essential, alcohol served.

$$$ Romero

Just off Al-Kulliyah al-Islamiyah St, 3rd Circle, Jebel Amman, T06-464 4227. Lunch 1300-1500, dinner 1930-2330.
Amman's premier Italian restaurant is a classy affair where the pasta is made in-house and there's no scrimping on quality. With quirky salads that will please vegetarians and mouth-watering dishes such as spinach and cheese tortellini served with cream and prosciutto, Romero's remains one of the city's best dining choices. Alcohol served.

$$$ Shams El Balad

69 Mu'ath Bin Jebel St, Jebel Amman, T79-969 2320, www.shamselbalad.com. Daily 1000-2400.
Located in a house of some character with a charming shaded open-air terrace, this eatery serves a wide range of fresh local cuisine and the bar is well stocked with cocktails, beers, *arak* and spirits. Highly recommended.

$$$ Sufra

28 Rainbow St, Jebel Amman, T06-461 1468. Open 1300-2330.
If you're going to splash out once on a meal in Amman, make it here. Behind the walls, with their colourful pots of geraniums standing guard, this restaurant serves up some of Jordan's best Levantine cuisine. It's a wonderfully ambient place to dine, set in a white-stone villa complete with restored tilework floors, chandeliers and plenty of antique bric-a-brac while during summer diners spill out onto the leafy terrace. The mezze section here is a delight to dip into while mains ramble from standard kebab fare to *tukharat* (slow-cooked clay-pot meals) such as *kibbeh* with tahini and citrus, and lamb stuffed with chickpeas. Alcohol served. Highly recommended.

$$ Abu Ahmad

Behind Amman Hospital, 3rd Circle, Jebel Amman, T06-464 1879. Open 1200-late.
This long-established place has a good reputation for Arabic food. It's a great place to try the Levantine speciality of *kibbeh nayeh* (raw lamb blended with crushed wheat and spices), but if you're not brave enough for that, the reasonably priced menu, with mezze dishes from 2-4JD, is extensive enough to have something for everyone.

$ Café al-Quds

Rainbow St, Jebel Amman.
Sat-Thu 1000-1800.
It's a big call but this may just be the best falafel sandwich in the city. They're tasty, filling and cheap as chips and the queues to order at lunchtime can be pretty long.

$ Hashem

Prince Muhammad St, Downtown.
If it's good enough for King Abdullah (who brought his family to dine here one evening) then it's good enough for us! Since 1954 this unpretentious street-side eatery has been serving up excellent falafel, hummus and *fuul* to the masses. Open 24 hrs a day, and always busy, it's an Ammani institution and should be visited at least once on your stay whatever your budget. Highly recommended.

$ Jerusalem Restaurant (Al-Quds Restaurant)

King Faisal St, Downtown. Open 0800-2200.
Walk past the sweet counters, to the humble diner-style restaurant out back which is nearly always full of locals looking for a cheap and filling dinner. You can get a half-chicken with plentiful sides or get stuck into the national dish of *mansaf* (boiled lamb in a delicately spiced yoghurt sauce). Service can be haphazard during busy lunch periods. They do have English-language menus, but you need to ask for them.

Cafés

Afra Restaurant and Café

King Faisal St, Downtown T06-461 0046, see Facebook. Daily 0800-2400.
This modern-style coffeehouse attracts a young crowd including plenty of local women who come here to relax with a coffee and *nargileh*. The decoration merges colourful Arabic lamps, exposed beams and a scattering of antiques with flatscreen TVs tuned into the sport channels for a truly contemporary coffeehouse experience. There's a good selection of snack food.

Al-Rashid

1st floor, King Faisal St, Downtown T79-948 1987. Sat-Thu 1000-2400, Fri 1300-2400.
You can recognize this place by its distinctive balcony, covered in painted flags. This is a friendly traditional coffeehouse where solo foreign women will feel comfortable. If you manage to get a seat on the tiny balcony you could happily whittle away a few hours mastering the art of *nargileh* smoking over a few cups of coffee or tea.

Crave Café

28 Rainbow St, Jebel Amman, T06-465 9292. Daily 0800-2200.
Some of the city's best cappuccino and espresso is served up at this bright café decorated with fragments of original tiles set in the polished concrete flooring and splashes of primary colour. They also serve inventive salads (the halloumi and strawberry salad is delicious) and sandwiches. Recommended.

Rumi Café

14 Kulliyat Al Shareeh St, Jebel al-Weibdeh, T06-464 4131, www.rumijordan.com. Sun-Thu 0700-2400, Fri-Sat 0900-2400.
A pleasant, friendly and leafy café serving an excellent range of international teas, coffee, cakes and snacks. A tranquil venue to kick back in.

Wild Jordan Center

Othman bin Afan St, 1st Circle, Jebel Amman, T07-9700 0218, www.wildjordancenter.com. Daily 0900-2330.

The place to head for healthy yet delicious food, fruit juices and snacks. Date smoothies, masala chai lattes and excellent carrot cake are just a few of the reasons to come here. Proceeds help the various RSCN (see page 178) projects around Jordan.

Bars

Books@Café

Omar bin Khattab St, Jebel Amman, T06-465 0457, www.booksatcafe.com. Daily 0900-0100.

Come here to lounge on the candy-pink and black sofas, listen to the cool music that's always on the stereo and down a couple of cocktails. There's an extensive spirit and wine list and the good-value menu offers a selection of light bites, sandwiches and pasta if you're peckish. The only downside is that service can be terribly slow.

Grappa

Opposite Fakhr el-Din restaurant, Ibrahim al-Muwaylehi St, Jebel Amman. Open 1900-late

This easy-going trendy bar has an excellent outdoor terrace that's great for warm summer nights. Don't come here for an intense conversation; the music is loud. There's a menu of pizzas and pastas if you get hungry.

La Calle

Rainbow St, Jebel Amman, T06-461 7216. Open 1300-late.

This little place draws a fashionable crowd but manages to have a chilled-out atmosphere nonetheless. The regular evening happy hours seem to keep punters content.

Festivals

Jul-Aug **Jerash Festival of Culture and Arts**, *www.jerash festival.jo.* Jordan's premier festival runs for 1 month with a diverse program of music concerts and theatre. Throughout Aug the festival is held at venues in Amman. Check the website for full schedule details.

Shopping

Handicrafts and souvenirs

Balian, *8 Rainbow St, Jebel Amman, www. armenianceramics.com. Sat-Thu 0900-1700.* This family-run business has been producing beautiful Armenian hand-painted ceramic tiles since 1922. Tiles start from around US$9 each, making them a unique and affordable gift or souvenir.

Homsi Mills, *King Faisal St, Downtown. Sat-Thu 1000-2000.* This is the place to stock up on *zaatar* (a spice mix of thyme, sumac and sesame seeds) and ground Arabic coffee.

Jordan River Designs, *off Rainbow St, Jebel Amman, T06-461 3081, www. jordanriverdesigns.com. Daily 0900-2200.* An absolute joy to browse in, with plenty of gorgeous embroidered and printed textiles on display. All items are made by craftspeople involved in the **Jordan River Foundation**'s (www.jordanriver.jo) income-generating projects.

Wild Jordan Center, *Othman bin Afan St, Jebel Amman, www.wildjordancenter. com. Daily 0900-1700.* A nature shop selling jewellery, soaps, ceramics and textiles based on traditional designs but with a contemporary twist. Many of the products on sale come from the RSCN's nature reserves.

What to do

Cooking classes

Beit Sitti, *16 Muhammad Ali As-Saadi St, Jebel al-Weibdeh, T07-7755 7744, www.beitsitti.com.*

If you fancy putting on a Jordanian feast for your friends when you get back home, Beit Sitti is the place to perfect your cooking skills. The fun and friendly courses take place in the family villa of the Haddad sisters who'll put you through your cooking paces. Highly recommended.

Hammams

Al-Pasha Turkish Bath, *Mahmoud Taha St, Jebel Amman, T07-9550 4471, see Facebook.* This excellent hammam may be modern but it's a faithful replica of a typical Ottoman bathhouse. There are separate bath times for men and women (call for details as times change) but mixed groups can be accommodated if they book ahead. The full works of sauna, scrub and oil massage is carried out by professional male and female therapists and is the perfect antidote to a hard day of sightseeing.

Hiking and nature

Wild Jordan Center, *Othman bin Afan St, Jebel Amman, T06-461 6523, www.rscn.org.jo.* This is the place to come in Amman to find out information and book accommodation, guides and activities at any of Jordan's **Royal Society for the Conservation of Nature** (*RSCN*) run reserves. Extremely well-informed staff can talk you through all your options and help with any queries you have.

Queen Alia International Airport (T06-401 0250, T06-500 2777, www.qaiairport.com), is approximately 35 km south of Amman along the Desert Highway. There are restaurants, cafés and ATMs in both the arrival and departure terminals. This is the main hub for **Royal Jordanian** (airport office T06-479 3170, www.rj.com, open 24/7), which also has an office in Abdali, on King Hussein St (T06-510 0000, open Sat-Thu 0800-1645).

The other airport is **Marka Airport**, officially known as Amman Civil Airport (T06-489 1401, www.jac.jo) in the district of North Marka ('Marka al-Shamaliyeh'), about 4 km northeast of Downtown. It's used for some **Royal Jordanian** flights to and from **Aqaba** and **Israel**.

To/from the airport The **Airport Express** bus (www.sariyahexpress.com) runs from outside the arrivals hall at Queen Alia International Airport to Tabarbour Bus Station (see page 44) every 30 mins between 0830 and 1800 and then hourly 1800-0800 (c45 mins, 3.30JD). **Taxis** run 24/7 from the airport and cost around 22-25JD for the 30-45 min journey to Downtown Amman.

Amman's bus terminals are spread throughout the city. There are 2 main stations: **Wahadat**, for heading south, and **Tabarbour**, which deals with all transport north. There are also a couple of minor bus stations that run services to towns near Amman. The private **Jordan Express Tourist Transportation Company** (JETT) (www.jett.com.jo) bus company offers a/c coach services, operating out of its office in Abdali – a 5-min walk from the King Abdullah Mosque.

Unless you're using JETT's scheduled buses, note that buses and minibuses depart when full and departures tend to be more frequent in the mornings. On Fri services are more sporadic.

Wahadat station (for transport to the south) This awkwardly placed station is a good 5 km from Downtown, 1 block to the west of Middle East Circle. It handles all bus/minibus services heading south from Amman. You can get here by taking a service taxi (No 19 and No 27). A private taxi from Downtown will cost around 2.50JD.

There are regular departures (about once an hour) to: **Ma'an** (3 hrs, 5JD); **Madaba** (45 mins, 90 piastres); **Kerak** (2 hrs, 2.20JD); **Tafila** (2½ hrs, 3.50JD); and **Aqaba** (4½-5 hrs, 7JD). There are less frequent departures (about once every 2 hrs) to **Wadi Musa** (**Petra**) (3 hrs, 3.45JD). You'll probably have to bargain for the ticket prices to Wadi Musa and Aqaba.

In the early morning there are also service taxis heading from here to **Aqaba** (10JD), **Ma'an** (5.50JD) and **Kerak** (3JD).

Tabarbour station (for transport to the north)

A good 7 km north of Downtown, Tabarbour controls all the transport heading north, and is also where to pick up a service taxi to the King Hussein Bridge border crossing with Israel. To get here you can use service taxi No 6. A private taxi from Downtown will cost around 2JD.

There are regular departures (about once an hour) to: **Jerash** (1 hr, 1.10JD); **Irbid** (1½ hrs, 1.50JD); **Suweileh** (25 mins, 30 piastres); and **Deir Alla** (1 hr, 85 piastres). In the morning there are a couple of services to **Ajloun** (1½ hrs, 1.15JD).

Service taxis north to **King Hussein** (**Allenby**) **Bridge** (1 hr, 5JD) leave in the morning from about 0600 and have finished running by mid-afternoon. On Fri and Sat (when the border shuts at 1200) there are only 1 or 2 services running in the early morning. There are also service taxis to **Jerash** and **Irbid**.

Muhajireen station

This station handles transport down to the **Dead Sea**. To get here take service taxi No 35, which passes close to Muhajireen station before heading up to 3rd Circle. There are departures about every hour to **Suweimah** (1 hr, 60 piastres) between 0600 and 1800.

Raghadan bus station

Not to be confused with New Raghadan station, see below, this one is about 3 km east of Downtown. For travellers, it's most useful for regular (about every half hour) buses to **Madaba** (90 piastres).

New Raghadan bus station

This station is just after the Roman theatre on Quraysh St. It operates bus services to nearby towns such as **Salt** and **Madaba**.

JETT bus station

The private **JETT** bus company (T06-566 4141, www.jett.com.jo) has its office/bus station on the northern end of King Hussein St. It operates comfortable a/c coaches to a few useful destinations. You need to buy your ticket the day before you travel.

To get to the **JETT** office, take service taxi No 6. A private taxi to the **JETT** office from Downtown should cost about 1JD.

To **Aqaba** (4½ hrs, 10JD), there are 6 departures daily at 0700, 0900, 1100, 1400, 1800 and 2100. To **Wadi Musa** (**Petra**) (3 hrs, 10JD), there is 1 departure daily at 0630. This bus leaves Petra at 1600 (1700 in summer), making a day trip possible. To the **King Hussein/Allenby Bridge border** (1 hr, 11JD) there's one bus daily at 0715. There is also a daily service to the Dead Sea (1 hr, 10JD, return 15JD), which departs Amman at 0830 and leaves the Dead Sea at 1700 for the return trip.

Taxi (local)

Private taxis are yellow (as opposed to the service taxis, which are white). All taxis have meters.

Don't bother using street names when telling your taxi driver where you want to go; most drivers don't know them. If the driver doesn't know your destination, name the suburb and, if possible, a nearby landmark (a big hotel, the nearest traffic roundabout, etc).

If you're heading to a destination in Downtown, tell your driver you want to go to 'al-Balad'.

ON THE ROAD

Service taxi routes

1 Starts from a small side street off Basman Street and travels past 1st, 2nd and 3rd Circles to 4th Circle.

2 Starts on Basman Street and travels via Omar Bin al-Khattab (Mango) Street up to 2nd Circle.

3 Starts from a small side street off Basman Street and heads up to 3rd and 4th Circles.

4 Starts from Omar al-Khayyam Street, and heads via Jebel al-Weibdeh to Al-Amaneh Circle.

6 Starts from Cinema al-Hussein Street, passing Abdali and JETT bus stations on its way to Interior Circle and Tabarbour bus station.

7 Starts from Cinema al-Hussein Street, passing Abdali bus station and King Abdullah Mosque, to Shmeisani.

19 Starts from Raghadan bus station to Wahadat bus station.

25/26 Starts from Italian Street and runs to Jebel al-Ashrafiyeh (for Abu Darwish Mosque).

27 Starts from Italian Street to Wahadat bus station.

29 Starts from Quraysh Street and heads along Al Quds (Jerusalem) Street, to the southern district of Ras al-Ain.

35 Starts from Quraysh Street and passes within walking distance of the Muhajireen Bus Station and Police Station (for visa extensions), before heading to 3rd Circle.

38 Starts from a small side street off Basman Street going via Prince Mohammad Street to Wadi Saqra Circle, then along Mecca Street and down Abdullah Ghosheh Street.

Short journeys generally come to around 50-70 piastres, while longer journeys within Amman are rarely more than 2-3JD. At late hours of the night most drivers expect at least double the standard fare. Alternatively, both **Careem** (www.careem.com) and **Uber** (www.uber.com) operate in Jordan and taxis can be booked via their apps.

Service taxi (local)

White service taxis (shared taxis) are the best cheap way of getting around, with numbered cabs running along fixed routes (see above) for set fares. All start from various points around Downtown, shuttling back and forth to the surrounding districts of the city, and dropping off or picking up anywhere along the way. Service taxis generally keep running until around 1 or 2 hrs after sunset, though much less frequently.

Jerash

Jerash may play second fiddle to Petra in the south, but only just. From the moment you enter, under the grand arch of Hadrian's gate, this old Greco-Roman city will weave a spell over you. The joy of a visit here is in the superb preservation of detail. Forgotten for centuries and left to be covered by sand and rubble, the graceful minutiae of this ancient metropolis have managed to survive.

Once a thriving centre of commerce, Jerash was one of the great cities of the Decapolis. Today, by sitting in the immense south theatre or taking a stroll through the imposing oval plaza and down the cardo maximus (its stones worn down by the carriage of chariots), you can still sense how splendid this city used to be.

Essential Jerash

Jerash is just 65 km (45 minutes) north of Amman and most people visit on a day trip from either the capital or Madaba.

Getting around

Public transport

There are regular minibuses direct to Jerash from Amman's Tabarbour station. They leave from the parking area in the middle of the station. Most of the bus drivers on this route will automatically stop at the ruins to let people out before heading onto Jerash bus station. Coming into Jerash keep an eye out for Hadrian's Arch (you can't miss it); this is where you want to be dropped off. Even from Jerash bus station, however, it is only a short walk back to the ruins.

Self-drive

If you're driving from Downtown Amman, follow King Hussein Street up past the old Abdali bus station and turn left at the Jamal Abd an-Nasir Interchange. Keep going straight at the Sports City Interchange, following signs for Suweileh, and then turn right at a large roundabout (14 km from the centre, signposted for Jerash) to join the motorway leading north. Take the motorway exit signposted for South Jerash and follow this road to arrive at Hadrian's Triumphal Arch. Adjacent to the arch is the south parking area and ticket office.

At the site

Within Jerash everything is easily accessible on foot with the exception of the Birketein reservoir and theatre, 2 km to the north of the main ruins. To get to this separate site you will need to negotiate a private taxi if you do not have your own transport.

Site information

The site and museum (T02-635 1272) are open daily 0800-1830 in summer, 0800-1600 winter, 0800-1730 April-May, and 0900-1700 during Ramadan. Admission is 10JD for adults; under 15s are free. The ticket office is accessed through the tourist souq attached to the south car park, adjacent to Hadrian's Arch. There are handicraft shops, toilets and a post office also within the souq. Multilingual guides (around 20JD for a two-hour tour, depending on group size) wait for customers just before the southern gate, where the visitor centre is also located.

When to go

If you can, come between March and May when poppies and wildflowers blossom between the marble stones creating a colourful addition to the site. From June to early September, try to visit early as from midday the ruins shimmer and swelter in the summer heat. If you're here in July, the **Jerash Festival of Culture and Arts** holds a series of evening concerts and performances at the site.

Jerash itineraries

With a two-hour visit you can easily visit the main highlights of the ruins but to do the site justice, a full or half day is preferable. If you're really stretched for time, make a beeline up to the Sanctuary of Zeus and south theatre first, then head through the oval plaza and down the cardo maximus (with a stop to admire the nymphaeum) to the monumental stairway. End your quick tour by walking up the stairs to sit atop the Temple of Artemis.

one of the classical world's best-preserved grand cities

Hadrian's Triumphal Arch

Approaching from the south, Hadrian's Triumphal Arch looms up impressively as the first of Jerash's monuments to come into view. Built to commemorate Hadrian's visit in 129-130 CE, it consists of a huge central gateway flanked by two side-portals. At a later date two side pavilions were added, the right-hand one being a reconstruction. Note the intricate carved decoration on the four semi-engaged columns flanking the gateway and side-portals. Unusually this is at the base of the columns, which stand on high pedestals. Above each side-portal is a recessed niche that would have held statues. Just inside the arch are numerous richly decorated architectural fragments laid out on the ground. The triumphal arch stands around half a kilometre to the south of the southern gate of the walled city and is linked to it by a long street. Clearly, the plan was to extend the city limits southwards, but this was never completed.

Hippodrome

Having passed through the gate, on the left, running along most of the length of the street, is the hippodrome. In the context of Jerash it seems huge, and indeed it was capable of holding up to 15,000 spectators, but it is in fact the smallest so far found in the Roman Empire. Exactly when it was built is not known for sure, though excavations by a Polish team point to the mid-second century CE. The hippodrome is now home to the **Roman Army and Chariot Experience Show**, which allows visitors a taste of how a hippodrome would have been used back in the Roman era. See page 60 for details.

Church of Bishop Marianos

A short distance up from Hadrian's Arch, to the right of the street, the foundations of the Church of Bishop Marianos can be seen. Discovered in 1982, only the outline of its plan is visible, although its floors were originally decorated with mosaics. It has been dated to 570 CE and pottery finds indicate that it continued to be used up until the earthquake of 747 CE. A little way beyond the church, also on the right, is a series of shafts with steps leading down to **rock-cut tombs**. These date originally from the Roman period, although they appear to have been reused during the Byzantine era. Further on, steps take the street down to a lower level that leads to the **Jerash Restaurant** (where there are toilets you can use) on your left and the visitor centre on your right. Just beyond these is the entrance to the main site, through the southern gate.

Southern gate

Though considerably smaller, the much restored southern gate mirrors exactly the style of Hadrian's Arch. As a result, it is thought to date from around the same time, although it may be earlier, and Hadrian's Arch a copy of it. Before passing through it, note on the right the well-preserved section of the city walls, with the different stones of the lower and upper courses representing the different stages of construction.

Once through the gate, immediately on your left, excavations have revealed a small area of shops and an underground room containing a huge olive press. These date from the third century CE. The press was made from reused columns and capitals. Deeper excavations uncovered pottery dating from the Middle Bronze Age (c1500 BCE) as well as evidence of construction dating from the second century BCE Hellenistic and first century CE Roman periods.

ON THE ROAD

The Decapolis

Meaning literally 'Ten Cities', the term Decapolis appears to have emerged in the early Roman period. According to Pliny, writing in 77 CE, the 10 cities of the Decapolis were Damascus, Canatha (Qanawat in southern Syria), Scythopolis (Bet Shean in Israel), Hippos (Qala'at al-Hosn in Israel), Dium and Raphana (both of which haven't been identified); and in modern-day Jordan, Philadelphia (Amman), Gadara (Umm Qais), Gerasa (Jerash) and Pella (Tabaqat Fahl). Not all later writers and historians kept to the same list. Writing in the second century CE, the geographer Ptolemy lists a total of 18 cities despite the literal translation of the word.

Although there are plenty of other literary references to the Decapolis, including in the Bible (*Matthew 4; 25, Mark 5; 20, 7; 31*) and Josephus (*Antiquities*), nowhere is its exact nature explained. It appears to have represented a federation or league of some sort, but what level this operated on – political/military, commercial or purely cultural – is not known. Early theories of a close political alliance have given way to ones suggesting a loose commercial relationship. The term may simply have been descriptive of a geographical area encompassing the cities or an administrative label, as perhaps suggested by one inscription found in Turkey detailing the posting of a Roman soldier to the 'Decapolis of Syria'.

Whatever its exact nature, the site clearly expanded and contracted, and its significance may have changed over time. With the administrative reorganization of 106 CE, which led to the creation of the new province of Arabia next to that of Syria, the cities of the Decapolis became divided between the two. Thriving on trade and agriculture, they were prosperous but essentially provincial towns that never played a major role in the affairs of the empire. The delight of Jerash is that it preserves such a complete record of the layout and architecture of a typical Roman city of this period.

From the southern gate the path splits, the left-hand branch running alongside the partly reconstructed supporting wall of the *temenos* (temple enclosure) of the Sanctuary of Zeus and under the steps leading up to it. Under the *temenos* is a long barrel-vaulted hall, inside which are various stone slabs bearing Greek inscriptions. The right-hand branch of the path slopes gently up to the oval plaza. To your right is a sign and path leading up to the museum.

Jerash Archaeological Museum
Admission and opening hours as per Jerash archaeological site.

Up on the hillside to the east of the southern section of the cardo maximus is a small museum which houses a collection of mosaics found at Jerash, along with various architectural fragments and items of pottery, glassware, metalware, coins and jewellery. It can be reached by a path from the oval plaza or by steps leading up from the southern section of the cardo and is well worth a visit if it's open (it doesn't always keep to its official opening hours).

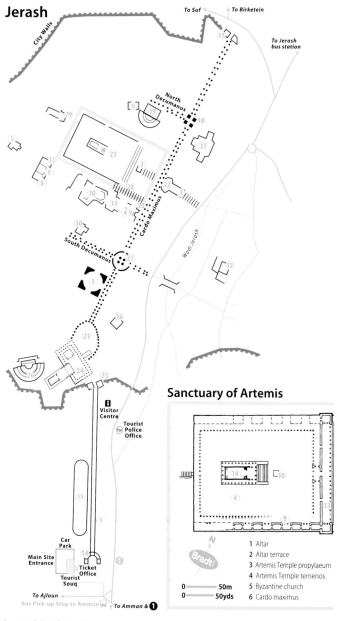

Jerash

City Walls

To Suf
To Birketein
To Jerash bus station

North Decumanus

Cardo Maximus

South Decumanus

Wadi Jerash

Visitor Centre
Tourist Police Office

Car Park
Main Site Entrance
Ticket Office
Tourist Souq

To Ajloun
Bus Pick-up Stop to Amman
To Amman & ❶

Sanctuary of Artemis

1 Altar
2 Altar terrace
3 Artemis Temple propylaeum
4 Artemis Temple temenos
5 Byzantine church
6 Cardo maximus

Bradt

0 — 50m
0 — 50yds

N

Bradt

```
0 ────── 100m
0 ────── 100yds
```

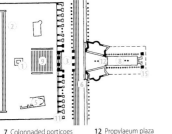

Sanctuary of Zeus

Climbing the stairs leading up into the Sanctuary of Zeus, you pass through the remains of an outer and inner wall. This formed a vaulted *peristyle* (or colonnaded corridor) running around the edge of the large rectangular paved area of the *temenos* (sacred enclosure) that preceded the temple. In front of you, on the slopes of the steep hillside, is a confusion of huge tumbled column sections, stone blocks and other architectural fragments, with the remains of the *cella* (temple inner sanctuary) itself at the top. The sight of such enormous and seemingly immovable chunks of fashioned rock scattered so haphazardly across the hillside is highly evocative – the story of the glory and decline of the Roman Empire captured in stone.

The existing sanctuary and temple dates from 162-166 CE. In the lower *temenos* (to your right as you enter) is a rather confused area of excavations. These have revealed an altar and parts of what is believed to have been an earlier Sanctuary of Zeus dating from the mid-first century CE. Traces of an earlier Hellenistic temple have also been found here, as well as a cave and altar that appear to have served as a pre-Hellenistic temple of some sort. A monumental staircase (its outline still just discernible) led up the hillside to the *cella*, with an upper terrace halfway up which, like the *temenos*, was supported by a long barrel-vaulted chamber. The *cella* occupies a platform at the top of the hill. It was surrounded on all sides by tall columns forming a *peristyle* around it. Three of these columns have been re-erected on the northwest side and one towards the rear of the southeast side.

South theatre

From the Sanctuary of Zeus you can conveniently walk across to the huge south theatre. This is the larger of the two

BACKGROUND

Jerash

The founding of Gerasa and Seleucid rule Despite evidence of settlement dating from the Stone Age onwards, the history of the city really begins during the Hellenistic period. Exactly when it was founded is not known though it appears to have been built on the site of a pre-existing settlement, known by the ancient Semitic name of Garshu which was Hellenized to Gerasa.

For more than a century after Alexander's death in 323 BCE, the region of Jerash was contested by his two main successors, Ptolemy and Seleucus. In 200 BCE the Seleucid emperor Antiochus III defeated the Ptolemids in the battle of Panium and Jerash fell firmly under Seleucid control. What had until then been just a small settlement of Macedonian soldiers from Alexander's armies soon began to develop into a substantial city, named Antiochia ad Chrysorhoam ('Antioch on the Chrysorhoas River'). Its prime function during the Hellenistic period would have been defensive, forming part of a chain of fortified cities protecting Seleucid territory from the nomadic desert tribes to the east. Almost nothing of the city during this period has survived, although it appears to have been centred round the hill on which the temple of Zeus stands.

The golden age – life under the Romans and Byzantines In 64 BCE the Romans, anxious to prevent the Parthians expanding westwards through the disintegrating Seleucid Empire, succeeded in bringing order to the area with the general Pompey establishing the Roman province of Syria. Roman rule brought peace and stability to the region – the famous *Pax Romana* – and Jerash began to flourish. Its success was founded primarily on commerce, standing as it did close to the important north–south trade route between Damascus and the Red Sea. The rich agricultural land surrounding the city likewise brought it prosperity.

From around the middle of the first century CE the Romans began to completely rebuild the city and by 76 CE the walls and basic city plan with its main colonnaded street, the north–south cardo maximus, and two intersecting east–west streets, the southern and northern decumanus, had been completed. In 106 CE Trajan annexed the Nabataean kingdom to the south and Jerash became part of the new Province of Arabia, with Bosra (in present-day Syria) as its capital.

theatres found at Jerash and has been extensively restored to provide a remarkably complete picture of its former glory. It was built in the late first century CE, during the reign of the emperor Domitian (81-96 CE) and was able to seat up to 3000 spectators. The lower half of the tiered semi-circular seating area or *cavea* was built into the hillside while the upper half rises above it. Greek letters can still be seen carved below some of the seats of the lower tiers, apparently part of a numbering system for the most desirable seats.

Two arched entrances lead via vaulted passageways into the semi-circular *orchestra* area between the stage and seating. The front of the stage is elaborately decorated with niches. The backdrop or *scaenae frons* behind was originally two storeys high, and is also elaborately decorated. There are three doorways in it, topped by triangular pediments,

An ambitious programme of building works continued under both Trajan (98-117 CE) and Hadrian (117-138 CE), the latter visiting the city in 129-30 CE. By the early third century CE Jerash boasted lavish temples, theatres, public baths, colonnaded streets, its unique oval plaza and all the other trappings of a thriving provincial Roman city. The Roman Empire, however, was starting to experience its own difficulties, with internal political instability and economic decline being matched externally by the rising Sassanid Persian threat from the east. Under Caracalla (211-217 CE), Jerash was made a colony and renamed Colonia Aurelia Antoniniana, but its most prosperous years were coming to an end.

Under Diocletian (284-304 CE), the city's fortunes were somewhat revived. By the time of Constantine's Edict of Milan in 313 CE, which officially allowed Christians to practise their religion, there was already a sizeable **Christian** community at Jerash. By the middle of the fourth century the city had its own cathedral and was the seat of a bishopric. It was represented at the Council of Seleucia in 359 CE and at the Council of Chaldecon in 451 CE. During the **Byzantine** era, particularly during the reign of Justinian (531-565 CE), many of Jerash's former temples were converted into churches. So far a total of 15 churches have been uncovered, although it is likely that there are more still to be found.

Decline, abandonment and rediscovery In 614 CE the **Sassanids** led by Chosroes II sacked the city and occupied it until 630 CE, when the Byzantines briefly regained control. With the decisive defeat of the forces of Byzantium at the Battle of Yarmouk in 636 CE, Jerash became part of the newly emergent **Islamic Arab Empire**. In 747 CE it was rocked by a serious earthquake and although it continued to be inhabited until the 12th century, the once glorious Roman city remained in ruins. By the 13th century it had been completely abandoned.

The ruins of the Roman city were made known to the outside world in 1806 by a German traveller named Ulrich Seetzen. In 1878 Jerash was resettled by a community of Circassian refugees from Russia, who planted gardens among the ruins and borrowed the Roman stones to build a new town on the eastern edge of the site. Serious excavations at the site began in the 1920s and are still continuing today, with current work focusing on the reconstruction and restoration of the existing monuments.

and between them four semi-circular niches with shell half-domes, each flanked by small columns supporting richly decorated triangular pediments.

The acoustics in the theatre are brilliant and a testament to the structure's clever design. Luckily on most days you can experience this ancient sound system at work yourself thanks to regular (and rather bizarre) performances by a Jordanian bagpiper band decked out in traditional Jordanian military costume, who belt out jaunty numbers such as 'Scotland the Brave' to demonstrate the acoustics. In case you're wondering, the bagpipe tradition is a remnant of the time Jordan was under British Mandate.

Oval plaza

Both the Sanctuary of Zeus and the south theatre make for good vantage points from which to look down on the oval plaza. In architectural terms this is the most distinctive feature of Jerash, being unique to this site. Surrounded by a full complement of re-erected Ionic columns and connecting *architrave*, and still with its original paving, it is very striking.

What has most interested scholars and archaeologists is its unusual oval shape, which was perhaps intended to provide a visual link reconciling the differing axes of the cardo maximus and Sanctuary of Zeus (this is best appreciated when approaching the plaza from the north along the cardo). In the centre is a pedestal, now topped by a column, which would originally have sported a statue. There are also traces of a building which surrounded it, later converted into a water cistern when the plaza area was built over during the late seventh century. The two lines cut into the plaza's paving slabs coming from the north and west conceal buried ceramic water pipes. At two points in the surrounding colonnade on the western side the columns are slightly wider apart and the connecting *architrave* slightly raised; streets led off from these points into the residential and commercial districts of the town.

Cardo maximus

The cardo maximus leads off from the oval plaza in a northeasterly direction. Lined with colonnades, this was Jerash's principal thoroughfare, and was laid out as part of the original Roman city plan of the early first century CE. Along the first stretch, on the left, note how the original Ionic columns are topped by Corinthian capitals. This dates from the late second century CE when the cardo as far as the north tetrapylon was widened. Also along this first stretch, on the right, you can see the small shops which lined the street behind the colonnade. The street is still paved with its original stone slabs.

Agora (Macellum)

A little way along on the left, four much taller columns mark the entrance to what is believed to have been the marketplace. This was first excavated in the 1970s and so identified because of the word *'agora'* found inscribed on one of the taller columns. Behind the four taller columns was a central portico and triple gateway, of which only the right-hand portal survives along with parts of two columns in front. Flanking the central portico and gateway on each side are four small cells, believed to have been shops. In front of the two northernmost shops is an area of fenced-off mosaic floor. Inside the northernmost shop there is another mosaic, though this has been reburied to protect it.

Passing through what remains of the triple gateway, the interior layout consists of a large central octagonal area surrounded by a colonnaded *peristyle*. In the centre there is an elaborate pond/fountain structure in what appears to be the shape of a Byzantine cross. Outside the octagonal *peristyle*, the four corners of the large square compound are marked by semi-circular *exedras* (or wall recesses), with square pilasters at either end of each semi-circle and two free-standing columns in between. It is only in recent years that a Spanish team have completed excavation and reconstruction work here, and their efforts have revealed an impressive and intriguing monument.

South tetrapylon

Returning to the cardo and continuing north, along the next section you can see traces of the ruts left by chariot wheels in the smooth and weathered paving slabs. You arrive next at the intersection of the cardo with the south decumanus, marked by a huge tetrapylon. The four large pedestals can still be seen, but the four granite columns and crowning entablature which would have stood on each of these are now all gone. During the

Byzantine period this junction appears to have been widened out into a circular plaza, the outline of which can still be seen, and surrounded by shops and houses. Turning left (west) at the junction, towards the end of the re-erected line of columns on the right there are the excavated remains of an **Umayyad house**. Turning right (east), the street slopes down before being interrupted abruptly by the site fence and beyond it the modern road. On the far side of the road, however, you can see a completely restored **bridge** that carried the decumanus over the small river running through Jerash, known today as the Wadi Jerash and in ancient times as the Chrysorhoas River (literally 'Golden River').

Nymphaeum

Continuing north along the cardo, you reach on the left the main group of ruins. Just beyond the monumental gateway and stairs leading up to the cathedral complex (see below) is a huge nymphaeum (a public fountain), dating from the late second century CE. You will come across the remains of many nymphaeums if you spend any time exploring Greco-Roman ruins in Jordan, but all consist of just the basic foundations with the rest being left to your imagination. Here at Jerash, however, you can appreciate what is a superbly decorated and remarkably well-preserved example. It consists of a towering recessed semi-circle flanked by side walls. Within the recessed semi-circular area are a series of niches, alternately rectangular and semi-circular, on two levels. The carved decoration on the triangular pediments above the niches of the upper level is particularly beautiful. In front of the nymphaeum is a huge shallow stone basin. Note also the drainage channel immediately below the front wall; the drainage holes in it are decorated with carved fish. The recessed area of the nymphaeum would originally have been covered by a semi-dome.

The cathedral complex

Cathedral The monumental gateway and stairs immediately to the south of the nymphaeum lead up to what became a cathedral during the Byzantine era. The gateway and stairs are believed to have originally formed the *propylaeum* (or monumental entrance) of the second century CE Temple of Dionysus. Four flights of stairs ascend to a small semi-circular niche with a shell-patterned semi-dome. This was a shrine dedicated to the Virgin Mary, probably dating from the fifth century when the cult of the Virgin Mary was gaining in popularity. The shrine is built against what is the eastern retaining wall of the cathedral. Worshippers had to walk around the sides to enter the cathedral via the opposite, western end. Built sometime during the second half of the fourth century CE, it is today completely in ruins, though its basic basilica shape can be made out and three of the columns separating the nave from the side-aisles have been re-erected.

Fountain court Immediately to the west of the cathedral is the fountain court. This was in fact the atrium of the cathedral, but a fountain/pool was built here at a later date, hence the name. The fountain appears to have been the venue for an annual feast celebrating the miracle of Cana, when Jesus reputedly turned water into wine at a marriage. The foundations of the polygon-shaped apse of the Church of St Theodore, which occupies the higher ground to the west, intrudes into the original plan of the atrium/fountain court.

Church of St Theodore On either side of the fountain court stairs lead up to the Church of St Theodore. Built between 494 and 496 CE, this is in better condition, with the base of the apse still intact, and two rows of seven re-erected columns marking the central nave and side-aisles. Like the cathedral, the entrance was via the western end, through a triple doorway which is still intact. Preceding the entrance was a large rectangular atrium. This would have been surrounded by a colonnade, parts of which have been re-erected.

Byzantine churches

To the west of the cathedral complex, reached via a path, is a group of three parallel churches sharing a common atrium. The most northerly (the one nearest you on the right as you approach from St Theodore's) is the **Church of SS Cosmas and Damien**, the middle one the **Church of St John the Baptist** and the southerly one the **Church of St George**. All three were built between 529 and 533 CE. You get a good view down onto them from the path as you approach.

The Church of SS Cosmas and Damien contains Jerash's best-preserved mosaic floor. Covering the central nave, it consists of alternating rows of squares and diamonds containing geometric patterns, inscriptions, animals, birds and portraits of benefactors. Immediately in front of the raised altar area is a large rectangular mosaic inscription in Greek which mentions Bishop Paul as the patron of the church and gives the date 533 CE. On either side of it are panels portraying the two saints Cosmas and Damien, each of them flanked by trees. Cosmas and Damien were twin brothers who gained fame as accomplished doctors who charged nothing for their services. They are thought to have been martyred by Diocletian and subsequently achieved cult status in the Byzantine era. You are able to view the mosaics from the walls of the church, which have been reconstructed to a considerable height. The gate is kept locked to prevent people walking on the mosaics.

The other two churches are open and contain small but impressive fragments of mosaics. The Church of St John the Baptist is interesting in that its layout is cruciform in shape, with semi-circular recesses extending out from the side-aisles to the north and south, and four columns forming a square in the centre.

From the churches you can walk across to the Sanctuary of Artemis, but to fully appreciate this awesome temple, and approach it as worshippers would have done, you should climb up to it from the cardo maximus.

Sarapion Passage

Returning to the fountain court, near the foot of the stairs joining it with the Church of St Theodore, a set of stairs on the left lead north to what is known as the Sarapion Passage, after an inscription dating from 67 CE found here that records its construction by Sarapion, son of Apollonius. At the top of the stairs, the path passes through what were once three gateways in succession, though the middle one is now missing. The passage brings you out on what is known as the **stepped street**, which runs east–west between the cathedral/fountain court complex and the Sanctuary of Artemis. Turning left into it, it climbs to the west, its long-interval steps subsided and leaning this way and that. On the right as you ascend is a long barrel-vaulted chamber built under the *temenos* of the Sanctuary of Artemis.

Sanctuary of Artemis

Returning to the cardo, note the sections of massive, richly decorated *architrave* lined up on the floor; these would once have crowned the colonnade on either side.

A little further to the north, past the nymphaeum, you come to four columns on the left that tower above those of the colonnade, marking the entrance to the Sanctuary of Artemis, the largest and most important temple sanctuary at Jerash. Built during the second century CE, probably between 150 and 180 CE at a time when the city was flourishing and expanding, the temple was dedicated to Artemis, the daughter of Zeus, sister of Apollo and patron goddess of the city. The glory of this sanctuary is not in its individual components, but rather in the way they combine to form a unified complex which would have unfolded before worshippers as they approached via a sacred way, monumental entrance and monumental staircase to arrive finally at the holy of holies, the temple itself.

Propylaeum plaza In fact, the approach to the sanctuary began to the east of the cardo, by the river. Turn right therefore and go as far as you can (the way is blocked by the apse of a Byzantine **church** built here in the sixth century) to get a view of the 'sacred way' as it would have looked. Beyond the church you can see the vague remains of a stairway which ascended from the river. By climbing up onto the apse of the Byzantine church you can get a particularly good view of the whole approach to the inner temple. From the apse of the church a colonnaded square extended to a propylaeum plaza (today a rather jumbled confusion of ruins), which in turn led out onto the cardo.

Monumental stairway and altar terrace After crossing the street and passing through the four taller columns of the colonnade, steps lead up through the **propylaeum gateway** of the complex. The gateway is of massive proportions, with four free-standing columns preceding a huge central portal flanked by smaller side-portals. Above each side-portal is an elaborate niche with a shell-patterned half-dome topped by a richly decorated triangular pediment. Only a fragment of the massive triangular pediment which once crowned the whole gateway remains in place.

Passing through the gateway a monumental stairway ascends in a series of seven flights, each of seven steps interspaced by a terrace, until you reach the **altar terrace**, with the foundations of a large altar in the centre. From here the monumental staircase, thought to have originally been over 100 m across, continues in three further flights up to the *temenos* of the temple itself.

Temple of Artemis A total of 22 Corinthian columns originally formed a colonnade along the top of the stairs, several of which have been re-erected, to your left as you ascend. Beyond this colonnade was a wall pierced by a doorway (of which almost nothing remains) which led through into the *temenos* proper, a large rectangular enclosure measuring 161 m by 121 m and originally surrounded on all sides by colonnades (some of the columns along the south side have been re-erected).

The *temenos* is dominated by the Temple of Artemis itself, described by CS Fisher, who excavated it in the 1930s, as "in all probability the finest single structure ever erected at ancient Gerasa". A modern set of steps lead up onto the platform on which the *cella* of the temple stood. In front of the *cella* itself was a massive portico supported by three rows of towering Corinthian columns, still standing after more than two millennia; six at the front (one of which is missing), followed by four, followed by two.

One of the columns (the middle one of the three along the south side) sways slightly in the wind. On a windy day you can actually see the movement with the naked eye, but even when the wind is very light, if you wedge some coins and a long flat object into the small gap at the base of the column (a favourite trick of tour guides here), you can see the movement.

Inside the *cella* itself, in the wall opposite the entrance, you can see the shrine that would have contained the sacred idol of the goddess Artemis. In front of the Temple of Artemis there are the remains of an altar. Excavations have revealed that this was partly covered over by a ceramics workshop dating from the late Byzantine to early Umayyad period. From the *temenos* it is possible to walk across to the Church of the Bishop Isaiah and north theatre to the north (see below).

North tetrapylon

Returning once again to the cardo and continuing north, you cross a dirt road leading up to the north theatre before arriving at the north tetrapylon, marking the junction of the cardo maximus with the north decumanus. It consists of four solid piers in each corner, with arches spanning the line of each road. This tetrapylon was added after the basic city plan had been laid out, probably during the late second century CE.

West baths

Immediately before the north tetrapylon, to the east of the cardo, are the west baths. Dating from the second century CE, the complex is huge (originally 75 m by 50 m) though now in an advanced state of ruin. Only the north pavilion with its domed roof is standing, along with one of the supporting arches of the central fridgidarium/caldarium complex.

North gate

From the north tetrapylon the cardo continues north for 200 m or so to the north gate of the city. Built in 115 CE during Trajan's reign, this gate is today largely in ruins; if you are hot and tired it can be skipped. More interesting is the last stretch of the cardo itself, which here retains the original colonnade with its Ionic columns and capitals, this part of the cardo (along with the section immediately to the south of the north tetrapylon) never having been widened.

North theatre

Following the north decumanus westwards from the north tetrapylon, you come to the north theatre on your left. This was preceded by a plaza and portico, both of which have been extensively restored. To the right (north side) of the street the plaza is marked by a series of six columns (two consisting of engaged columns and pilasters, and all but one re-erected) standing on huge pedestals and crowned by Corinthian capitals and plain interconnecting *architrave*. To the left, steps lead up to the portico, from where two doorways lead through to the stage of the theatre. The *scaenae frons* (a reconstruction) is much simpler than that of the south theatre. The marble paving decorating the orchestra is a modern reconstruction of the original design. Climbing up from here via the steps between the tiered seating of the *cavea*, you can gain access to a vaulted tunnel which runs beneath the uppermost tiers of seating. Doorways lead out from the tunnel onto the higher ground between the theatre and the Temple of Artemis, while at the eastern end steps lead steeply down to an entrance beside the stage.

Excavation of the north theatre only began in 1982-1983, carried out by British, American and Australian teams and restoration of this monument only finished in the late 1990s. In its original form, the theatre appears to have been completed around 164-165 CE, at which time it was much smaller, really only counting as an *odeon* rather than a full-blown theatre, and probably also serving as a civic centre. During the early third century CE it was enlarged, although it still remained much smaller than its southern counterpart, seating only around half as many spectators.

Sights outside the main ruin complex

Birketein reservoir and theatre Just over 2 km to the north of the main ruins of Jerash is a large reservoir and the remains of a theatre. To get here, head north along the main road running alongside the ruins. Go straight across the first roundabout you come to and then take the left turn signposted to 'Suf'. Very soon after, more or less opposite the north gate of ancient Jerash, bear right where the road forks to arrive at the reservoir and theatre on the left. The name Birketein means literally 'double pool' or 'two pools' and the large rectangular reservoir has a dividing wall sectioning off one portion of it. The reservoir is still in use today, although in summer it gets rather stagnant and smelly.

Above it on the hillside are the remains of a small theatre, today rather worn and eroded, not having undergone restoration or reconstruction work of any sort. Both the reservoir and theatre date from the late second or early third century CE.

East baths The remains of the east baths sit amid the crowded press of the modern town, providing a stark contrast with the ruins within the site. Originally even larger than the west baths, they are today in an advanced state of ruin. The baths have never been closely studied and the date of their construction is not known.

Tourist information

Jerash Visitor Centre

Within the site grounds, adjacent to the southern gate (which gives access to the main body of the ruins), T02-635 1272/4653.
You can pick up a copy of the free **Jordan Tourism Board** map/pamphlet about the site here. There's also a small but nicely presented exhibit of finds from excavations within the site and some excellent explanation boards about the history of Jerash (in English and French).

Tourist Police

Headquarters are outside the site on the main road, nearly directly opposite the visitor centre, T02-635 0670.

Where to stay

Jerash can be easily accessed as a day trip from Amman and the following 2 hotels are among the best in the town.

$$$ Olive Branch Resort

6 km west of Jerash (signposted at turn-off) on the road to Ajloun, T02 634 0555, see Facebook.
Surrounded by forests of Aleppo pine this family-friendly hotel located high up in the hills has stunning views out over the surrounding countryside. The hotel offers comfortable, if a bit generic, rooms fitted with fan, satellite TV and heater. With a tempting swimming pool and lots of easy hikes available in the surrounding area, it's a nice place to relax for a day or 2. Camping (10JD own tent, 12JD resort's tent) is possible in the resort garden and campervans are also welcome. Restaurant, breakfast included.

$$ Hadrian's Gate Hotel

Main Rd, opposite Hadrian's Arch, T02-7779 3907, www.hadriangatehoteljerash.com.
This welcoming, family-run place with 5 rooms, all with a/c, is in a prime position, with a terrace overlooking the ruins. Spotlessly clean, simple rooms come with fan, satellite TV, fridge and electric heater and share 2 large, nicely appointed baths. An excellent choice if you want to savour your time over the ruins, though it's a bit expensive considering the facilities. Breakfast and Wi-Fi included.

Restaurants

There are several cheap and cheerful eateries surrounding the roundabout on the Main Rd, about 700 m further north of the site entrance. All offer a standard selection of Arabic dishes.

$$$ Lebanese House

Main Rd, about 400 m south of the site entrance, T07-7999 9400, see Facebook. Daily 1200-2300.
Extremely popular with locals and visitors alike since it opened in 1977, Lebanese House serves up an excellent and varied menu of Arabic cuisine accompanied by equally excellent customer service. Highly recommended.

Entertainment

The Roman Army and Chariot Experience (RACE), *The Hippodrome, www.jerashchariots.com. Performance times Sat-Mon and Wed-Thu at 1100 and 1400, Fri at 1000, tickets sold at Hippodrome, 12JD, under 12s 2JD (note that during the quietest tourism months of Dec-Jan, the performance is usually cancelled).* If you've ever tried to imagine how these crumbling ruins would have been used in the time of the Romans then this performance is for you. Bringing the hippodrome to life with a 45-min performance involving Roman Legionnaires, a gladiator fight and an impressive chariot race, the RACE project aims to re-create a little piece of Imperial Rome in its proper setting. Children, military-buffs and history lovers will especially enjoy it.

Festivals

Jul-Aug **Jerash Festival of Culture and Arts**, *www.jerash festival.jo*. Jordan's premier annual festival runs from mid-Jul to mid-Aug with a line-up of performances featuring both local and international singers and musicians, as well as theatre events. The Jul scheduled events take place amid Jerash's atmospheric ruins while most of the Aug concerts are held at venues in Amman. Check the website for full schedule details.

Transport

Bus and minibus

Regular buses and minibuses (about every hour) run from Jerash to **Amman**'s Tabarbour station (1 hr, 85 piastres) throughout the day 0600-1700, with only a few operating after sunset. The bus picks up passengers on the right-hand side of the main intersection just south of Hadrian's Arch. Service taxis to **Amman** (2JD) usually hang around the left-hand side of the intersection. A regular taxi from Amman to Jerash should cost around 20-25JD.

From Jerash's bus station there's also regular services to **Ajloun** (40 mins, 60 piastres); **Irbid** (40 mins, 1JD); **Mafraq** (40 mins, 50 piastres); and **Zarqa** (40 mins, 50 piastres). All services depart when full and peter out before nightfall, so make sure you get to the bus station a little beforehand.

Dead Sea
& the King's
Highway

Dead Sea

First named the Dead Sea by the Crusaders, this bizarre natural phenomenon sits at the lowest point on earth (more than 400 m below sea level) and contains the highest salt content in the world; some 10 times greater than the oceans. Apart from a dozen or so halophilic microorganisms that thrive in saline water, the Dead Sea is devoid of all normal marine life. Stretching for more than 80 km, it's a shimmering blaze of blue made all the more dramatic by the austere barren cliffs that rise from its shoreline.

For travellers, a dip in the water here is always a surprise. The surreal sensation of floating without having to make any effort is astounding no matter how many times it's described to you beforehand. These days there are plenty of places where you can take a dip. From the luxurious confines of one of the world-class resorts that surround the northern shore (where you can indulge in all manner of spa treatments as well), to the highly popular Amman Beach Resort, which caters for both local day trippers and travellers on a budget.

Getting around

Given the importance of the Dead Sea as a tourist attraction, public transport facilities are pretty appalling. If you want to explore the area, hiring a car/driver for the day is the best option. A full-day taxi tour of the Dead Sea sites can be arranged from Madaba or Amman and costs around 50-65JD.

Public transport

From Amman, minibuses to Suweimah leave from Muhajireen bus station (one hour, 60 piastres) on a when-full basis meaning you might be in for a long wait. From Suweimah you have to take a taxi to get to the resort beaches and other sights. Getting transport back to Amman from Suweimah can also be problematic.

From the King's Highway, there are buses from Madaba to Suweimah and from Kerak to Safi, but as services really trail off later in the day there's no guarantee that you'll be able to find a service to bring you back. If you're determined to visit the Dead Sea basin by public transport be prepared for long waits and the probability that you're going to have to do some hitching.

If you just want to visit for the obligatory float, the best public transport option is to take the **JETT** bus (www.jett.com.jo) to Amman Beach Resort. This operates daily, leaving the **JETT** station in Amman at 0830 and returning at 1700 (one-way 10JD, return 15JD).

Dead Sea swimming tips

Refrain from shaving at least two days beforehand, check for open wounds on your skin (even the tiniest scratch can sting like crazy) and whatever you do, don't put your head under the water. The pain after getting even the tiniest bit of water into your eyes is indescribable. If you are unfortunate enough for this to happen, head immediately to the freshwater showers and rinse like crazy.

Most digital cameras don't deal well with salt, so try not to handle them without rinsing your hands first. Remember the sun here is fierce – pack your sunblock and bring along a hat. Insect repellent is particularly useful as the flies on the beach can be atrocious.

When to go

Due to the Dead Sea basin being below sea level, this region has its own microclimate. From May to September it can be unbearably hot and humid and the flies around the Dead Sea are a force to be reckoned with. If you can, visit from October to April when the heat is not so fierce.

Time required

In a one-day trip (either self-driving or on a taxi tour) you can easily fit in Lot's Cave Monastery, an hour or so at Amman Beach Resort and a stop at the Dead Sea Panoramic Complex.

The resort area of the Dead Sea stretches along its northern edge. There are luxury spa resorts in abundance to be found here and this is also where you'll find the much less luxurious Amman Beach Resort, which provides day access to the Dead Sea for those on a budget. If you've hired a taxi or have your own car, don't miss the RSCN's Dead Sea Panoramic Complex, which has excellent views over the surrounding area and an informative museum about the Dead Sea.

Dead Sea Panoramic Complex

T07-8248 8880, www.panoramadeadseacomplex.com, daily 0900-2200 winter, 0900-2300 summer, adults 2JD, under 12s 1JD, under 6s free.

Driving from the north on the Dead Sea Highway, pass the resort complexes on your right beside the Dead Sea and take the left-hand turning (signposted 'Panoramic Complex'). Follow this road up the hill until you reach the complex. There is no public transport. If taking a taxi from Madaba or Amman, it's easy to combine a visit here with visits to **Amman Beach Resort**, Hammamat Ma'in and Mount Nebo. The cost would depend on your itinerary and the waiting time at each site.

On the edge of the Zara mountain range, this excellent RSCN complex is just a short drive off the Dead Sea Highway. From here there are incredible views over the surrounding landscape of the Dead Sea basin, particularly beautiful at sunset. There's also the small but well-thought-out Dead Sea Museum (T05-349 1133, daily 0900-1700, free).

Essential Northern Dead Sea

Getting around

Driving from Amman, turn left at 7th Circle (signposted for the airport) and around 6 km afterwards, take the exit signposted for the Dead Sea. Keep following this road, past an exit signposted for Madaba, and then through an almost lunar landscape of barren hills as you begin the descent to the Dead Sea.

Look out for a marker to the right of the road indicating sea level; soon after you'll pass an exit signposted for South Shunah. About 5 km further on is the small village of Al-Rameh, clustered around a junction. Continuing straight on, a further 5 km or so brings you to a T-junction. Turn left here to head to the Dead Sea's resort area.

Fact...

The high salt content of the Dead Sea, around 10 times greater than normal sea water, is due to high evaporation rates. The Dead Sea is fed by the Jordan River, which drains into it from the north, and by the various *wadis* (valleys) and springs that drain into it from the east and west. Being below sea level, the Dead Sea has no outlet and water only leaves the lake by evaporating under the heat of the sun, particularly in the summer when as much as 25 mm is lost every 24 hours, which leaves the salts brought in with the water behind.

BACKGROUND

Dead Sea

Jordan's most striking and unusual topographical feature, the Dead Sea is actually a huge inland lake whose salt-laden waters lie at some 431 m below sea level, making it the lowest point on the earth's surface. About 60,000-70,000 years ago, following the shearing and slumping that formed the **Rift Valley**, rainwater washed large quantities of limestone down from the mountains on either side, partially filling the rift and creating a large freshwater lake (the **Lisan Lake**) which covered the Jordan Valley. About 15,000 years ago, following the end of the last ice age, much of the lake's water evaporated and became saltier, eventually separating into three independent bodies of water: Lake Tiberius (the Sea of Galilee), Bisan Lake (which was located in the Beit She'an Valley in modern-day Israel) and the Dead Sea.

As well as common salt (sodium chloride), the waters of the Dead Sea are rich in magnesium chloride, calcium chloride and potassium chloride, the latter providing the raw material for the industrial production of potash, used in the manufacture of fertilizers, soaps and glass (a huge industry on the southern shore of the lake). These salts, together with a wide range of other trace elements, also give the water (and the mud below) significant therapeutic properties, adding another aspect to the Dead Sea's tourist appeal.

Visiting the complex The main building has a nature shop containing products and crafts produced by the many RSCN projects around Jordan, meeting rooms and the Dead Sea Museum, which gives a thorough overview of the history of the Dead Sea (including some excellent multimedia displays) and the environmental issues that the area faces.

Outside the main building, the landscaped terrace leads to the edge of the cliff where there are sweeping views. To the right is the **Panorama** restaurant (see page 71), where you can have a bite to eat while admiring some of the best vistas in Jordan.

Amman Beach Resort

Resort Area, Dead Sea Highway, T05-356 0800, daily 0900-2000, 25JD, 4-12 years 15JD, under 4s free. Entry fee gives you use of the swimming pools and the beach for the day. There is a small kiosk beside the first swimming pool selling cold drinks, ice cream and snacks as well as nargileh.

If you don't want to pay the prices charged by the resorts to sample the Dead Sea experience and don't fancy the public beaches along the highway (which can be dirty, crowded and not particularly pleasant for females) then this complex is a good compromise. Note that the resort can get crowded on Fridays and Saturdays when families from Amman come here for a day out. This can be loads of fun but if you're after a quieter experience then try to come on a weekday.

Tip...

Women should note that although wearing a swimsuit is acceptable within the resort, local women will go into the water fully clothed and (especially on a Friday and Saturday) you will probably feel more comfortable if you wear a T-shirt/sarong over your bathers.

Visiting the resort The complex is built on a series of terraces. From the car park you enter the main terrace, which comprises a freshwater swimming pool with shaded seating. To your left a shop sells Dead Sea products and there's a large air-conditioned restaurant (see page 72), and to your right are the changing rooms and toilets.

Dead Sea

From behind the swimming pool you walk down to another terrace that holds a smaller swimming pool and then down some more stairs to the actual beach. The beach here is nothing to write home about (gravelly grey sand), but it's clean and has shaded (though rather tatty) picnic table seating available and plenty of freshwater showers. The 'lifeguards' here can also cover you with Dead Sea mud, though females should be warned to watch for wandering hands when they enthusiastically help in applying it.

Ain Zarqa

If you have your own transport, the hot sulphur springs at Ain Zarqa (or 'Zara'), 13 km south from the **Mövenpick Resort and Spa**, are worth a visit. Look out for the distinctive blue fencing by the road on the left; there are usually also several cars parked here, and people offering camel rides. Here, the hot springs of Hammamat Ma'in (see page 89) finally drain into the Dead Sea. At the point where one spring emerges from the rocks, the stream below has been landscaped into three shallow pools with mini-waterfalls between them.

On weekends (Friday and Saturday) it can get very busy. Hot spring soaking here is unfortunately a male-dominated activity; Jordanian women are rarely seen bathing, and if so are always fully clothed. This is a good free option for a float in the Dead Sea, since afterwards you can wash off the salt in the hot springs.

Where to stay
Dead Sea Marriott
Resort & Spa **1**
Kempinski Ishtar Resort
& Resense Spa **2**

Mövenpick Resort
& Zara Spa **3**
Mujib Chalets **4**

ON THE ROAD

One of the world's unique natural features is under threat. For around 15,000 years the flow of water into the Dead Sea was balanced by the high rates of evaporation from its surface, maintaining a stable water level, but in the past 60 or so years this delicate equilibrium has been damaged. During the early 1960s the surface of the Dead Sea was around 395 m below sea level, but today this vast lake sits at 431 m below sea level. The Dead Sea is dying; shrinking by approximately 1 m every year. It has already lost a third of its surface area and the fight is on to find the solution.

The reasons behind this damaging decline are threefold. Although a decrease in annual rainfall has contributed to the lake's contraction, the main reasons are due to human intervention. The ever-expanding potash and mineral extraction industries on both sides of the southern section of the lake have taken a massive toll on the Dead Sea, with industrial solar extraction ponds directly responsible for 30-40% of the total evaporation. While in the northern section, the unchecked ongoing construction of large-scale luxury hotels is also contributing to the demise. But the main reason for the lake's reduction is due to our change in water usage. The Jordan River is the main water source for the Dead Sea, but this resource is now being pumped away before it reaches it, drained away for irrigation and other urban and agricultural usage by both Jordan and Israel. Today only one fifth of the original quantity of water from the river actually gets to the Dead Sea.

So how to maintain the Dead Sea? Both the Jordanian and Israeli governments are huge advocates of the Bahrain Canal Project: a hugely ambitious and highly controversial plan to build a pipeline that would let the water of the Red Sea feed into the Dead Sea. The project has an estimated price tag of between US$5-10 billion. In 2015 Jordan and Israel signed an agreement to begin working on the first stage of the project by building a desalination plant near Aqaba.

However, serious questions have been raised on the unknown environmental impacts of replacing the Jordan River's inflow into the Dead Sea with Red Sea water and the effect it could have on the Red Sea's corals. Environmental agencies, such as EcoPeace Middle East, believe it could have potentially disastrous effects on the delicate ecosystem of the Dead Sea. They are calling instead for the inflow of the Jordan River into the lake to be brought back to its original capacity; a difficult goal considering the fresh water scarcity issues in both Jordan and Israel, but one they believe can be achieved if government stopped focusing its sights on the canal project.

For now the future of this unique area hangs in the balance. Let's hope it can be solved before the Dead Sea disappears forever. For more information on this issue visit the EcoPeace Middle East website, www.ecopeaceme.org.

Bethany Beyond the Jordan (Al Maghtas)

Less than 10 km north of the Dead Sea, Bethany is one of the most significant recent archaeological finds in the Middle East and of paramount importance to the Christian faith; the site where Jesus was baptised by John the Baptist. Set amid a barren landscape, its excavations were only made possible following the 1994 peace treaty with Israel; prior to this the area was a closed military zone. A UNESCO World Heritage Site since 2015, Bethany is a noteworthy addition to any travellers' Jordan itinerary.

Visiting the site

T05-359 0360, T07-9595 8960, www.baptismsite.com, daily 0800–1600 winter, 0800–1800 summer, 12JD, under 12s free. Entry fee includes a local guide and shuttle bus service, which operates around every 30 minutes from the ticket office to the site. Refreshments and toilets are also available at the site.

This desolate plain may not be one of Jordan's most architecturally illustrious attractions, but the site still has plenty of appeal for its historical context and continued reverence by Christian pilgrims. Since archaeologists took over the area, a large number of important finds have been unearthed, including caves, churches, mosaics, wells, baptism pools, and a number of designated walking trails guide you around the various places of interest. One of the principal attractions here is **Elijah's Hill (Tell Mar Elias)**, the place where the prophet Elijah is assumed to have ascended to heaven on a chariot. It contains a reconstructed **arch** from 1999 that stands over the foundations of a church probably dating from the fifth century. Beneath the arch is where the site was given its blessing by the late Pope John Paul II (1920-2005) during his visit in 2000. North of the arch is the Byzantine-era **Rhotorios Monastery**, with a prayer hall and some mosaic remains nearby, and to the west

Essential Bethany Beyond the Jordan

Getting around

At the time of writing there is no bus service to the actual entrance of the site itself; buses will drop you off 5 km away at the Al Maghtas junction, where you will need to either hitch a ride, flag down a taxi or walk the remainder of the way. If you are arriving from Amman, the Dead Sea or Madaba, hotels can often arrange return transport by taxi or as part of a more wide-ranging tour of the region. There is a JETT bus stopping service (via Madaba and Nebo) from Amman to Bethany Sun-Fri, departing the capital at 0800 (15JD).

If you are self-driving, Bethany is around a 50-minute drive from Amman and a 3-4 hour picturesque drive north from Aqaba along the King's Highway. A taxi from Amman costs about 40JD one-way and around 80JD return (including 1-2 hour waiting time while you view the site).

Tip...

Ensure you pack plenty of water as in summer temperatures can reach north of 40°C. Also be aware that the flies around the site can be horrendous.

of the hill is a cave where John the Baptist resided. Other areas of interest include the **River Jordan** itself, where, by giving at least 24 hours' notice, it is possible for visitors who wish to confirm their Christian faith to be baptised in the river by a local priest. Other must-see sites include the **Pilgrims' Station** dating from the Byzantine period, hermits' caves, the **Church of John the Baptist** (as well as a series of more modern places of worship tastefully dotted around) and the site of **Mary the Egyptian**, who repented her life of sin by living out the remaining decades of her life in prayer and fasting close to the area where Jesus was baptised.

A free brochure and map of the site is available from the ticket office; allow approximately 1-3 hours for your visit depending on your interests and the amount of detail you require.

Listings Northern Dead Sea *map p68*

Where to stay

$$$$ Dead Sea Marriott Resort & Spa
Dead Sea Highway, T05-356 0400, www.marriott.com.
This is a mammoth resort featuring a huge range of facilities: several swimming pools, a selection of restaurants, private beach, gym, spa and a whole host of activities. The elegant rooms all come with Wi-Fi access and gorgeous views.

$$$$ Kempinski Ishtar
Dead Sea Highway, T05-356 8888, www.kempinski.com.
The height of luxury, the Kempinski Ishtar has been decked out with a grand Babylonian theme and stretches over a massive area of landscaped gardens planted with palms and olive groves, and sprinkled with hidden waterfalls and pools. The 345 rooms and suites are modern and even the cheaper categories all boast terraces and all the complimentary goodies (Wi-Fi, minibar, etc) that the Kempinski are known for. Families after a luxurious escape should check out the **Ishtar Royal Villas**, which offer direct beach access along with your own personal butler and chauffeur. Restaurants, bars, swimming pools, fitness

centre, private beach and the **Resense Spa** (see page 72).

$$$$ Mövenpick Resort & Spa
Dead Sea Highway, T05-356 1111, www.movenpick.com.
A classy hideaway of traditional stone buildings set around lush gardens and a large sweep of private beach dotted with sunshades. The 346 rooms and suites are stylish and contemporary with the white and neutrals theme creating a bright and breezy feel. Each room boasts all the usual mod cons and most come with balcony. Restaurants, bars, swimming pools, gym and the acclaimed **Zara Spa** (page 72).

Restaurants

$$$ Panorama
Dead Sea Panoramic Complex, T07-8248 8880. Daily 0900-2330 summer, 0900-2200 winter.
The menu here is a well-thought-out range of Arabic dishes that are slightly overpriced. However, you're really paying for the privilege of the views, which from the outdoor terrace truly are 5-star. If you don't want to spend the cash for a full meal, it's a great place for a sunset drink. Alcohol served.

$$ Amman Beach Resort

Dead Sea Highway, T05-356 0800.
Daily 1100-1700.

If you can put up with the tour bus groups who descend on the resort restaurant every day, what you get is actually one of the best lunch buffet offers in Jordan. For 14JD there's a massive table of salads and a selection of hot mains (usually 1 meat, 1 fish and a rice dish). During winter don't miss their dessert selection, which includes a delicious version of *Umm Ali* (an Arabic speciality similar to bread-and-butter pudding).

Festivals

Apr **Dead Sea Ultra Marathon**, *www. runjordan.com*. If you've ever wanted to run to the lowest point on earth then this is the race for you. Held annually in Apr, the Dead Sea Marathon is the main fundraiser for Jordan's Society for the Care of Neurological Patients (SCNP) and is backed by the royal family with HRH Prince Raad bin Zeid as its patron and HM Queen Rania competing in the race in 2003. The race attracts approximately 5000 participants from numerous countries. If you'd like to take part you can download an application form and find out more Information on the website.

What to do

Spas

Resense Spa, *Kempinski Ishtar hotel, Dead Sea Highway, T05-356 8888, www.kempinski. com. Daily 0900-2000.* Indulge yourself in some well-earned pampering among intoxicatingly regal surroundings. The Resense Spa is the height of chic where no expense has been spared. There's a huge range of treatments for both body and face including hammam facilities, traditional Arabian-style massages, and plenty of full scrub, massage and facial combinations utilizing Dead Sea products.

Zara Spa, *Mövenpick hotel, Dead Sea Highway, T05-356 1111, www.movenpick.com. Daily 0830-2030.* For the ultimate in spoiling yourself you'd be hard pressed to beat the award-winning Zara Spa. Non-guests can have full use of all the facilities (Dead Sea pools, hydropool, infinity pool, indoor and outdoor relaxation lounge, beach access and gym) for 40JD per day or for free if they book a spa treatment worth over 100JD. There's a huge range of treatments and the therapists here are top-notch. The Dead Sea Spa Journey is what they're famous for – the package includes a salt scrub, full-body mud mask, Swedish massage and mud facial (250JD) – but there are plenty of other options, ranging from couple's massage (199JD) and healing mud facials (85-90JD) to traditional Turkish hammam (70JD). It's the perfect place to scrub off that layer of travelling dirt and be renewed for the rest of your journey.

Transport

There are services to **Amman**, **Madaba**, and **South Shunah** from **Suweimah**, though they're all pretty irregular and peter out by mid-afternoon. There are always a few taxis hanging about waiting for fares if you do find yourself stuck in Suweimah with no public transport running.

The southern section of the Dead Sea is much less picturesque. The shoreline is given over to banana and tomato fields while the ugly potash factories, right at the southernmost tip, dominate the landscape. For travellers with some time up their sleeves though, there are some gems to discover here. In particular, Mujib Biosphere Reserve is an adventure-enthusiast's dream, while the sustainable tourism project run by Zikra for Popular Learning in Ghor al Mazraa allows you a peek into traditional Jordanian village life.

Mujib Biosphere Reserve
Individual trail fees are stated on page 74 for each hike. Trail fees for the Ibex Trail include a guide; life jackets are provided. The Ibex Trail should be booked at least 24 hrs in advance through the RSCN's Wild Jordan Center in Amman, T06-461 6523 or 79-700 0086, www.rscn.org.jo (see page 43) or through Mujib Biosphere Reserve, T79-720 3888, mujeb.reserve@rscn.org.jo. Guides are not available during Ramadan. Accommodation is available within the reserve (see page 76).

If your idea of fun is hiking through a river and getting soaking wet, then don't miss Mujib Biosphere Reserve. This excellent RSCN reserve offers a couple of hiking trails that combine walking, scrambling and rock climbing; all assured to provide the necessary adrenaline buzz.

Straddling an area of 212 sq km between the King's Highway and the Dead Sea, Mujib Biosphere Reserve holds the proud title of lowest-altitude nature reserve in the world. It incorporates a huge diversity of habitats, with five different vegetation zones and around 550 species of plants. Most of the action takes place along (or in) the river, so a hike here is the perfect antidote to the heat and a great fun-filled activity for anyone who loves the water.

Hiking in the reserve
There are currently two trails within the reserve, ranging from moderate to hard (a 100m zipline has also been added). One, the Siq Trail, can be walked without a guide and

Essential Mujib Biosphere Reserve

Getting around

There is no public transport to Wadi Mujib Bridge. A return taxi from Madaba costs around 50JD (including four-hour waiting time); a little more from Amman. If you're driving, follow the Dead Sea Highway until you reach Wadi Mujib Bridge.

Site information

Wadi Mujib Visitor Centre, right beside Wadi Mujib Bridge, Dead Sea Highway, T07-9720 3888, www.rscn.org.jo. The visitor centre is the starting point for all the hikes.

Hiking tips
- Prepare to get wet: wear a swimsuit under your clothes and walking shoes (hiking sandals are best) that you don't mind getting wet.
- Bring an extra set of clothes to change into after the hike.
- If you're bringing your camera, don't forget a waterproof bag.

BACKGROUND
Mujib Biosphere Reserve

Established in 1987, the Mujib Biosphere Reserve is one of the largest in Jordan. The reserve begins around 18 km downstream from where the King's Highway crosses Wadi Mujib and extends westwards, tumbling from 900 m above sea level to around 400 m below, where it finally emerges from a narrow canyon to drain into the Dead Sea.

North–south it extends for more than 20 km to incorporate a number of other perennial *wadis*. Like Dana Biosphere Reserve to the south, Mujib incorporates a huge diversity of habitats. Rare mammals found here include the golden jackal, grey wolf, Egyptian mongoose, Blandford's fox, honey badger, striped hyena, caracal, Nubian ibex and rock hyrax. Others, such as the leopard and mountain gazelle, once existed here but are now believed to be extinct.

For a time the Nubian ibex seemed condemned to the same fate due to excessive hunting, but a captive breeding programme has so far proved highly successful, and some are now being released into the wild. Mujib is also home to nearly 200 species of birds, including the extremely rare griffin vulture, lesser kestrel and Egyptian vulture.

doesn't need to be pre-booked. Due to the nature of the trails, participants must be aged at least 18 years old and be confident in water. The minimum number of participants for the guided hike is six people. If you're a solo traveller enquire at the RSCN's **Wild Jordan Center** in Amman to see if you can join up with a group.

Siq Trail ⓘ *No guide or advance booking necessary, trail fee: 23JD, open Apr-Oct, 2-3 hrs, rating: moderate.* This trail leads you into the main gorge, enclosed by grand sandstone cliffs. Prepare to get wet as the walk follows the river's course until arriving at a large waterfall. Depending on the season you can be hiking through water up to your waist (or higher) at times and being pulled by the water currents.

Ibex Trail ⓘ *Guided only, trail fee: 23JD, open Nov-Mar, 3-4 hrs, rating: moderate.* This hike begins with a steep and sweaty walk just south of the gorge entrance, providing stunning views of the Dead Sea. The trail levels off to lead towards a ranger station passing interesting rock formations along the way and providing more excellent views over the basin. There is also the chance of seeing some of the reserve's ibex population along the path. The trail then returns to the visitor centre at Wadi Mujib Bridge.

Zikra for Popular Learning
Ghor al Mazraa, on the Dead Sea Highway, see Facebook. Private tours 35JD per person for group of 3 or more; enquire for solo rates. Book at least 48 hrs in advance.

The farming village of Ghor al Mazraa is home to a unique community-tourism initiative where visitors can learn traditional skills still practised in rural Jordan, including cooking, bread-making, crafts and kohl (eyeliner) making. Run in partnership with local residents, all tour fees are used on community development projects within the village. This eye-opening and thoroughly worthy tour provides visitors with an open door into the culture of Jordanian daily life that is otherwise very hard to access. During tomato harvesting season, tours that allow visitors to help with the harvest can be arranged. Local hiking trips are also organized.

Deir Ain Abata (Lot's Cave)
Daily sunrise-sunset, free entry.

Perched on a steep hillside a little to the north of Safi are the ruins of a Byzantine church, built over the cave that pilgrims believe to be the site to which Lot retreated after the destruction of Sodom and Gomorrah. Below the church a circular building houses the aptly named 'Lowest Point on Earth Museum' which does a thorough job of showcasing finds from both excavations at Lot's Cave and the surrounding sites, such as Bab adh-Dhraa.

Lowest Point on Earth Museum *T07-9629 4923 or 03-230 0405, daily 0800-1900 summer, 0800-1600 winter, 2JD.* The interesting exhibits here include fragments of the pulpit and one of the mosaic floors from the Lot's Cave excavations, and some of the clothing textiles (dated between the first and fourth centuries) found during archaeological work at the nearby Khirbat Qayzun cemeteries.

Lot's Cave Monastery From the museum, a narrow road snakes up the mountain to a stairway where 300 steps climb steeply up to the site. Here you can see the remains of a triple-apsed **basilica church.** The outline of the church is clearly visible with two rows of four re-erected columns separating the central nave from the side-aisles. The northern (left-hand) side-aisle, the nave and the raised chancel area in front of the altar all have mosaic floors but these have been covered up for preservation reasons. As a restoration project has added a protective roof to the site, it's hoped that the mosaics will be uncovered at some stage in the future.

The apse at the end of the northern side-aisle contains a doorway that leads through into a **cave**. The lintel of the doorway to the cave is carved with a cross and two rosettes. Interestingly, excavations in the cave have revealed evidence of occupation and burials dating not just from Byzantine and later times, but right back through the Hellenistic, Middle Bronze Age, Early Bronze Age and Neolithic periods.

To the south (right) of the church is a large 7-m-deep **water cistern** in two

Essential Lot's Cave

Getting around

Public transport
Minibuses from Kerak, headed for Safi, pass right outside the signposted turn-off for Lot's Cave. From the turning, it's a 2-km walk to the site. Leave plenty of time for the return trip as minibuses back to Kerak can be thin on the ground in the afternoon.

Self-drive
If you're driving to Lot's Cave (heading south along the Dead Sea Highway), 4 km after passing the huge 'Arab Potash Company' factory, take the left turn signposted 'Cave and Monastery of the prophet Lut (Lot)'. After 1 km, branch off to the left along a rough track (signposted 'Lot's Cave') for approximately 700 m, until you arrive at a parking area below the site.

BACKGROUND

Lot's Cave

Although local people had long known of the existence of this site, it was only officially reported in 1986. The church is depicted on the Madaba Map, but until then the attempts of scholars to locate it had proved fruitless. Excavations began in 1988, sponsored by the British Museum, and the Byzantine basilica church and monastery complex were uncovered in 1991, with finds unearthed during the archaeological work clearly dating the building to between the fifth and seventh centuries CE.

sections, with steps leading down into it and a feeder channel coming from the west. Originally the whole cistern was covered by a roof supported on cross arches. To the north (left) of the church is a **Byzantine tomb**, a **bread oven** and perhaps a later **Abbasid children's tomb**. Beyond these, the foundations of a series of rooms can be seen, thought to be part of the **monastery** complex.

Bab adh-Dhraa (Sodom and Gomorrah)

First identified in the early 1920s by a team led by Melvin Grove Kyle, a Doctor of Divinity at Jerusalem, evidence of a huge Bronze Age settlement, dominated by a fortress and surrounded by ramparts up to 4 m thick in places, have been uncovered by excavations here. Occupied from approximately 3200-1900 BCE, the settlement subsequently appears to have been abruptly abandoned, with no evidence of further occupation until the Byzantine period, a sequence that certainly makes it a viable contender to be the site of Sodom and Gomorrah. The Israelis, of course, have their own contender for this title, on their side of the Dead Sea, a little further south. However, the conclusive identification in recent years of the Byzantine Lot's Cave Monastery gives added weight to the Jordanian site's credibility.

Visiting the site The gate in the site's perimeter fence is kept locked, but it's fairly easy to scramble underneath. Inside, the basic outline of the ramparts can be seen, but otherwise there are only mounds of earth and stone, the excavations long since having been all but erased by the elements. Across the road is the site of a large graveyard dating from the same period, which yielded thousands of flint artefacts and pottery shards. Today absolutely nothing can be seen of this.

Listings Southern Dead Sea

Where to stay

$$$ Mujib Chalets

Wadi Mujib Bridge, Dead Sea Highway, T07-9720 3888 (Wadi Mujib), T06-461 6523 (RSCN Amman), www.rscn.org.jo.

If you're planning on spending some time exploring Mujib Biosphere Reserve, you couldn't get closer than this. Set on the shore of the Dead Sea, these 15 simple chalets provide unimpeded views across the lake, perfect for admiring spectacular sunsets. They're spartan for the price, but are kept spotlessly clean and all come with their own private terrace and a/c (single 80JD, double 90JD, triple 105JD). Bathrooms are shared and located nearby and a restaurant serves meals (lunch/dinner 14JD). Room rate includes breakfast and conservation fee.

Transport

Services between **Aqaba** and **Kerak** all stop in **Safi** on the southern edge of the Dead Sea. Unfortunately there is no public transport from Safi up the Dead Sea Highway. From here you'd have to hitch.

King's
Highway

Ancient and ruggedly beautiful, the King's Highway stretches from Amman to Petra, snaking through some of Jordan's most spectacular scenery. Running along the eastern edges of the Great Rift Valley, descending precipitously every so often to cross the deep wadis that drain into the Dead Sea from the east, this road has seen empires rise and fall. Moses led the Israelites towards the Promised Land along here, the Nabataeans were able to grow rich by controlling the caravan trade on this route, and during the Roman period this causeway was used as part of their Via Nova Traiana, linking Damascus with the Red Sea.

Today the King's Highway is a quiet alternative to the Desert Highway and boasts an array of fascinating sites. There's Madaba with its stunning mosaics; Mount Nebo with its sumptuous views out over the Dead Sea; the hot springs at Hammamat Ma'in; Herod's mountain-top stronghold at eerily beautiful Mukawir (ancient Machaerus); the rambling ruins and well-preserved mosaics at the World Heritage Site of Umm ar-Rasas; the mighty Crusader castles of Kerak and Shobak; and the breathtaking Dana Biosphere Reserve, to name but a few. There are also several points at which you can descend from the King's Highway to the Dead Sea – a special experience in itself.

Getting around

From Madaba there are fairly regular minibuses as far as Dhiban, and from Kerak you can pick up minibuses to Tafila (from where you can also get onward transport to Qadisiyyeh, a couple of kilometres from Dana Village). The section of road between Dhiban and Ariha, across the deep Wadi Mujib, though, is a public transport black hole.

Best places to stay

Mosaic City Hotel, see page 85
Mariam Hotel, see page 86
Dana Guest House, see page 100
Feynan Ecolodge, see page 101

Best restaurants

Haret Jdoudna, see page 86
Hekayet Nebo, see page 86

If you're going to hire a car/taxi once on your Jordan trip, this is the time to do it. A taxi for a full day of sightseeing along the King's Highway starting from Madaba and finishing at Petra (with three or four stops) will cost around 100JD.

Alternatively, Madaba's **Black Iris Hotel** (see page 85), runs shuttle services that leave Madaba at 1000, with stops at Kerak and the lookout point over Wadi Mujib, before finishing at Petra. Tickets cost 20JD.

Madaba

famed mosaics and remnants of Byzantine glory

Quieter and prettier than Amman, Madaba – named capital of Arab tourism in 2022 by the World Tourism Organisation (WTO) – is fast becoming a favourite base for travellers who want to explore the north of the country without staying in the capital. The Dead Sea and sites along the King's Highway, the Jordan Valley and even Jerash are within easy day trip reach of the town, while the excellent standard of accommodation and good eating options here make it a great place to rest up for a few days.

Madaba may be small but it boasts some of the best-preserved and most beautiful Byzantine-era mosaics in the Middle East. During this period the town flourished to become one of the most important centres of Christianity to the east of the Jordan River, and today it still has a large Greek Orthodox community. The most famous relic of this period is the 'Madaba Map', interred in the floor of St George's Church, but there are many other examples of fine mosaic work to be seen in the town.

St George's Church and the Madaba Map
King Talal St, Mon-Thu and Sat 0800-1800, Fri 0900-1800, Sun 1030-1800, 1JD. The church is also open to all visitors for Mass every Sun 0700-1000. Note that the Madaba Map is kept covered up during Mass.

The Greek Orthodox St George's Church was built in 1896 over the foundations of an earlier Byzantine church. The full extent of the famous Madaba Map, parts of which had been

ON THE ROAD

The world's oldest continuously used communication route, the King's Highway, has been traversed for millennia. Nearly as old as the land it passes through, it finds mention in the Old Testament when Moses, leading the Israelites towards the Promised Land, requests free passage from the king of the Edomites and the king of the Amorites (*Numbers 20; 14-17, 21; 22*). Though the origins of this road's name remain obscure, it may stem from an even earlier biblical account, when an alliance of kings advanced along this path on their way into battle with the sinful cities of Sodom and Gomorrah (*Genesis 14*).

It was a vital trading route, so any upstart empire worth its salt recognized the significance of controlling this road, which linked the biblical seaport of Ezion-Geber (present-day Aqaba) on the Red Sea with Syria to the north. It was by taxing (and plundering) the trade along this path that the wily Nabataeans acquired the fantastic riches that enabled them to build the city of Petra. The Romans may have named it part of Trajan's grand Via Nova Traiana, and the Muslim Arabs may have modified its ancient biblical name, referring to the road as the Tariq as-Sultani (the 'Sultan's Road'), but the importance of this route remained unchanged as empires rose and fell. To hold control over the King's Highway was to hold control over the region.

Today the King's Highway is a sleepy shadow of its former self. A road that winds and dips through a staggeringly beautiful landscape, it is scattered with the remnants and ruins of earlier empires' glories, which attest to its once-vital role.

traced by a local priest in 1890, was only revealed when the floor tiles of the new church were being laid. The map originally depicted an area extending from the Egyptian delta in the south to the Levantine coast in the north, including the cities of Tyre and Sidon in modern-day Lebanon. Although only a quarter of the original has survived, this includes most of the all-important city of Jerusalem as well as the Jordan River flowing into the Dead Sea and sections of Sinai. As such, it still represents perhaps the most significant mosaic discovery in the whole of the Middle East, and the historical and geographical information it contains continues to fuel research and debate to this day.

Visiting the map   The glory of the map is in the detail, and in the remarkable geographical accuracy it achieves. Essentially a document of biblical geography, it was most probably intended as a guide for religious pilgrims to the Holy Land. A total of 157 captions in Greek identify important religious sites as well as indicating the 12 tribes of Israel. The map is oriented to the east, with the Jordan River and Dead Sea forming the central axis. The highlight is the detailed bird's-eye view plan of the Holy City of Jerusalem. The walls and gates of the city, its cardo maximus running north–south (left to right on the map) through the centre, and its principal buildings are all clearly discernible, including the Constantinian complex of the Holy Sepulchre halfway down the cardo and two large basilica churches towards its southern end. The detail elsewhere is just as meticulous: fish swimming in the Jordan River, two boats on the Dead Sea, palm trees at the oasis of Jericho, with tributary rivers and mountains, are all displayed.

Madaba Archaeological Park

Abu Bakr as Siddeeq St, Sat-Thu 0800-1900 summer, 0800-1700 winter, Fri 1000-1600, 3JD (combined ticket covering the Archaeological Park, Madaba Museum and the Church of the Apostles).

Included in the Madaba Archaeological Park are the Church of the Virgin and Hippolytus Hall, the Church of the Prophet Elias, and a section of the Roman decumanus. Entering the 'park', an impressive selection of mosaics discovered in the Madaba region are displayed: from the first century BCE Herodian fortress at Machaerus (the oldest in Jordan); the upper mosaic Church of Massuh (3 km east of Hisban, sixth century); the Acropolis Church at Ma'in (early eighth century); and the hall of the Seasons in Madaba (sixth century).

The highlight is the Church of the Virgin and the surviving parts of the Hippolytus Hall, housed within a large modern structure with walkways around the inside.

Church of the Virgin Dating from the late sixth century CE, the church was built over a late-second- to early-third-century CE Roman temple to which a further hall had been added in the early sixth century CE (the Hippolytus Hall). There's a beautiful mosaic covering the floor of the circular central nave of the Church of the Virgin, which corresponds with the platform of the Roman temple. The floral designs around the outer border of the mosaic date from the late sixth to early seventh century CE, while the central square enclosing a circular medallion was added later, during the early Umayyad period by the then bishop of Madaba, Theophane. The inscription in the centre reads: "If you want to look at Mary, virginal Mother of God, and to Christ whom she generated, Universal King, only Son of the only God, purify mind, flesh and works! May you purify with prayer the people of God." The date accompanying the inscription is incomplete, but is believed to correspond with 662 CE.

Hippolytus Hall The hall contains a beautifully preserved rectangular mosaic, one part of which formed the floor of a private house until it was fully excavated in 1982. The border consists of acanthus scrolls and hunting scenes, with personifications of the Four Seasons at each corner. Along the east wall, outside the border of the main mosaic, the cities of Rome, Gregoria and Madaba are personified as three Tyches, each seated on a throne and holding a cross on a staff. To one side of them is a small medallion with two sandals surrounded

Essential Madaba

Public transport

Madaba is a 20-minute taxi ride (c20JD) from Queen Alia Airport. Madaba's bus station is a chaotic yard just off the King's Highway, about 1 km from the centre of town. Buses and minibuses from Amman's Wahadat and Raghadan stations pull in regularly throughout the day. A taxi from the bus station to the centre should cost around 1-2JD.

Self-drive

If you're driving, the easiest way to join the King's Highway from Amman is to head west along Zahran Street and, around 8 km from Downtown, turn left at 7th Circle to head south (signposted for the airport). Around 6 km further on, take the exit signposted for the Dead Sea. After another 7 km, take the exit signposted for Madaba. You are now on a small, relatively quiet road that leads directly to Madaba, 13 km further on.

by four birds, while on the other side are monsters and birds. The central section of the mosaic consists of three panels. The bottom one contains flowers and birds. The central one contains characters from the Greek tragedy of Phaedra and Hippolytus (as recounted in Euripides' *Hippolytus*, hence the hall's name), although parts of it were destroyed when the hall was divided into two rooms at a later date. The top one contains various scenes from the legends of Adonis and Aphrodite, who are seated on a throne and surrounded by a number of Cupids and Graces.

Decumanus The Church of the Virgin and the Hippolytus Hall borders the Roman period decumanus, a section of which has been excavated revealing the large flagstones with which it was paved. Running roughly east–west, this would have originally linked two of the city's gates and would have been lined by a colonnade.

Church of the Prophet Elias On the other side of the decumanus is the Church of the Prophet Elias. The church was first discovered in 1897 and a fragment of mosaic flooring was uncovered near the steps leading to the presbytery that included a dedicatory inscription referring to the Prophet Elias and giving a date for the church of 607–608 CE.

Madaba Institute for Mosaic Art and Restoration
Abu bakr as Siddeeq St, T05-324 0723, www.mimarjordan.org, Sun–Thu 0800-1500.

Next door to the archaeological park is the Madaba Institute for Mosaic Art and Restoration, a joint Italian-Jordanian project to train people in the art of making and conserving mosaics. Visitors with a keen interest in the process can arrange a visit and tour of the workshops by booking with the administration office here.

Madaba

To Amman via Tell Hisban

Al-Quds St

To Mount Nebo

Yarmouk St

Al-Quds St

Palestine St

Tourist Police Station

Al-Malik Hussein St

St George's Virgin Mary Mosaic & Handicrafts

Burnt Palace & Church of El Khadir

Abu Bakr as Siddeeq

To Main Bus Station (150 m) & Amman (direct)

Al-Malik Abdullah St

Talal St

Madaba Archaeological Park

Madaba Institute for Mosaic Art & Restoration

P

Dar al-Saraya

Shrine of the Beheading of St John the Baptist

Balqa St

To Hammamat Ma'in

Madaba Regional Archaeological Museum

Rocks bin Zayd al Uzayzy St

King's Highway

To Umm ar-Rasas

N

Church of the Apostles

Bradt

0 ___ 100m
0 ___ 100yds

To Kerak

Where to stay
Black Iris 1
Mariam 2
Mosaic City 3

Restaurants
Adonis 1
Ayola 2
Bawabit 3
Haret Jdoudna 4

BACKGROUND

Madaba

The earliest evidence of settlement at Madaba goes back to the late **Early Bronze Age** period (around 3100 BCE). The town finds mention in the Bible on several occasions, where it is referred to as *Medeba*. It is first recorded as being among the cities of **Moab** conquered by the Israelites.

In 106 CE Madaba became part of the **Roman** province of Arabia and under Roman rule developed into a small but significant provincial town laid out along typical Roman lines with colonnaded streets, baths and temples. It soon became a focus of Christian activity and during the persecution of Christians carried out by Diocletian (284-305 CE), several of Madaba's inhabitants were martyred.

Throughout the **Byzantine** period Madaba continued to prosper, becoming the seat of a bishopric by the mid-fifth century, as mentioned in the Acts of the Council of Chalcedon of 451 CE. The height of the town's prosperity came during the rule of Justinian (527-565 CE) and it was from this period onwards that all the great mosaics were laid.

The present town dates from the 1880s, when Christians from the nearby town of Kerak were settled here following disturbances between the Christian and Muslim inhabitants.

Burnt Palace
Hussein bin Ali St, Sat-Thu 0800-1900 summer, 0800-1700 winter, free.

When part of this complex was first uncovered in 1905, it was thought to be a church. However, excavations since 1985 have confirmed that it was a lavish complex, probably secular in nature, dating from the late sixth to early seventh century. It was destroyed by fire (hence the name), perhaps as a result of the earthquake around 749 CE.

The palace consists of a central courtyard surrounded by rooms with walkways allowing you to view the mosaics. Preserved in the first room is a mosaic of the bust of the goddess Tyche (complete), along with a fragment of a personification of one of the seasons. The second room contains a mosaic of scale patterns framed within a plaited border. On the west side is a long room containing three square mosaic panels with geometric designs. Between the northernmost and central panel is a strip of mosaic depicting a lion attacking a bull. The southernmost panel actually belongs to a separate room.

To the west again of these mosaics is a further complex of rooms, and also a deep water cistern. It's in the large hall on the east side of the central courtyard that the most impressive mosaic has been uncovered. It consists of a broad border decorated with birds, fish, animals, plants and trees. Within this is a large panel depicting pastoral and hunting scenes, each encircled within an acanthus scroll.

On the south side of the Burnt Palace, another section of the Roman decumanus has been excavated (this would have joined up with the section across the road in the Archaeological Park).

Church of El Khadir

Immediately to the southeast of the Burnt Palace is the sixth-century Church of El Khadir (literally Martyrs' Church), enclosed under a protective roof. The semi-circular apse and altar area are clearly discernible, while two rows of Corinthian columns separate the nave from the side-aisles.

The mosaic floors of the church suffered damage from iconoclasts in the eighth century but despite this, much of the intricate mosaic decoration, depicting hunting and pastoral scenes, still survives.

Dar al-Saraya

Talal St, T07-9008 3436, see Facebook.

Beautifully restored in recent years, Dar al-Saraya functioned as Madaba's administrative centre during the Ottoman period and later served as the British administration's headquarters in 1922. The planned new hotel and restaurant should hopefully be open by the time you read this.

Shrine of the beheading of St John the Baptist

Talal St, daily 0900-1900 summer, 0900-1700 winter, 1JD, under 12s free.

Dating from 1913, this Catholic Church was built on top of the town's ancient acropolis and, after careful excavations, the warren of rooms under the building have been opened up for tourism.

On entry into the church compound, a small museum displays interesting black-and-white photographs of Madaba from the early years of the 20th century.

Acropolis A small door leads under the church and down a staircase to a Moabite-era well, thought to be around 3000 years old, which would have been the main water source for the acropolis. It still draws water today. After walking back up the staircase, there are six small vaulted stone-cut rooms, a tunnel and some fragments of Byzantine mosaic, which were all once part of earlier buildings on this site. A set of stairs then brings you into the church itself.

Church The present-day church holds some lovely paintings and stained-glass window details but the real attraction for visitors is climbing up to the bell tower, which is the highest point in Madaba. Walking up the narrow metal stairways to the top, ducking between the bells and bell ropes along the way, brings you to a lookout platform with panoramic views across the town.

Madaba Regional Archaeological Museum

Off Balqa St, www.madabamuseum.org, Sat-Thu 0900-1700, 3JD (combined ticket covering the Archaeological Park, Madaba Regional Archaeological Museum and the Church of the Apostles).

The Madaba Regional Archaeological Museum hosts an eclectic collection displayed over a series of interconnecting courtyards scattered with column capitals and mosaic pieces. There is very little in the way of information but the location, with views over Madaba's rooftops from the courtyards, and higgledy-piggledy nature of the exhibits has a certain charm.

One room is built around the mosaic floor of a sixth-century house, with panels depicting a Bacchic scene, with a lute-playing satyr still discernible, and a scene containing Achilles and Patroclus. Two other rooms also contain mosaic floors; one large room given over to floral and geometric designs and a small one with a central medallion of a ram nibbling at a tree. The dusty room that holds the folklore section includes traditional jewellery, costumes and headdresses, while the archaeology section contains a range of artefacts including 'ballistic missiles' (Byzantine slingshot stones) and a copy of the Mesha Stele.

Church of the Apostles

Rocks bin Zayd al Uzayzy St, Sat-Thu 0800-1900 summer, 0800-1700 winter, Fri 1000-1600, 3JD (combined ticket covering the Archaeological Park, Madaba Regional Archaeological Museum and the Church of the Apostles).

Located on the southern edge of the town, the Church of the Apostles is enclosed by a modern protective building. First discovered in 1902, an inscription in a room at the eastern end of the church (now gone) identified the church as having been dedicated to the Apostles and built in 578 CE.

The nave is covered by a large mosaic consisting of a border of acanthus leaves enclosing a geometric pattern of birds and plants. In the centre is a medallion with a personification of the sea represented as a woman, Thetis, emerging from the waves and surrounded by fish and sea monsters. The inscription around the edge of the medallion reads: "O Lord God who has made the heavens and earth, give life to Anastasius, to Thomas, to Theodore and to Salamanios, the mosaicist".

Listings Madaba *map p82*

Tourist information

Madaba Visitor Centre
Abu Bakr as Siddeeq St, on the same road as Madaba Archaeological Park, T05-325 3097, T07-9652 5011. Sat-Thu 0800-1600.
One room displays information boards about Madaba's history. If the centre is staffed (it's sometimes unmanned) you can also pick up a range of free pamphlets and maps on Madaba and nearby sites.

Tourist Police
Based in a little shack on Yarmouk St, just before the entrance to St George's Church.

Where to stay

There are no luxury hotels in town, but the mid-range options are some of the best in Jordan and offer good value. All hotels below include breakfast and Wi-Fi.

$$$ Mosaic City
Yarmouk St, T05-325 1313, www.mosaiccityhotel.com.
With 50 spacious rooms, this hotel has tasteful neutral decor (a/c, satellite TV, fridge) with lovely modern baths. Ask for one of the rooms on the 2nd floor, which come with private balcony. The gracious owners are helpful and efficient and despite being on the main street it manages to be wonderfully quiet inside, guaranteeing a restful sleep.

$$ Black Iris
Off Al-Mouhafada Circle, T05-325 0171, www.blackirishotel.com.
This sociable backpacker favourite has plenty

of cosy appeal and the friendly manager Diana goes out of her way to help. The 40 rooms have been spruced up in recent years and are looking spiffy with new paint, carpets and comfortable new mattresses on the beds. A double is 35JD.

$$ Mariam
Aisha Um al-Mu'meneen St, T05-325 1529, www.mariamhotel.com.
The Mariam's reputation as a homely traveller haven is well deserved. Charl, the owner, is a fount of knowledge about the local area and ready to help with any query. The reason for this hotel's popularity is not just for the 57 decent-sized rooms (a/c, satellite TV, some with balcony) and comfortable beds, or for the courtyard swimming pool (a welcome retreat in the summer), but for the genuine welcome you get here. They also offer some of the best taxi fares for full- and half-day trips in Jordan. A double is 42JD. Recommended.

Restaurants

For cheap eats take a walk down Yarmouk St, which has some great little falafel and shawarma places.

$$$ Haret Jdoudna
Talal St, T05-324 8650, www.haretjdoudna. com. Daily 1100-2400.
This atmospheric restaurant was where Bill Clinton chose to eat when he sauntered into town. It certainly has a picturesque setting in a restored Ottoman house centred round a tranquil courtyard where you can dine under a leafy fig tree. There's a tasty selection of local specialities on offer, from the wonderfully tangy *treedah* (a mousakka-like dish of mince and aubergines topped with lashings of yoghurt) to the *sawani* dishes (such as delicately spiced chicken and potatoes oven-baked in the serving tray). Alcohol is served.

$$ Adonis
Balqa St, T07-7733 8448. Daily 1000-2200.
Particularly popular with Ammanis out for an evening meal on the weekends, Adonis serves up a decent range of Middle Eastern dishes with good-value mezze (around 30JD for 2 people) and lots of meaty grills. There's also an excellent wine list.

$$ Bawabit
Talal St, T05-324 0335, www. bawabitmadaba.com. Daily 1000-2345.
Satisfying local and international diners since 2007, Bawabit, with its floor-to-ceiling windows looking down onto St George's Church, is a terrific place for a lunch (or dinner) stop in between sightseeing. The menu is varied and includes a good mix of Arabic favourites such as *mansaf* and international cuisine including steak, pasta, grills, spaghetti bolognese and burgers. The bar is well stocked with a range of alcoholic beverages including local wine and beer, cocktails and spirits, and *nargileh* is also available; all backed up by the excellent service. Highly recommended.

$$ Hekayet Nebo Restaurant
Prince Hussan St (5 km west of Madaba, on the road to Mount Nebo), T05-324 1119 , T07-9156 5752. Open 1000-1700.
If you're heading out to Mount Nebo this large restaurant, upstairs from the La Storia Museum complex, is a fine place to stop for lunch. The huge outdoor terrace has panoramic views over the rolling countryside and the menu delivers on tasty mezze and salads and Arabic mains including less well-known Jordanian dishes such as chicken *sajieh*. Alcohol served (beer, wine and arak).

$ Ayola
Talal St.
A travellers' favourite, the Ayola is a top spot for *nargileh* smoking. They also offer a range of cheap sandwiches and burgers (1-2JD) with lots of different fillings. Fresh juice costs

1-1.5JD and the beer here is considerably cheaper than anywhere else in town.

Shopping

Most of Madaba's shops are on, or around, Hussein bin Ali St. Predictably, mosaics are in abundance here and there's a vast selection from cheap and cheerful to beautiful high-quality pieces.

Haret Jdoudna, *Talal St, www.haretjdoudna. com, daily 1215-0030*. Inside the restaurant (see opposite) there's a boutique-style shop selling gifts and local handicrafts. Quality is high but so are the prices.

Virgin Mary Mosaic & Handicrafts, *Hussein bin Ali St, T05-324 8650, T07-7765 5217, see Facebook*. A small, friendly store run by female mosaic artist Khuloud Abu Daqar, who is passionate about Madaba's mosaic heritage. Khuloud also runs mosaic-making workshops.

Bus and microbus

Madaba's bus station is about 1 km from the centre of town, just off the King's Highway. Buses leave to **Amman** (Wahadat station and Raghadan station) roughly every 30 mins throughout the day (1-1½ hrs depending on traffic, 90 piastres). The last bus leaves between 2000 and 2100.

Fairly regular minibuses operate to **Dhiban** (1 hr, 1JD). For **Mukawir** (Machaerus) there are around 5 minibuses daily (40 mins, 1JD), but these only take you to Mukawir town and not direct to the ruins. From Mukawir town you'll have to hire a taxi or bargain with your minibus driver to take you the extra distance (most minibus drivers are more than willing to do this). For **Umm ar-Rasas** (30 mins), there are a couple of minibuses that leave the bus station early each morning.

Mount Nebo (Siyagha) and around

historic holy site where Moses saw the Promised Land

On Mount Nebo, 8 km to the west of Madaba, is the Memorial Church of Moses, in which are preserved some beautiful mosaics, now cared for by Franciscan monks. The mosaics themselves are reason enough to visit, however the hilltop on which they are situated offers truly stunning views across the Jordan River and Dead Sea towards the Palestinian West Bank territory (biblical Judaea and Samaria).

Mount Nebo consists of several peaks, the highest reaching 800 m above sea level (if you take into account the altitude of the Dead Sea, you're looking at around 1200 m). The Memorial of Moses is on a peak known as Siyagha, while at Khirbet Mukhayyat (identified as the ancient town of Nebo) are the Church of St George and the Church of SS Lot and Procopius.

One of Jordan's principal holy sites, resonating with Christians, Jews and Muslims alike, Mount Nebo remains an

Tip...

The area around Madaba holds enough sights to keep you occupied for a good few days but if you've got your own vehicle or charter a taxi, you could fit four sites into a full day's tour. Travellers should note that, as well as the sites listed on page 88, if you've got your own transport Madaba also makes a good base for visiting the Dead Sea and Jerash. Madaba taxi drivers also tend to quote slightly less for full- and half-day fares than their compatriots in Amman.

Essential Mount Nebo

Self-drive

Head northwest out of Madaba along Palestine Street, following the signs for Mount Nebo. The road passes through the small village of Faissaliyeh (4 km) before arriving, after another 2 km, at the monastery and Memorial of Moses on the right.

Taxi

A private taxi from Madaba will cost in the region of 10JD for the return trip, including waiting time.

important monastic refuge and pilgrimage site to this day. In March 2000 Pope John Paul II visited and planted an olive tree while in 2009 Pope Benedict XVI, like Moses, spied Jerusalem and remarked that 'the ancient tradition of pilgrimage to the holy places also reminds us of the inseparable bond between the Church and the Jewish people'.

Visiting Mount Nebo

Daily 0800-1800 summer, 0800-1600 winter, 3JD. Shoulders and knees should be covered when entering the site and smoking and eating is not allowed.

From the car park and entrance gate, a short stroll up the hill brings you to a modern sculpture built to mark the millennium and bearing the legend "Unus Deus, Pater Omnium, Super Omnes" ("One God, Father of all, above all others").

From here a large courtyard opens out. The small site **museum** ⓘ *entry included in Mt Nebo ticket*, is nearby and contains excellent information panels documenting the history and biblical significance of Mount Nebo.

There is a pathway leading from the museum to a **viewing terrace** where there are stunning views out over the Dead Sea and beyond to the West Bank. On a clear day, in the morning before the haze has settled, it's possible to see Jerusalem from here.

By the terrace is a modern sculpture portraying a snake wrapped around a cross. Known as the **serpentine cross** it represents the bronze snake that Moses carried into the desert with him to protect the Israelites from the plague and the cross that Jesus was crucified upon. Just behind the viewing terrace are the grounds of the Memorial Church of Moses.

Memorial Church of Moses The Memorial Church of Moses ⓘ *entry included in Mt Nebo ticket*, was originally built in the second half of the fourth century as a small triapsidal church with a vestibule in front and two funeral chapels on either side, although little of this remains today. Various additions over the years culminated in the construction of the full three-aisled basilica incorporating the earlier church (in the second half of the sixth century, in the time of the Bishop Sergius of Madaba). In the meantime the monastery surrounding it steadily grew in size, giving rise to a substantial complex which would have been able to accommodate several hundred monks and pilgrims at its height.

Entering the main church, to the left (north) of the central nave, is a walkway overlooking an earlier baptistry (the 'Old Diaconicon'), dominated by a large panel of mosaic which is beautifully preserved and perhaps the most impressive in the church. Depicted on it are scenes that appear to chart the progression of man's relationship with animals from primitive hunting to domestication: lions, a bear and a boar being hunted; sheep and goats grazing from trees; and finally an ostrich, a zebra and a camel being led by two men.

BACKGROUND

Mount Nebo

The ridges of Mount Nebo are littered with traces of settlement dating back as far as the **Stone Age** but it's most famous as the scene of the final vision and **death of Moses**.

By the fourth century CE Mount Nebo was an important pilgrimage site marked by the Memorial Church of Moses and several accounts of pilgrims visiting it can be found in the writings of the late **Roman** and **Byzantine** periods. Exactly when the monastery and town were abandoned is not known, but it was only in 1864 that the ruins of Siyagha were brought to the attention of the outside world.

In 1933 the land was bought by the Franciscan Custody of the Holy Land order (www. custodia.org). By 1937 excavations had uncovered the Memorial Church of Moses with its mosaic floors, and the surrounding monastery complex. Work on the preservation and further excavation of this site continues to this day.

An inscription in Greek gives the date of the mosaic as 530 CE and the mosaicists' names: Soelos, Kaiomos and Elias. Dotted around the church are various other mosaics, either in situ or mounted on the walls, the detail on some of them being equally impressive.

La Storia Museum
Prince Hassan St, on the main road to Mt Nebo, 5 km west of Madaba, T05-324 1119 daily 0900-1700, 2JD, under 15s free.

This new museum complex presents dioramas of religious scenes and Jordanian cultural heritage including a mock-up of a traditional Jordanian village. Upstairs is **Hekayet Nebo Restaurant** (see Madaba listings, page 86).

Hammamat Ma'in
recharge your batteries with a soak in the hot springs

Nestled in a sheer ravine as it plunges down from the Eastern Plateau towards the Dead Sea are the hot sulphur springs of Hammamat Ma'in. Both the setting and the springs themselves are dramatic, with hot water cascading down from the cliff-side waterfalls and feeding the pools below. The excellent road to Hammamat Ma'in leading from Mukawir (Machaerus) to the hot springs and then all the way down to the Dead Sea makes visiting all three sites in one day entirely possible.

Visiting the springs
Daily 0800-2300, 15JD, changing rooms are provided beside the main waterfall hot pools.

On the left, as you head down into the resort from the entrance gate is the somewhat run-down **Roman bath complex** with separate (rather murky

Tip...
You'll notice that Jordanian women, if they are bathing at all, do so fully clothed. It is acceptable for foreign women to bathe just in their swimsuit here, but during the busier periods women will probably feel more comfortable if they wear a sarong (or T-shirt and shorts) over the top.

Essential Hammamat Ma'in

Getting around

Self-drive

Hammamat Ma'in is 30 km southwest of Madaba. To get there, head southwest out of Madaba on Ibn Kuthayr Street. After 8 km, go straight on at the roundabout in the village of Ma'in (right for the village centre). Around 4 km further on the Dead Sea and the barren moonscape of hills leading down to it come dramatically into view. The road runs along the side of a ridge before arriving at two viewpoints close together (18 km from the roundabout in Ma'in). Immediately after the viewpoints, the main road descends precipitously to arrive at the resort entrance. On the way down you can see another road which climbs equally precipitously from the resort up towards Mukawir.

Taxi

A taxi from Madaba to the hot springs including one-hour waiting time will cost somewhere between 25 and 40JD.

Tip...

On Fridays, Saturdays and public holidays it can get very busy. Try to avoid these times if possible.

looking) pools for men and women, a sauna and treatment rooms. Further on down, there is a **family spring** consisting of a small waterfall feeding a bathing pool, complete with its own cave, as well as an outdoor cold water **swimming pool**.

Skip past all these and follow the road down to veer off onto the right-hand path that leads to the hot springs' primary attraction, the **main waterfall**, just before the entrance way to the Ma'in Hot Springs Resort & Spa.

With steam rising off it, the waterfall cascades down over rocks rounded smooth and caked with the accumulated deposits of millennia, like a thick sludge dripping slowly down. At the bottom there is a pool in the stream where you can immerse yourself in the hot water (45°C) and treat yourself to a high-powered, pummelling sort of 'massage' from the waterfall above.

There are changing rooms just before you get to the waterfall and there's a pleasant shaded seating area beside the waterfall itself. There is another waterfall (strictly men only) on the turn-off to the main waterfall. The water here is a scorching 65°C.

If you want extra privacy for your hot springs soaking you can book a range of treatments at the spa, inside the grounds of the **Ma'in Hot Springs Resort & Spa** ⓘ *just after the main waterfall, T05-324 5500, www. mainhotsprings.jo.*

BACKGROUND

Machaerus

The earliest defensive stronghold at Machaerus dates from the rule of the Hasmonean (Jewish) King Alexander Jannaeus (103-176 BCE), when it formed an important frontier post on the border with the Nabataean kingdom to the south. Following the arrival of the **Romans**, it was destroyed in 67 BCE by Pompey but later rebuilt by Herod the Great (37-34 BCE). It was under Herod the Great's son, **Herod Antipas** (4 BCE-39 CE) that **John the Baptist**'s execution took place.

Mukawir (Machaerus)

Herod's mountaintop eyrie with views over the West Bank

The lonely mountain stronghold of Machaerus is one of the most atmospheric sites along the King's Highway. Today this barren mountaintop provides a fittingly eerie experience for the few travellers who come to see where John the Baptist was beheaded. Those who do venture here are rewarded with some of the best views in Jordan. The detour off the King's Highway to here takes you through rugged, striking countryside that tumbles down to the Dead Sea basin.

Visiting the site
Sunrise-sunset, 1.5JD.

It's a 15- to 20-minute walk from the car park, down and then up to the summit along a good path. As you descend the stairway from the car park to the low saddle that joins with the conical hill of Mukawir, at the bottom on your right is a doorway of cut stone

Essential Mukawir

Getting around

Public transport
The minibuses running from Madaba come only as far as Mukawir village. It's an easy walk from there to the ruins, or you can negotiate with the driver to take you the rest of the way for a small fee. Check what time the last minibus back to Madaba leaves; they are much less frequent in the afternoon, and stop operating altogether well before nightfall.

Self-drive
The turning for Mukawir (signposted both for 'Mukawir' and 'Memorial of John the Baptist') is 14 km south of Madaba, in the small village of Lib. Fork right immediately after taking the turning and follow the winding road down to the modern village of Mukawir. Just over 2 km past the village, the road ends in a parking area a short walk from the ruins of Machaerus, which are perched on top of a distinctive conical-shaped hill visible from some distance away.

Tip...
Plan to visit in the early morning when the air is free of haze and you'll easily see Jerusalem shimmering faintly in the distance.

blocks leading into a cave with a side room. Further on, if you branch off to the right on a rough path (instead of following the main track around to the left), you come to a series of caves cut into the side of Mukawir hill itself. Some of these have been carefully hewn out into square rooms, others have doorways of cut stone blocks and traces of mud plaster on the walls, and in one case, a square supporting pillar in the centre. According to local legend, it was in one of these caves that John the Baptist was beheaded.

Nearing the top, there's a restored section of the original defensive walls and glacis. Of the original buildings there's very little to see; just the outlines of their foundations and a few low walls. In the centre of the hilltop the main palace complex has been restored with the newly paved courtyard and new columns surrounding it, all smooth and immaculate, looking rather incongruous. However, the reason for coming to this lonely outpost is for the views. The surrounding hills are strikingly patterned with the swirling shapes of folded rock formations that tumble down to the shore of the Dead Sea. In the morning the light here is magnificent and you can see for miles over to the West Bank.

Umm ar-Rasas

intricate Byzantine mosaics amid slumping ruins

A detour east from Dhiban takes you to the sprawling UNESCO World Heritage Site of Umm ar-Rasas with its incredibly well-preserved Byzantine mosaics. Easily comparable with anything on display at Madaba or Mount Nebo and well worth the extra effort involved in coming out here, the World Heritage status attached to the site indicates the level of importance these beautiful mosaic works have for our understanding of Byzantine art.

Visiting the site
0800-sunset, free entry.

Church of St Stephen   From the entrance gate a short stroll to your left will bring you to the large green corrugated-iron hangar which protects the mosaic floors of the Church of St Stephen. A raised walkway has been constructed so that you can view the mosaics.

Essential Umm ar-Rasas

Getting around

Public transport
There are only a couple of minibuses daily that run from Madaba via Nitil to Umm ar-Rasas; check what time the last one leaves for the return journey. Alternatively, there are more regular minibuses to Dhiban, from where you will have to negotiate with either the minibus driver to take you onward to Umm ar-Rasas, or for a private taxi to take you out to Umm ar-Rasas and back.

Self-drive
Head south along the King's Highway then take the left turn immediately after the roundabout in the centre of Dhiban (clearly signposted for Umm ar-Rasas). After around 12 km take another signposted left turn and 4 km further on, the low, sprawling ruins are clearly visible.

BACKGROUND

Umm ar-Rasas

Umm ar-Rasas has been identified with the site of **Kastron Mefaa**, an important Roman/Byzantine settlement. According to Eusebius, a unit of the Roman army was stationed here, and he goes on to identify the site with the Old Testament city of Mephaath. The identification with biblical Mephaath remains to be confirmed, although it seems likely and excavations have revealed evidence of settlement during the **Iron Age II** (seventh to sixth century BCE). The site appears to have been abandoned until the **Roman** period, when it developed as a military outpost and went on to flourish during the **Byzantine** era.

The main mosaic covering the central nave of the single-apsed church depicts men, animals and birds in various hunting and rural scenes, although it suffered damage at the hands of iconoclasts. The borders are the most interesting. The inner border depicts a river with boats and people fishing, along with 10 cities of the Nile Delta: Alexandria, Kasin, Thenesos, Tamiathis, Panau, Pilousin, Antinau, Haraklion, Kynopolis and Pseudostomon.

Along the north side, between the spaces where the columns separating the nave from the side-aisles would have stood, eight Palestinian cities are depicted: Jerusalem, Neapolis (Shechem), Sebastis, Caesarea, Diospolis (Lydda), Eleutheropolis (Beth Guvrin), Ascalon and Gaza. Along the south side seven Transjordian cities are shown: Kastron Mefaa, Philadelphia (Amman), Madaba, Esbounta (Heshbon/Tell Hisban), Belemounta (Ma'in), Aeropolis (Rabba) and Charach Mouba (Kerak).

The great detail with which all these cities are depicted, amounting to a plan in the case of Kastron Mefaa, represents a source of information of equal importance to scholars and historians as that of the more famous Madaba Map. The two dedicatory inscriptions confirm the identification of Umm ar-Rasas with Kastron Mefaa and date the church to the eighth century. One indicates that the mosaic around the presbytery was completed in 756 CE by two mosaicists from Heshbon, Staurachios and Euremios, while the other indicates that the full mosaic decoration was not completed until 785 CE.

Also preserved within the hangar is part of the mosaic floor of the adjacent **Church of Bishop Sergius**. Only a rectangular panel of mosaic in front of the altar has survived. In the centre of the panel is a circular medallion containing a dedicatory inscription dating the church to 586 CE, flanked on either side by rams and pomegranate trees. The mosaics of the central nave were largely destroyed by iconoclasts, although a particularly striking personification of one of the seasons has survived, having been hidden under the foundations of a pulpit which was added at a later date.

Outside the protective hangar, on its northwest side, is a courtyard that was later converted into a church (the **Church of the Courtyard**), and, adjoining it, another church, dubbed the **Church of the Niche**. Together, these four churches formed an integrated liturgical complex surrounded by a wall.

Outer ruins Heading southwest from the hangar, towards the ruins of the castrum (fortified camp), you come to the remains of another church. Its basic structure is well-preserved, with the semi-circular apse clearly discernable, along with doorways, pilasters, niches and various architectural elements bearing carved decorations. Adjacent to it is a complex of rooms, some with mosaic floors (covered for protection against the elements), as well as stone basins and deep cisterns.

Further on, close to the northeast corner of the castrum, are the remains of a larger, triple-apsed church with impressive mosaic floors. An interesting feature of this church's mosaics is the depiction of two lions facing each other (hence its name; the **Church of the Lions**), along with a pair of gazelle, both these motifs being usually associated with synagogues.

Castrum From here it is a short walk to the large rectangular walled castrum, which represented the main Roman/Byzantine settlement. It's possible to scramble through the ruinous walls, though inside is a scene of almost total dereliction, with numerous arches and the occasional outline of a building rising out of the rubble of what must have been a densely packed town.

Tower Just over 1 km to the north of the hangar housing the Church of St Stephen there is a 14-m-high tower standing in a courtyard along with the remains of a small church. The tower, which had a small room on top and no stairs, is believed to have been a stylite tower in the tradition of St Simeon in Syria.

Wadi Mujib Viewpoint
a great spot to admire the spectacular gorge scenery

Continuing south along the King's Highway from Dhiban, the views from the top of Wadi Mujib's massive gorge are spectacular. Where the road begins its descent, there is a parking area and viewpoint. This is the biblical *Arnon*, which formed the border between Moabite and Amorite territories at the time of the Exodus.

The road hairpins its way down to the bottom; the scenery of bare earth and rock giving way to lush green vegetation the lower you go.

Kerak
Jordan's finest Crusader castle; worth a detour

Although now peacefully sitting on Kerak's hilltop, some 900m above sea level, the town's famous Crusader castle was once the site of bloody battles between the Arab hero Salah ud-Din and the vile Reynald of Chatillon. Things have calmed down somewhat since then, with Kerak more famous these days for its shopping bargains that tempt crowds of locals to the town from all over the surrounding area. For travellers though, it's all about the castle with its fortifications – still an imposing presence that dominates the town.

Kerak Castle
Castle plaza, at the end of Al-Qala'at St, T03-235 4263, daily 0800-1800 summer, 0800-1600 winter, 2JD. Bring a torch to explore the darker recesses of the castle.

Upper court Heading up the ramp from the entrance, you find yourself in the upper court of the castle. Along with the northern and eastern walls and towers, this dates mostly from the Crusader period, with some later additions. Running along the northern wall of the upper court are two **barrel-vaulted galleries**, one above the other. Towards the end of the lower gallery, steps on the left lead down to the **Crusader gate**. Further along there is a reused stone block in the wall featuring a carved torso (now headless) of Nabataean origin. The complex of rooms in the northeast corner served as **barracks**, **kitchens** (complete with an olive press and a huge brick oven) and **storerooms**.

Mamluk-era fortifications Working your way south from here, you come next to a complex of buildings, which includes a **Crusader church** and sacristy. Further on is a **Mamluk palace** and **mosque** complex (this can also be reached from the north via a long underground passage which brings you to the entrance court of the palace). The south end of the upper court is dominated by the **Mamluk keep**, its massive fortifications providing improved defenses against attack from the south – the castle's most vulnerable point.

Lower court The lower court can be reached either by doubling back the way you came and following the ramp/steps down from the entrance, or via a set of stairs leading down through the castle's inner wall. This part of the castle dates almost entirely from the Mamluk period, with traces of Crusader foundations in places.

Essential Kerak

Getting around

The main bus station is an open parking lot just off Salah ud-Din Street below the town. From here it's a 20-minute walk uphill to the castle. Regular buses and minibuses run to Kerak from Amman's Wahadat station and less regular buses and minibuses from Ma'an, Aqaba and Tafila. There are also reasonably frequent minibuses shuttling between the Dead Sea town of Safi and Kerak. See Transport, page 97.

Kerak is small enough to be easily explored on foot, although the layout of town, being strung across the hillside, does mean that there's a fair whack of ascent and descent involved. If you're driving, be aware that Kerak has a rather confusing one-way system and traffic congestion is a real problem within the town.

> **Tip...**
> If you've got the time, venture down the hill into the lively shopping streets. Lined with atmospheric and decaying Ottoman-era buildings, the streets of Kerak throng with local Bedouin selling produce, groups of women buying kitchen supplies and young boys checking out pirate DVDs. It's a colourful and vibrant commercial hub that few travellers bother to see.

At the northern end of the lower court is a long, narrow vaulted hall that probably served as soldiers' barracks and now houses the **Kerak Archaeological Museum** ⓘ *T03-235 1216, daily 0800-1800 summer, 0800-1500 winter, entry included in castle ticket*, which has a small but interesting collection of artefacts from the Neolithic period through to the late Islamic era arranged around the walls (work your way round anti-clockwise for a roughly chronological tour, with a few anomalies).

Kerak Castle

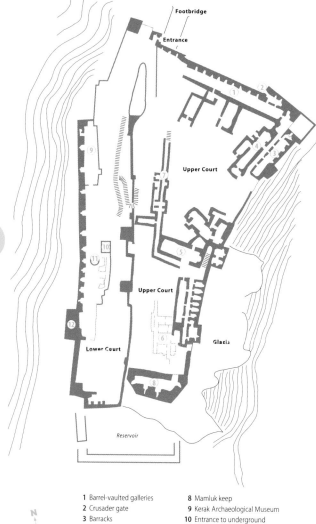

Footbridge

Entrance

Upper Court

Upper Court

Lower Court

Glacis

Reservoir

N

0 ———— 30m
0 ———— 30yds

1 Barrel-vaulted galleries
2 Crusader gate
3 Barracks
4 Kitchens & storerooms
5 Crusader church & sacristy
6 Mamluk palace
  & mosque complex
7 Underground passage

8 Mamluk keep
9 Kerak Archaeological Museum
10 Entrance to underground
   vaulted galleries
11 Domed skylight
12 Monumental west gate
   & bastion

BACKGROUND
Kerak

The present castle dates from the **Crusader** period, built in around 1140 by Payen de Bouteiller. It was one of the largest and best defended of the string of castles which stretched from the Gulf of Aqaba all the way to Turkey, protecting the Crusader states from attack from the east, and controlling movement along the King's Highway. Standing halfway between Jerusalem and Shobak, Kerak served as the capital of the Crusader administrative district of Oultre Jourdain (part of the Seigneury of Montreal).

Perhaps the most colourful (or at least, most notorious) period of its history was under the governorship of Reynald of Châtillon, a rather gruesome character who made a habit of tossing prisoners over the walls. Despite its strong fortifications, it was eventually taken in 1188 by Salah ud-Din's forces, more than a year after the battle of Hattin. From 1264, having wrested control of it from the Ayyubids, the **Mamluk** Sultan Baibars, and later his successor Sultan Qalaun, carried out extensive modifications and rebuilding work on both the castle and the city's outer walls. Subsequently, however, it fell into relative obscurity.

Back on ground level, towards the southern end of the lower court, is the **monumental west gate** and **bastion**. The full dimensions of this structure are difficult to appreciate from up the castle itself, but if you drive down to the Dead Sea from Kerak, you get an excellent view of the whole western wall and its fortifications.

Listings Kerak map p96

Restaurants

For cheap eats head down the hill to Umari St, at the centre of town, where you'll find several down-to-earth traditional Arabic diners offering *fuul*, hummus, falafel and *shawarma*.

$$ Kir Heres
Qala'at St, T07-9658 5500, daily 1030-2100.
The only place in town offering something different from the usual fare, Kir Heres is a cheerful little place with a floor covered in bright *kilims*. The mezze selection is tasty and inventive and even old favourites like hummus have an extra flavour-kick here.

$ Shehab
Castle plaza, T03-951 3803, daily 1200-2000.
Good for dishes like *shish tawook* and *kebab*, a filling meal here shouldn't cost much more than 6JD. The helpful owner, Trad, can help arrange onward travel.

Transport

Bus and minibus
Buses and minibuses run from the main bus station below the town. They leave (when full) pretty regularly to **Amman** (2 hrs, 2JD). In summer the last service is about 1900 and in winter about 1600. There are also services to **Tafila** (1 hr, 1.5JD, change for Dana Biosphere Reserve here); **Ma'an** (2 hrs, 2.5JD, change for Petra, Aqaba and Amman here); and **Aqaba** (3 hrs, 5JD) running approximately 0800-1400.

There's a small minibus station, on the corner of Maydan St, which deals with all transport to the **Dead Sea**. It has fairly regular minibuses to **Safi** (for Lot's Cave).

Dana Village is picturesquely rustic. Old crumbling stone buildings back onto winding alleys. The nearest they get to a traffic jam here is a shepherd herding his small flock down the street. At night the silence is all-encompassing, broken only by the occasional braying of a lone donkey.

For nature lovers, or anyone who simply enjoys a stupendous vista, Dana is surely among the highlights of Jordan. Covering around 292 sq km of land, Dana also spans a variety of biodiversity zones; beginning in the heights of the craggy highlands and then tumbling down to the Dead Sea basin.

The big attraction here is the hiking. Even the most reluctant walker couldn't help but feel enthused by the big-sky scenery of Dana. The RSCN have opened up a range of walks, so there's something for everyone, from serious treks to casual ambles. If you're really not the active type Dana should still be on your must-visit list. There's a tranquil atmosphere

Essential Dana Biosphere Reserve

Getting around

There are erratic minibuses that shuttle between Tafila and Qadisiyyeh (the small village 1 km or so south of the Dana Village turning). Either ask to be dropped off at the Dana Village turning and walk down from there, or it is usually possible to negotiate a ride from Qadisiyyeh. Coming from the south, you'll have to charter a private taxi from Wadi Musa (20JD).

Park fees and accommodation

You don't need to pay to enter or stay in Dana Village, only if you wish to hike any of the reserve trails. The reserve fee is 10JD.

Tip...

Guide fees are per group, if you're a solo traveller you can enquire at the Dana Visitor Centre (see page 100) to see if there are any groups that you can join. If you're staying at one of the two budget hotels in the village, you can usually pick up other keen hikers who are looking for someone to share costs with.

Tip...

There's no ATM, bank or grocery store at Dana Village so bring enough money with you.

Fees are paid at the **RSCN Dana Visitor Centre** (see page 100). If you're planning to stay the night at any of the RSCN's accommodation within the reserve (one hotel in Dana Village and the campsite at Rummana) it is strongly recommended you book in advance.

Guides

If you want to do a guided hike it's also recommended to book in advance. Note that guides are not available during Ramadan. Guide fees are: one to two hours 10JD; three to four hours 13JD per person, for a minimum of four people. Bookings can be made through the reserve directly: T07-9911 1434, dhana@rscn.org.jo, or through the RSCN's **Wild Jordan Center** in Amman: T06-461 6523, T07-9700 0086, tourism@rscn.org.jo, www.rscn.org.jo (see page 43).

BACKGROUND
Dana Biosphere Reserve

The Wadi Dana drops from 1200 m above sea level to 100 m below sea level as it plunges from the eastern plateau of the Great Rift Valley down to the lowlands of the Wadi Araba. With this massive diversity of environments, it contains a remarkable variety of habitats, ranging from Mediterranean semi-arid forests through to subtropical *wadis* and desert dunes. With this comes an equally remarkable variety of flora and fauna, bringing together in one area species from Europe, Asia and Arabia.

The reserve covers what was the heartland of the ancient Edomite kingdom and contains hundreds of sites of archaeological interest, including **Wadi Feynan** (down in the lower Wadi Araba part of the reserve), where evidence of occupation dates back as far as the seventh millennium BCE.

that's hard to find these days, making it the perfect place to rest up from your travels and enjoy the solitude.

Hiking in the reserve

Though you can get a taste of the unique beauty of Dana from the viewpoints, to really appreciate the richness of this natural environment you have to head into the reserve itself. The RSCN has established 10 main hiking trails, a selection of which are detailed below; for five of the routes a guide is mandatory and some walks also require a private transfer either to the walk starting point or from the finish.

Village Tour Trail (starts from Dana Village) ⓘ *No guide necessary, open all year round, 2 km, 30 mins-2 hrs, cost included in reserve entry fee, rating: easy.* This short ramble around the village is a good time filler if you arrive in Dana in the afternoon. The path takes you along the terraced gardens of the village and up to the viewpoints where you have a bird's-eye view of Wadi Dana.

Wadi Dana Trail (starts from Dana Village) ⓘ *No guide necessary, open all year round, 14 km, 6-7 hrs, 20JD, rating: easy to moderate.* This spectacularly scenic walk begins at the end of the village and traverses all the way to Wadi Feynan through the beautiful and serene sandstone gorge of Wadi Dana. It's downhill all the way so go easy on your knees – they'll have suffered a bashing by the walk's end. The path is easy to follow as it winds downward through rugged mountains, past bizarre rock formations sculpted by the wind, and through lush sections of palm towards the end. There's also a Bedouin encampment 10 minutes before the end, where the friendly locals will invite you to sit and drink a refreshing tea. The hike finishes at **Feynan Ecolodge in Wadi Feynan**. Before beginning the walk you will have to arrange a private transfer back to Dana Village (or you can stay the night at the lodge).

Fact...
There are just over 700 species of plants to be found in Dana Biosphere Reserve, over 90 of which are rare, and eight of them endemic. The reserve also contains some 250 species of bird and is the location for the world's largest cluster of the Syrian Serin (*Serinus syriacus*).

Transfers can be arranged at the Dana visitor centre or through your hotel and cost around 60JD. It's a good three-hour drive back to Dana Village from here through breathtaking desert and then mountain scenery. If you want to move on after the walk, you could also arrange to have the transfer driver bring your bags in his car when he picks you up and drop you at Petra as you have to pass near there on the way back to Dana Village.

Rummana Mountain Trail (starts from Rummana Camp) ⓘ No guide necessary, open Mar-Oct, 2.5 km, 1-2 hrs, cost included in reserve entry fee, rating: moderate.
If you're staying the night at Rummana Camp, this is a wonderful walk to do by yourself. Starting from the campsite, the trail winds up to the summit of Rummana Mountain. The views on the way up are great and there are plenty of surreal sandstone rock formations to stop and admire. This is also an excellent choice for birdwatchers, with lots of potential for bird-spotting. On the summit you are greeted with grand views over Wadi Araba. From there it's all downhill back to camp.

White Dome Trail (starts from Dana Village or Rummana Camp) ⓘ Guided only, open Mar-Oct, 8 km, 12JD, 3-4 hrs, rating: moderate.
This trek takes you through the gently sloped gardens of Dana Village before heading onto the escarpment of Wadi Dana. The views over the surrounding countryside are the highlight here. From your high vantage point you're able to see for miles across the nature reserve as the *wadi* plunges dramatically down to the Dead Sea basin. The hike finishes at **Rummana Camp** where you can stay the night. If you want to head back to Dana village you'll need to book a private transfer beforehand, with either the visitor centre or through your hotel. Transfers cost around 10JD. This trek can be done in reverse.

Feather's Canyon Trail (starts from Dana Village) ⓘ Guided only, open all year round, 8 km, 2-3 hrs, 12JD, rating: moderate to hard.
This trail isn't one for those who have a fear of heights. Starting near **Dana Guest House**, this circular route takes you to the stunning Shaq al-Reesh (Feather Canyon). On the way you also pass by some Nabataean tombs.

Listings Dana Biosphere Reserve

Tourist information

Dana Visitor Centre
Inside the Dana Guest House complex, the 1st left-hand turning as you come into Dana Village, T03-227 0497/8, T07-9911 1431, www.rscn.org.jo.
The helpful staff here can give you information on all the hikes and treks. This is also where you come to book a guide. Inside is a shop selling locally made produce and gifts, a craft workshop, and a small museum about the reserve. Don't forget to walk up to the lookout point terrace to admire the expansive views over Wadi Dana.

Where to stay

Dana Village

$$$ Dana Guest House
1st left turning as you come into Dana Village, T03-227 0497 (Dana), T06-461 6523 (RSCN Amman), www.rscn.org.jo.
There are 23 rooms at this intimate stone-walled guesthouse that's built into the

cliff side to blend into the surrounding countryside. The sun-filled rooms are simply furnished with beds and other furnishings made from recycled iron. Bathrooms are communal (except the deluxe rooms, which have private bathrooms). They are all kept exceptionally clean and have by far the best showers in the country. The real reason for staying here though are the views: the rooms boast huge glass doors that lead onto balconies where you can admire the sweeping vistas of Wadi Dana at your leisure. Waking up to this kind of scenery is a sheer joy. A non-deluxe double room costs 80JD (deluxe 100JD), which includes the 10JD reserve entry fee, breakfast and conservation charge. Lunch/dinner available upon request (15JD).

$$ Dana Hotel
On the left in the middle of the village, T07-7238 7787, T07-9559 7307, see Facebook. Owned and operated by the **Dana Local Community Cooperative**, this is a friendly choice and the 40 spotlessly clean rooms come with plenty of rustic charm, all set round a pretty central courtyard. Cheaper rooms come with shared bathrooms. A double room costs 25JD. During summer you can sleep on the roof (6JD). Meals are provided upon request. Breakfast and Wi-Fi included. Recommended.

$ Dana Tower
On the left at the end of the village, T07-9568 8853, www.dana-tower-hotel.com. The endearingly eccentric Dana Tower is a rambling conversion of old stone buildings quirkily connected together. With tons of rooftop space on different levels there's plenty of relaxation room for exhausted hikers. The 20 rooms are small and basic (and some of the private baths tiny) but cheerful local textiles brighten them up. Nabil, the friendly owner, is a fount of knowledge on

the local area. Breakfast and a communal dinner are included in the room rate.

Around Dana Biosphere Reserve

$$$$ Feynan Ecolodge
Follow the Dead Sea Highway until the left-hand turn-off for Gregra village, follow this road (14 km) until you reach Gregra, from here there is a sign-posted turn-off for Feynan, which will take you to Rashaydeh village (this is as far as you can come without a 4WD); local Bedouin can meet you here and shuttle you the rest of the way to the lodge (book transport at same time as accommodation), T06-585 0333, www.ecohotels.me/feynan.
A little piece of rustic chic in the middle of nowhere, the 26 rooms at Feynan Ecolodge offer travellers a complete getaway from modern life. In a true attempt to be self-sustaining, the water here is all heated by solar power, and at night your simple rooms are lit by flickering candlelight. Breakfast included. Meals upon request. No alcohol served.

$$ Rummana Campsite
From the King's Highway, look for the turn-off, signposted for the campsite, 4 km after Buseira, T07-9911 1434 (Dana), T06-461 6523, T07-9700 0086 (RSCN, Amman), www.rscn.org.jo. 15 Mar-31 Oct.
Perched high up in a secluded spot, this campsite has 20 tents offering superlative views over the surrounding rural landscape. It's quite basic with no electricity (bring a torch), shared toilets, solar-heated showers and a large communal Bedouin-style tent for dining. Extremely hospitable and perfect for those seeking a tranquil escape. A dbl costs 60JD per night including breakfast and conservation fee. Lunch/dinner (15JD) upon request.

Strikingly situated on top of a conical hill, Shobak Castle has a more romantic setting than Kerak and is also less visited. The castle's walls and fortifications have mostly crumbled away and the aura of general dilapidation make Shobak an atmospheric and fascinating place to explore. For most of the year the surrounding hills are barren and stark, but if you come in spring they are carpeted in grass and wildflowers.

Visiting the site
Daily 0800-sunset, 1JD, the caretaker is usually on hand to show you around for a tip, bring a torch if you want to explore the darker recesses of the castle.

The Arabic inscription on the large rectangular tower to the right of the entrance gate dates from the Mamluk-period modifications; during the Ottoman period, this tower served as a **prison**. After you go through the entrance gate, turn left to follow the path running between the inner and outer walls of the castle. On your left, steps lead down into a chamber with two holes in the floor giving access to a large water cistern below. This chamber leads in turn to a small **church** with a vaulted ceiling.

Returning to the path, note the water channels that fed the wine presses. You come next to a cross-vaulted **entrance hall** which gives access to the inner castle. Once through it, on your left is the partially restored **south tower**, with a series of rooms each containing arrow slits built into arched recesses. Follow the path from the entrance hall, around past the entrance to a large hall on the right, to arrive at a long flight of slippery stone-cut stairs leading down to the castle's main water **cistern**. No one seems to count the same number of stairs (anywhere between 350 and 375), but it is certainly a long way down. A good torch and sure footing are required if you want to go to the bottom.

Doubling back from here and going through the entrance to the large hall, you pass the remains of a sizeable olive press before joining a street lined on either side by what are thought to have been shops. Going through any of the entrances to the left, you can get a good view of the walls and bastions of the castle on this side. At the end of the street is a building on the left, believed to have been a **madrassa** (religious school) with three arched entrances. Above the third entrance arch is a large Arabic inscription attributing the building to Hosam ud-Din (Salah ud-Din's brother).

Essential Shobak

Getting around

From the signposted turning off the King's Highway it is around 3 km to the castle of Shobak. Unless you have your own transport, the best option is to catch a taxi out here as an excursion from Petra.

If you go through the remains of the madrassa (only two barrel-vaulted rooms survive) and turn right, you come to a long rectangular bastion containing barracks and stables. A long passageway leads from here past rooms with arrow slits to the castle's **north tower**, consisting of a single room with four arched recesses containing arrow slits.

BACKGROUND

Shobak

Like Kerak, Shobak formed part of the chain of Crusader castles along the King's Highway. Known as Mont Realis (or Montreal) to the **Crusaders**, it was originally built by Baldwin I in 1115 when he founded the Seigneury of Montreal. Baldwin appointed Peyen de Bouteiller as lord of this Seigneury, and Payen resided here until moving to Kerak around 1140 and building the larger castle there. In 1187 the castle was besieged by **Salah ud-Din** after the battle of Hattin, but it only fell to him two years later in 1189.

From here, loop round to follow the eastern wall of the castle, then climb up to what is generally referred to as the **palace complex**. This dates originally from the Crusader period, though it was largely rebuilt by the Ayyubids.

Petra,
Wadi Rum & Aqaba

Petra

Massive façades cut into the cliff face soar upwards to
dizzying heights. Around every corner are gallery-worthy
masterpieces of vibrantly coloured and swirled rock faces
formed by nature rather than paint and palette. Ancient
staircases, cut into the rock, lead to silent summits where
the grand vistas of jagged mountains spread out before
you. This is the Nabataean capital of Petra – undoubtedly
the Middle East's most impressive historical sight and, due
to its inclusion as one of the world's new seven wonders,
definitely its most famous.

Rediscovered to the West by the Swiss adventurer and
Arabist Johann Ludwig Burckhardt in 1812, this 'lost city'
of the Nabataeans has been feted by visitors ever since.
David Roberts immortalized the city in his paintings,
Agatha Christie set one of her books here and the mighty
Treasury became a movie icon after posing as the home
of the Holy Grail which a swashbuckling Indiana Jones
fought the Nazis for.

Today, Petra is firmly stamped upon the tour bus circuit.
However, off the main tourist trail it is still amazingly
easy to escape the crowds. The Petra back roads are
filled with jaw-dropping beautiful views, little-visited
monuments, and flocks of sheep and goats being
herded by their Bedouin shepherds between the
ruins. If you want to discover these, linger longer than
the usual one day and trek out into the hills where the
real magic of this grand site lies.

Petra Museum

Tourism St, near visitor centre, T03-215 6044, www.petramuseum.jo, daily 0830-2030 Apr-Oct, 0830-1930 Nov-Mar, free, museum galleries and toilets wheelchair friendly, free audio guide.

Spread over eight galleries, this fairly recent addition to the site of Petra's ancient wonders takes visitors on a fascinating journey through the very foundations, history, economy, life and peoples of Petra. The quality of the numerous exhibits, enhanced by the informative multimedia displays, make this museum a must-see during your visit to Petra.

The Siq

Having passed through the ticket gate, you follow the course of a wide, dry *wadi* bed (part of Wadi Musa), down towards the Siq. First you pass, on the right, three large free-standing rock cubes known as **Djinn Blocks**. There are more than 20 of these carved rock cubes dotted around Petra, some of them up to 9 m tall and hollowed out inside. Their exact purpose is not clear, although they are believed to have been created as the dwelling places of Nabataean spirits.

A little further on, on the left, there's a double monument, the Obelisk Tomb (above) and the Bab as-Siq Triclinium (below). The **Obelisk Tomb**, so called because of the four obelisks each originally over 7 m high carved above the entrance, dates from the first century CE and shows an interesting mix of Egyptian and classical influences in the use of obelisks alongside the standard pilasters, niches and pediments. Immediately below it is the **Bab as-Siq Triclinium** ('Gate of the Siq Triclinium'), a façade with two heavily weathered tiers of pediments and a large cave chiselled out of the rock in the lower tier. A *triclinium* is a banquet hall in which feasts were held, usually in honour of the dead. Immediately opposite the Obelisk Tomb, about 5 m up in the cliff side, there is an **inscription** in both Nabataean Aramaic and Greek announcing a Nabataean burial place.

Beyond the Obelisk Tomb, the path swings round to the right, before entering the Siq proper. A **dam** blocks the *wadi* at this point, its purpose to divert the flow of water through a tunnel off to the right in the event of flash floods. For those staying an extra day at Petra, the tunnel to the right is the beginning of the Petra back road through Wadi Muthlim (see page 126). Crossing over the dam and entering the narrow Siq, if you look up you notice the remains of a **triumphal arch**, now collapsed, but still intact 100 years ago, as shown by the watercolours of David Roberts. Much of the floor of the Siq has now been consolidated with concrete to prevent further erosion. Originally, the full length of the Siq would have been

Fact...

The Siq is an entirely natural feature, a narrow cleft produced by earth movements that literally split a solid section of mountain in two. In places you can clearly match the cross-section patterns in one cliff side with those opposite. The effects of weathering and erosion, meanwhile, have carved fantastic shapes in the rock higher up. The Siq runs for a length of 1.2 km and in places is just 3 m wide, while the walls tower up to a height of 200 m. The overall effect of walking through this remarkable natural feature is truly awe-inspiring and is half the magic of approaching the great monuments of Petra.

Finding your feet

All visitors to Petra will pass through Wadi Musa, the closest town to the archaeological site. The town sprawls for 5 km and has three main parts. **Ain Musa (Musa Spring)** is right at the top of the hill on the highway into town with a few hotels dotting the road. Following the road downwards for 2.5 km brings you to the modern village of **Wadi Musa**, with the bus station, shops, banks, cheap restaurants and plenty of budget and mid-range hotels. A further 1.5 km down the hill is a line of tourist-orientated shops and restaurants, tucked between hotels, with more accommodation hidden on the side streets shooting off from the main road. Right at the bottom of the road is the visitor centre and entrance to **Petra** itself.

From the visitor centre/entrance gate it's still a 10-minute walk (just under 1 km) to the beginning of the Siq (the narrow canyon that you enter Petra from).

Getting around

From Amman, the **JETT** bus departs daily at 0630 from Abdali station (10JD) or catch any Wadi Musa minibus service from Wahadat station. Alternatively, hop aboard one of the more regular Ma'an-bound minibuses and change there.

If you're heading to Petra from Aqaba there are supposed to be about five minibuses per day, but services sometimes don't run. Hiring a taxi (around 2 hrs, c45-75JD) is an easier option.

There's no shortage of private unmetered taxis shuttling between Wadi Musa town and the visitor centre/entrance to Petra. This short trip usually costs an inflated 'tourist price' of 2JD. You'll have to be a consummate haggler to get them down to the fairer 1JD (and even a consummate haggler can be too exhausted to attempt this after a long day trekking around the ruins).

Nearly all the hotels in Wadi Musa town and along the road up as far as Ain Musa offer free transport to and from the visitor centre/entrance to Petra. Be sure to agree clearly in advance a time in the afternoon/evening for them to pick you up when you emerge from the site.

A taxi to nearby Al-Barid (Little Petra) should cost around 10JD return.

Inside Petra

Petra is massive but there are ways of cutting down some of the walking involved. From the entrance gate, you can ride a horse down to the dam at the start of the Siq (included in the price of the entrance ticket whether you ride or not). From the beginning of the Siq to the first monument (the mighty Treasury) you can hire a rickety horse and cart (two people for around 20JD).

The trouble with both of these forms of transport is that not only do you miss seeing the surrounding landscape and small monuments along the way but also, despite brilliant efforts by the animal welfare clinic here, some of the horses remain poorly treated.

Tip...

Once you're inside the site of Petra it's important to note that there's not much food on offer. The **Basin Restaurant** (T07-9720 3384, daily 1200-1530, US$22pp) and the **Nabataean Tent Restaurant** (1000-1600, high season only) just opposite, offer buffet-style lunches. There are also plentiful Bdoul-run shacks offering tea, coffee and cold drinks. The best idea for lunch in Petra though, is to pack a picnic and find your own dining spot among the ruins.

Once through the Siq and inside the site proper, donkeys and camels can be hired. Prices are negotiable but expect to pay around 15JD for a camel ride from the Treasury to the Qasr al-Bint monument and 15JD for a donkey ride from the **Basin Restaurant** to the Monastery.

Site information

The site and visitor centre (T03-215 6044, www.visitpetra.jo) are open daily 0600-1630 in winter and 0600-1800 in summer. Entry fees are 50/55/60JD for a one-/two-/three-day pass which must be paid in Jordanian dinars or by credit/debit card, and you must show your passport at the visitor centre when buying tickets. Children under 12 are free. If visiting Petra on a day trip from Israel the entry fee is 90JD. For holders of the excellent-value Jordan Pass (page 172), entry to Petra is included. Optional multilingual guides can be booked at the visitor centre.

When to go

To beat the heat, March to early May and late September to October are the prime times to visit. Due to a lack of shade, large distances and high temperatures, hiking around the site can be extremely tiring during summer. From September to March be aware that flash floods can occur in the wadis. Check weather reports and seek advice at the visitor centre before venturing out onto Petra's lesser-used trails. December to February can be bitterly cold and snow isn't uncommon. Then again, the site covered in a dusting of snow is a spectacle itself and travelling at this time is fantastic if you want the ruins all to yourself. Budget travellers in winter should make sure that their accommodation has adequate heating.

Time required

With a lot of walking, in one full day you can see all the major sights along the main

Best viewpoints

Jebel al-Khubtha To look down on the Treasury from above.
Jebel al-Habees View over the central city ruins backed by the Royal Tombs.
The Monastery Hike an extra 10 minutes from the Monastery for panoramic views of Wadi Araba.

tourist route, along with the steep staircase trail to the Monastery. Two days allows you to slow down the pace and tackle some of the Bedouin back roads with their lesser-seen monuments and panoramic views. With an extra half day, visit nearby Little Petra. Keen hikers with a full three days could also hike up Jebel Haroun.

Safety

The greatest risk is from dehydration, so make sure you bring plenty of water. Adequate protection against the sun is also vital; take sunblock and wear a hat and loose-fitting clothes that cover the skin, including the back of the neck.

Exploring the site on your own is perfectly safe providing you are sensible, but if you intend to do any climbing or to venture very far from the central ruins, the normal hiking advice to go with at least one other person is very sound.

As well as the official guides you can hire at the visitor centre, many of the Bdoul who work inside the site (see page 124) can also act as guides. As they've lived all their lives at Petra, most make extremely good guides and are usually cheaper than the official guides at the visitor centre. A word of caution must be stated, though, if you are a solo female traveller: Petra is a vast site with many isolated and lonely spots and hiking off into the hills with an unofficial guide cannot be recommended.

paved, and sections of this paving, dating from the Nabataean and Roman periods, can be seen at various points, along with traces of heavily weathered niches carved into the cliff sides.

The Treasury (Al-Khazneh Pharon)

The numerous twists and turns bring you suddenly to your first glimpse of the Treasury, one of Petra's best-preserved and most impressive temple façades, framed between the narrow walls of the end of the Siq. The contrast of bright light after the gloom and the sheer improbability of the scale of this monument combine to challenge your sense of reality. The morning is the best time to see the Treasury (between around 1000 and

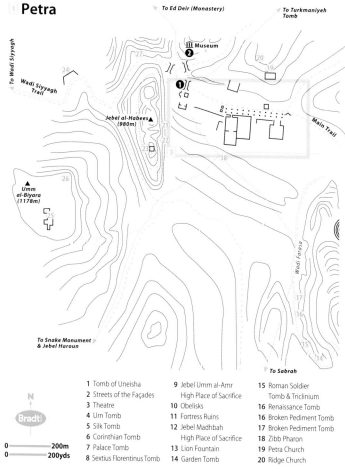

Petra

1 Tomb of Uneisha
2 Streets of the Façades
3 Theatre
4 Urn Tomb
5 Silk Tomb
6 Corinthian Tomb
7 Palace Tomb
8 Sextius Florentinus Tomb

9 Jebel Umm al-Amr
   High Place of Sacrifice
10 Obelisks
11 Fortress Ruins
12 Jebel Madhbah
   High Place of Sacrifice
13 Lion Fountain
14 Garden Tomb

15 Roman Soldier
   Tomb & Triclinium
16 Renaissance Tomb
16 Broken Pediment Tomb
17 Broken Pediment Tomb
18 Zibb Pharon
19 Petra Church
20 Ridge Church

1100 in summer and 0900-1000 in winter), when the sun falls directly on its façade, illuminating the warm hues of the rock.

The Treasury towers to a height of over 40 m and is comprised of two tiers. The lower tier consists of six huge Corinthian columns topped by ornate capitals, with a frieze running in a band above them, decorated with pairs of griffins each flanking a vase with plant tendrils. A

→ **Petra maps**
2 Petra Siq, page 112
3 Petra central city ruins, page 115

→ **Petra maps**
2 Petra Siq, page 112
3 Petra central city ruins, page 115

21 Unfinished Tomb
22 Columbarium
23 Crusader Fortress
24 Nabatean Quarry
25 Edomite Excavations
26 Cisterns
27 Painted Room

Restaurants 🍴
Nabataean Tent 1
The Basin 2

Tips…
- Wear sturdy walking shoes – your feet will thank you for it later.
- Don't forget to pack a hat, sunscreen and plenty of water. A picnic lunch and snacks are also a great idea.
- Tour group buses usually arrive around 0800 and leave by 1500. Get there early and leave late to experience Petra without the crowds.
- Take time to sip tea and banter with the Bdoul souvenir and tea shop vendors in the site. Most speak multiple languages and love to chat.

pediment sits over the four central columns and is decorated with plant designs. The upper tier consists of two side pavilions and a central *tholos*, or small circular shrine. Each pavilion is supported by Corinthian columns and contains barely discernible carved figures. On top of each are the end-wedges of a broken pediment. The *tholos* rises up in the centre, topped by a dome and then a Corinthian capital surmounted by a 4-m-tall urn. Surprisingly little is known about the Treasury. Locally it is referred to as Al-Jerrah, meaning 'the urn', a reference to the huge solid-stone urn that sits on top of the central *tholos* of the upper storey. Local legends told that this urn was filled with gold, hence its rather reduced state, chiselled and shot at countless times over the centuries by hopeful treasure hunters. Hence also its name Al-Khazneh, 'the Treasury', or Al-Khazneh Pharon, 'the Pharaoh's Treasury'. According to one variation of the legends it was the very same pharaoh that pursued the Israelites from Egypt in the Old Testament book of *Exodus* who stored his treasures here.

Various theories exist as to its true origins and purpose. Perhaps it was the tomb of King Harith IV or King Aretas III, thus dating to somewhere between 86 and 62 BCE, or else the tomb of King Aretas IV, which would put it as late as 25 CE. Others suggest that it was not a tomb at all, but a temple dedicated to the goddess Al-Uzza, equated with the Egyptian goddess Isis. The statue contained within the central *tholos* is recognized by some as being of Isis, although it has been badly damaged and is today only just discernible as female. Another theory suggests that it was dedicated to the Nabataean god of caravans and caravaneers, She'a-alqum.

The Treasury to the theatre

Continuing past the Treasury, walking along the main trail (known as the Outer Siq), after a couple of hundred metres you pass on your left three large, heavily weathered tombs (the central one incomplete) and a fourth smaller one, while on your right is a series of tombs ascending in size. The *wadi* here begins to open out and ahead of you on the left is the theatre. To your right, up on a higher level around the corner, is the **Tomb of Uneisha** and, further away, the Royal Tombs, ascending in a series along the base of Jebel al-Khubtha. To your left, just past a tent for souvenirs and refreshments, steps mark the start of the route up to the Jebel Madhbah High Place of Sacrifice (see page 121). Just beyond the steps, also to the left before the theatre, are the **Streets of the Façades**, cut into the cliffs on four levels.

Tomb of Uneisha

The Tomb of Uneisha is strictly speaking one of the Royal Tombs. Reaching it involves a bit of a scramble. An inscription suggests that Uneisha was either the brother or a minister of Queen Shaqilat, wife of King Aretas IV. The internal chamber is of interest in that it demonstrates the complete layout of a royal tomb. There are a total of 11 recesses, four in the side walls and three in the rear, each of which would have held a sarcophagus. Once up here you can explore a number of other unnamed tombs and caves, as well as getting some good views down onto the theatre.

Streets of the Façades

The Streets of the Façades consists of more than 40 tombs (although, in fact, the majority were probably dwellings rather than tombs), their façades carved into the cliffs on four

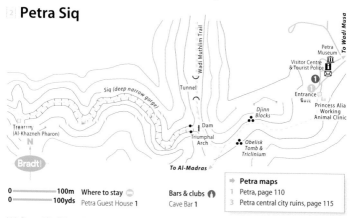

Petra Siq

Wadi Muthlim Trail

To Wadi Musa

Petra Museum

Visitor Centre & Tourist Police

Tunnel

Siq (deep narrow gorge)

Entrance Gate

Princess Alia Working Animal Clinic

Djinn Blocks

Treasury (Al-Khazneh Pharon)

N

Dam

Triumphal Arch

Obelisk Tomb & Triclinium

Bradt!

To Al-Madras

0	100m
0	100yds

Where to stay
Petra Guest House 1

Bars & clubs
Cave Bar 1

➡ Petra maps
1 Petra, page 110
3 Petra central city ruins, page 115

BACKGROUND

Petra

Pre-history to the Edomite period Petra has been a focus of settlement since prehistoric times, as confirmed by the excavation of Neolithic settlements at Al-Beidha and Basta, which date back to the seventh millennium BCE.

The Nabataeans Petra's most famous period though begins with the Nabataeans; a nomadic Bedouin people who gradually settled in the region and relied on trade to support themselves.

From around the third century BCE, the Nabataeans began to abandon the tents of their nomadic roots and build a city at Petra. The trade passing through brought with it great wealth and a synthesis of Hellenistic and Egyptian architectural influences, along with the indigenous styles (which themselves stemmed largely from former Assyrian and Babylonian influences) of these increasingly sophisticated Arabs.

The collapse of the Seleucid Empire in 64 BCE left the two great regional powers, Rome in the West and Parthia in the East, struggling for control of the Middle East. Like Palmyra, the other great caravan city to the northeast, Petra took advantage of this state of affairs to increase its autonomy. Under **King Aretas II** (110-96 BCE) the Nabataeans, by now relatively powerful in their own right, were able to carve out an independent kingdom for themselves, which under Aretas III (84-56 BCE) was briefly extended as far as Damascus. Pompey responded by sending Scaurus to lay siege to the city in 63 BCE. The Nabataeans were able to hold out and subsequently bought him off.

The Nabataeans in the Roman period At the same time, Rome was exerting an increasingly strong influence on Petra, both culturally and politically. Thus Strabo records how the succession of Aretas IV to the throne after the death of King Obodas in 9 BCE was officially confirmed by the Roman Emperor, despite the supposed status of Petra as an independent kingdom. King Aretas IV was highly successful in pursuing a diplomatic policy of close allegiance with Rome, even obtaining possession of Damascus from Caligula. Nevertheless, the power of Rome continued to increase until finally in 106 CE Trajan was able to incorporate Petra into the newly established Roman Province of Arabia.

Byzantine period to rediscovery Petra continued to be inhabited well into the Byzantine period, as attested by the conversion of some of its monuments into churches or monastic retreats, such as the Petra Church and Ridge Church to the north of the Colonnaded Street. By the fourth century CE, Petra had its own bishop, although its life-blood in the form of trade had ceased to exist. The Byzantine occupation probably continued well into the sixth century, but Petra appears to have fallen steadily into obscurity, certainly disappearing from the historical records. It next reappears during the **Crusader** period when, between 1108 and 1116, Baldwin I built two fortresses here (Wu'eira and Al-Habees). However, following the victory of Salah ud-Din over the Crusaders, these fortresses were abandoned and this time Petra fell into total obscurity for nearly 800 years, its existence known only to the local Bedouins who guarded their secret jealously from outsiders. Finally, in 1812, the Anglo-Swiss explorer **Johann Ludwig Burckhardt** 'rediscovered' it.

levels (or 'streets', hence the name). They are thought to be early examples of Nabataean workmanship, classified as Assyrian I and II in style after the strong Assyrian influence shown in the crow-step decoration of the façades.

Theatre

The theatre dates originally from around 25 CE and was constructed by the Nabataeans. After 106 CE, however, it was greatly extended by the Romans to seat a capacity of between 7000 and 8000 spectators in 40 rows of concentric semi-circles. The construction cut into an earlier street of tombs which can be seen above. The devastating earthquake of 363 CE, and the subsequent removal of materials for other building works have severely damaged the theatre, leaving it a poor reflection of its former state.

Royal Tombs

The Royal Tombs, as with so many of Petra's monuments, are so called with little firm basis. Only one, the Tomb of Sextus Florentinus, is definitely a tomb; the others may have been tombs, temples or royal houses. To reach them, continue along the valley floor past the theatre until you reach a good stairway on the right, just past a large restaurant and souvenir stall. This leads directly up to the Urn Tomb.

The **Urn Tomb** is distinctive for the two tiers of arched vaults below the main façade. The main façade consists of four huge pilasters topped by an enormous lintel, followed by a pediment with an urn on top. Between the four pilasters there are three niches, the central one still containing a heavily weathered bust. Inside is a large chamber with arched and square recesses in the walls. An inscription in the rear wall tells of its conversion into a church in 446/447 CE, while holes in the floor mark the placement of the chancery screen, altar and pulpit.

To the left of this, past a badly weathered façade with crow-step decoration, is the **Silk Tomb**, its façade also badly weathered and rather plain looking, but interesting for the colourful swirling patterns in the carved rock. These are among the best examples in Petra of the striking colours and patterns in the grain of the rock.

Continuing along the line, you come next to the **Corinthian Tomb**. The upper section of this monument, although heavily weathered, is unmistakably modelled on the Treasury. The lower section is unusual in that the three surviving doorways between the pilasters are each in a different style.

Next to it on the left is the **Palace Tomb**, among the largest of the monuments in Petra, its façade consisting of three tiers. The first tier has pilasters separating four large doorways that lead into individual chambers (unfortunately the two on the left side are heavily eroded). The second tier consists of another row of pilasters, while the third has largely collapsed or been eroded away. A little further on, around the corner, you come to a stairway that is the beginning of the Jebel al-Khubtha back road that allows you absolutely fantastic views of the theatre and the Treasury from above, see page 110. Just beyond this is the **Tomb of Sextus Florentinus**. A Latin inscription above the doorway identifies Sextus Florentinus as a Roman soldier who served in the early second century CE, retiring in 127 CE from his position as Governor of Arabia. Most probably, however, the tomb is much older, having been acquired by him at a later date.

Central city ruins

Returning to the valley floor and following the course of the *wadi* bed, the main path swings round to the left soon after the turning up to the Urn Tomb, bringing you to the central basin, where Petra's main urban centre was located.

Colonnaded street, nymphaeum and 'upper market' The remains of the **colonnaded street** to be seen today are of Roman origin, dating either from the time of Trajan when Petra became part of the Roman province of Arabia, or else later, during the reign of Antoninus (138-161 CE) – a period of intense building works throughout the empire. Further excavations have revealed the existence of a much older, gravel-surfaced roadway of Nabataean construction lined with one- and two-storey buildings dating from the third century BCE. Much of the original limestone paving still remains, along with many of the pedestals of the columns which once lined the street.

Following the street westwards towards the Qasr al-Bint, you pass first a stairway on the left (originally graced by a monumental arch over it) leading up to a terrace generally referred to as the **'upper market'** or 'upper court' (of which there is little to see). Some of the **shops** on either side of this stairway have now been partially restored; the one to the right of the stairway gives a good idea of their layout, though it was modified during the Byzantine era, perhaps after the earthquake of 363 CE. Between the 'upper market' and the Great Temple are two further terraces, largely unexcavated, known as the middle and lower markets.

Great Temple Just before the monumental gateway, a set of steps on the left leads up into what is termed the Great Temple. Covering more than 7500 sq m, this vast structure was originally thought to be the town's *agora* (marketplace). In 1921 the archaeologist W Bachmann suggested that it might be a temple, and in 1993 when work by archaeologists

3 **Petra central city ruins**

➡ **Petra maps**
1 Petra, page 110
2 Petra Siq, page 112

Wadi Musa

N

Not to scale

1 Qasr al-Bint Pharon	6 Byzantine Tower	12 Lower Market	18 Pillar
2 Altar	7 Nymphaeum	13 Propylaeum Steps	
3 Temenos	8 Shrine	14 Great Temple	
4 Temenos Gate	9 Colonnaded Street	15 Small Temple	
5 Temple of the Winged Lions	10 Upper Market	16 Roman House	
	11 Middle Market	17 Faroun Ruins	

from Brown University began, this theory was confirmed. However, the discovery of a theatre-like structure in the 'temple' itself has forced archaeologists to admit that its exact nature remains something of a mystery.

Clearly this was once one of the main architectural components of Petra. Centrally located, rising to a height of nearly 20 m and decorated with red and white stucco, it must have contrasted strikingly with the surrounding monuments. The complex comprised of a *propylaeum* (monumental entrance), a lower *temenos* (sacred area) and a monumental stairway leading up to the upper *temenos* where the 'temple' itself was located. The complex is believed to have originally been constructed in the late first century BCE, during the reign of Malichus I (62-30 BCE) and/or Obadas II (30-9 BCE). Sometime during the late first or early second century CE it was completely rebuilt and enlarged to its present form. Exhibiting a mixture of local Nabataean and Classical styles, it was lavishly decorated and included some unusual features such as capitals with carved elephant heads.

Ascending the stairway from the colonnaded street (originally this would have been topped by a *propylaeum*), you find yourself in the **lower temenos** of the temple, parts of which are still paved with large hexagonal flagstones. On either side of the *temenos* were triple colonnades that ended in semi-circular *exedrae* (or wall recesses). On the eastern (left-hand) side some of the columns of the triple colonnade have been re-erected, and the *exedra* partially reconstructed.

Two stairways next to each of the *exedra* lead up to the forecourt of the **upper temenos**, from where a broad central stairway flanked by two narrower ones lead up to the *portico* of the 'temple' itself. Some of the huge columns of the portico have been partially re-erected, though perhaps more evocative are those that still lie fallen in neat lines like dominoes, the victim presumably of the great earthquake of 363 CE.

It is the '**temple**' itself, standing in the centre of the upper *temenos*, which is the most unusual feature of the whole complex. Originally this was thought to follow the standard plan of a *cella*, or inner sanctuary, in which the 'holy of holies' (a statue of the temple god) would have been housed. However, the excavations carried out in 1998 revealed instead what appears to have been a small theatre (a *theatron* or *odeon*). Five tiers of seating from the theatre's semi-circular *cavea* have survived (and have now been restored), and the excavators believe that originally there may have been as many as 20 tiers, which would have accommodated somewhere between 550 and 630 people.

Monumental Gateway The Monumental Gateway at the western end of the colonnaded street originally consisted of a triple-arch, although all that remains today are the four piers that once supported the arches. Excavations have revealed that the gateway was built in the second century CE, after the colonnaded street had been completed. Originally it was believed that the gateway formed the western entrance to the town, but it has since been demonstrated that it was the entrance to a large *temenos* which preceded the Qasr al-Bint.

Qasr al-Bint Pharon The Qasr al-Bint Pharon towers impressively at the far end of the open *temenos*, offset slightly to the left. Built to a huge scale with its basic structure still standing, it is possible to reconstruct in the imagination the four massive pillars at the top of the wide stairway that would have supported the entrance portico. Behind this is an enormous single doorway (still standing) to the inner temple. Inside, the dividing walls of a central altar-chamber (*adyton*) flanked by two side-chambers are still tied into the rear wall. In front of the entrance is the base of a large, square altar. The outer walls, particularly the east one which faces you as you approach from the monumental gateway, are well-preserved, with two sections of crowning *entablature* still in place.

The name Qasr al-Bint Pharon means literally 'Palace of the Pharaoh's Daughter', a reference to a local legend which relates how the princess who lived in the palace (the Pharaoh's daughter) vowed to marry the first man to successfully supply the palace with running water. According to the legend, eventually one man succeeded, with the help of 'men, camels and God'. The story is slightly suspect in that the building was clearly a temple; according to one fourth-century writer it was dedicated to Dusares (Dhu-Shara) and his virgin mother Al-Uzza, a theory confirmed by Greek inscriptions and a fragment of an eye-idol discovered in the temple. On the other hand, such temples might also have served as royal palaces (a number of Nabataean rulers were after all deified).

Petra basin

From here the main trail turns to the right, crossing a bridge to bring you to the **Basin Restaurant** and the old Petra Museum on your right. This former museum's collection has been moved to the new museum near to the visitor centre (see page 129). From the museum the trail then continues on (turning into a rough, rocky track) until it finishes at the start of a rock-cut staircase in the side of the mountain. This is the beginning of the route to the Monastery.

Popular trails

discover the ancient site at your own pace

The Monastery (Ed-Deir)

Alongside the Treasury, this is certainly among Petra's most impressive and best-preserved monuments. It takes around 45 minutes to one hour to get there, including side trips, but the long steep climb involved is well worth the effort. The best time to arrive is in the late afternoon when the sun falls directly on the Monastery façade, illuminating the rock to a rich golden yellow. Late afternoon is also when most of the climb is in shade, making the going that much easier in summer.

The trail The path leads past the **Basin Restaurant** on the right, soon giving way to rock-cut steps as it enters the Wadi ed-Deir. After a short distance there is a signpost indicating the **Lion Triclinium** down a narrow cleft to the left of the main path. Some scrambling over rocks is needed to reach this monument, so called because of the large, now severely weathered, lions carved into the rock on either side of the entrance. The entrance itself consists of an odd keyhole-shaped crack in the rock, a result of weathering on what was originally a separate doorway and window. Above this is a frieze, with carved faces at either end, and symbols in between, followed by a pediment.

Back on the main path, the trail continues to climb steeply through more spectacular rock formations and, shortly before reaching the summit, passes a steep-sided pinnacle on the left with a number of caves carved into the rock. Dubbed the **Hermitage**, there are various crosses carved into the walls of the cells, indicating that they were occupied during the Byzantine era, although nothing is known about their origin or precise function.

The Monastery A short way further on is the Monastery, or **Ed-Deir**. The climb may have seemed interminable and you might be thoroughly exhausted, but the spectacle that greets you is more than worth the time and effort spent slogging your way up there. This is the largest of Petra's monuments, towering to a height of over 40 m and measuring nearly 47 m in width. The doorway alone measures 8 m in height, dwarfing any figure framed within it into insignificance.

Given its enormous size, the Monastery must have played an important role in the religious life of the Nabataeans. The temple façade has been carved deeply into a shoulder of the mountain to give a large courtyard area in front, presumably to accommodate a large congregation, and it seems likely that the climb up to it represented an important aspect of the rituals and ceremonies associated with the temple.

Stylistically, the Monastery mirrors closely the Khazneh and the Corinthian Tomb, differing only in that it has none of the detailed decoration found on the latter two. This simplicity of style serves to emphasize the grandeur and boldness of its scale. It is generally dated to around the middle of the first century CE, perhaps between 40 and 70 CE, making it in effect a culmination of the Hellenistic styles first developed in the Khazneh and Corinthian Tomb. The inside consists of a large single chamber with a large niche in the rear wall. Steps lead up to the niche on either side, and above it is a segmented arch.

Opposite the Monastery there's a tea and cold drinks stall offering refreshments and shade from which to appreciate the Monastery's grandeur. You can climb up onto the rock hillock behind for a better vantage point. Continuing west past the Monastery brings you to a wide ledge with dramatic views out across the Wadi Araba; the small white sanctuary of Nabi Haroun is also visible from here.

Al-Habees and its monuments

Just beyond (west of) the **Qasr al-Bint**, and towering above it, is the mountain of Al-Habees. At the northern edge a short stairway climbs up the slope and loops around to the west, snaking around the mountain. Cut right into the side of the mountain, this path has wonderful views over Wadi Siyyagh down below. The path then bends, turning into a wide plateau. To your right, just below, is a complex of buildings dug into the sandstone cliffs, surrounding a courtyard. Named the **convent**, opinion varies on this building's function. One suggestion is that this was where the temple priests lived (hence the name), but it seems more likely that these buildings were simple tombs. To your left is the cave home of **Mofleh Bdoul** with its colourful courtyard of plants. Mofleh is one of Petra's last Bdoul residents, resisting the call to leave the site when the Bdoul were resettled at Umm Sayhoun in the mid-1980s. Mofleh's courtyard serves as a tiny, welcoming tea-shop where you can take a break and enjoy a cuppa with your genial host.

From Mofleh's house, there are two routes up to the Crusader fort on the summit. You can continue along the path around the mountain which leads you to the bottom of the mountain, behind Qasr al-Bint. Here, a sign marks the spot where a set of restored staircases begin. Near the summit you cross a small wooden bridge and then climb up another small flight of stairs. This is also the way back down (see below). If you're feeling fit you can take a more tiring (but more interesting) route. This other trail is reached by walking up the rocky slope between Mofleh's house and a **tomb façade** cut into the mountain. At the top of the slope, to your right, is a steep staircase built into a narrow cleft in the cliff (if you're unsure of directions Mofleh is happy to point them out to you). The natural rock colours along this staircase are particularly stunning: one patch at the top, on the right, is a shimmering purple and shaped like zebra-stripes. At the top of the staircase you have to scramble onto the ledge to your left and then up a small, partially worn away staircase to your right. At the top of this set of steps, it's an easy walk along an exposed ridge to the **Crusader fort**. The ruins here are sparse and pretty uninteresting but the views across the central city ruins to the Royal Tombs are spectacular.

To descend, keep walking around the ridge until you reach a set of stairs that leads you to a small wooden bridge. From here there are rock-cut stairs leading you all the way down the mountain until you arrive at the bottom behind Qasr al-Bint. As you walk back to Qasr al-Bint and the central city ruins, there are two interesting monuments carved into the base of Al-Habees' eastern face. The first of these you will encounter is the **Columbarium**, the Latin name given to a place where cremation urns are stored, usually in niches. The exterior of this simple rock-cut chamber, as well as the interior walls, are completely covered in small niches, giving rise to the name, although the niches appear to be far too small and impractically shaped to have ever held urns. One theory is that mourners for the dead would collect their tears in small jars and this was the place those tear jars were stored. Another theory is that it was used as a dovecote in Byzantine times. After this you come to the **Unfinished Tomb**, which is interesting for the insight it gives into the way in which the façades of Petra were carved, working from the top down. Thus the upper half of this monument, including all the entablature and the capitals of the pillars, has been completed, while the lower half is bare rock except for a small doorway cut into it at ground level, probably at a much later date since its positioning interferes with one of the uncompleted columns.

Temple of the Winged Lions and the Petra churches
This short, easy walk is reached by crossing the *wadi* by the bridge directly opposite the Qasr al-Bint.

Temple of the Winged Lions If you turn right and then bear off to the right again up a slope, you reach the excavated remains of the Temple of the Winged Lions (also known as the Northern Temple or Temple of al-Uzza) up on a hillock. First identified by Bachmann and others in 1921 as a gymnasium, detailed excavations carried out since 1974 by Dr Hammond of Utah University have revealed it to be an important temple.

It is named after the intricately carved capitals decorated with floral patterns and winged lions that once topped every column. A road once crossed the *wadi* from the colonnaded street and led up to the temple, which consisted of a *temenos* surrounded by colonnades in the centre of which was a *cella*, also colonnaded (many of these have been re-erected).

Originally the temple was lavishly decorated with painted plaster, but after a fire in the early second century CE partially destroyed it, it was clad in white and brown marble. It was finally completely destroyed by the earthquake of 363 CE. At the time of writing, the temple was undergoing further restoration by a team of archaeologists.

Petra Church Continuing east from the Winged Lions Temple towards the Royal Tombs and then bearing off slightly to the left brings you to the rather unimaginatively named Petra Church. These remarkable remains were first discovered in 1990 by Dr Kenneth W Russell, and subsequent excavations here revealed a large triple-apsed basilica church measuring some 26 m by 15 m, with an atrium and baptistry. Impressive mosaics were found in both the side-aisles of the church, prompting the archaeologists to erect a protective structure over it. The site was only opened to the public in 1998.

The church is thought to date originally from the late sixth century CE. During the early sixth century CE it appears to have been enlarged, with most of the mosaics being dated stylistically to this period. The mosaics paving the north and south side-aisles are beautifully preserved. The north aisle consists of three parallel rows of *roundels*, or medallions (84 in total), depicting various animals, birds and objects such as vases and water jars, as well as some human figures, all enclosed within a geometric border. The eastern end of the south aisle consists of six larger-sized *roundels* depicting animals enclosed within a border. The rest of the south aisle consists of three rows of geometric panels, the central one containing personifications of the four seasons, the ocean, earth and wisdom, while those flanking it on either side contain various birds, animals and fish. Traces of the original paving of the central nave can be seen, though most of it is a modern reconstruction.

Ridge Church Continuing uphill from the Petra Church, up onto the ridge to the north, you arrive at the Ridge Church. Excavated between 1994 and 1998, this church is much smaller and simpler than the Petra Church, perhaps reflecting the fact that it stood at the outer limits of the city centre. Only the foundations of the church remain, and there are no surviving mosaics. However, the panoramic views from up here are spectacular and well worth the climb.

Jebel Madhbah High Place of Sacrifice

The Nabataeans had a fondness for high, exposed rock summits on which they would carry out ritual sacrifices. There are numerous examples of these 'High Places' all around Petra. The largest and most famous of these is on the summit of Jebel Madhbah. After the trail to the Monastery it has to be Petra's second most popular route off the main path.

The trail After passing the **Treasury** and before arriving at the **theatre**, a signpost indicates the start of the rock-cut staircase that leads up to the High Place of Sacrifice. At least 1½ to two hours are needed to go and come back by the same route. Alternatively you could descend via the much less-trodden path on the other side of the mountain. This is one of the Petra back roads, but for ease of continuation the route has been included below.

The ascent to the High Place takes around 30 minutes, following clearly marked rock-cut stairs. Near the summit are various seasonal souvenir and tea/cold drinks stalls, followed soon after by two stone **obelisks** up on a small plateau to your left, perhaps meant to mark the approach to the High Place. These have been created by chiselling away all of the surrounding summit, which must have been a monumental task. It has been suggested that they represent the two main Nabataean gods, Dushara (Dusares) and Al-Uzza. If you climb up the slope opposite the obelisks (to your right when they first come into view), you pass the heavily ruined remains of a **fortress**. This is generally believed to be of Crusader origin, although some suggest it might be Byzantine, Roman or even Nabataean in origin (according to the latter theory, it was built from the stone that was chiselled away to create the obelisks).

High Place of Sacrifice Beyond the fortress ruins, rock-cut steps take you out eventually onto the flat, exposed summit of Jebel Madhbah, and the High Place itself. From here there are spectacular views in all directions, including southwest to Jebel Haroun, west to Umm al-Biyara and northeast to Jebel al-Khubtha.

The High Place consists of a large rectangular sunken courtyard with a small raised platform within it and, just to the west, a large rectangular altar platform. Three steps lead up to the altar platform, which has a square hole cut into it, perhaps to hold a representation of a deity. Just to the left (south) of the main altar platform there is a second, circular platform with a circular basin carved into it. There is a small drain in the basin, and a channel leading from it; this was perhaps used for ritual washing. The large sunken courtyard was most probably used as a congregational area for those witnessing the ritual sacrifices which were taking place.

You can continue north along the ridge from the High Place and, if you scramble far enough, it is possible to get good views down onto the whole area of the central city ruins.

Wadi Farasa back road from Jebel Madhbah
Returning to the gully that runs between the two obelisks to the south and the fortress ruins and High Place to the north, if you keep the obelisks to your left, you can pick up the path that leads down the western face of the mountain via the Wadi Farasa. At first the route is a little unclear, although small stone cairns mark the way and soon there is a clear path as well as rock-cut stairs in places. Following this route, you pass first the **Lion Fountain** on your left, consisting of a heavily weathered but clearly discernible lion carved into the rock.

You come next to the **Garden Triclinium** with a large **cistern** next to it. The *triclinium* opens onto a platform of rock, while the area in front of this was seen to resemble a garden plot, giving rise to the name. According to the sign it is a tomb, but the monument almost certainly served as a *triclinium* (a banqueting hall in honour of the dead). The design is simple, consisting of four columns, two of them free-standing, supporting a lintel. This forms a portico (the area in which the banquets were held), beyond which there is a small shrine. The cistern is lined and would have been used to store water channelled from the Braq springs 4 km to the south, right into the centre of Petra.

A little further along, on the left, is the **Roman Soldier Tomb**, and opposite a **triclinium**. These two features once formed part of a single complex, with a central courtyard surrounded by a colonnaded portico joining the two. The Roman Soldier Tomb consists of four tall pilasters with a low-pitched pediment above. The central doorway has its own small pilasters (largely eroded away) supporting an entablature and pediment. In the upper level, between the four pilasters, are three niches each holding heavily weathered statues. It's from these statues that the tomb gets its name, with the central one, although headless, clearly being clad in Roman armour. Inside there are two large chambers, with the main one having a series of arched recesses in the walls, presumably to accommodate sarcophagi.

Although the *triclinium* is distinctly unimpressive from the outside, the interior is particularly interesting since it is the only one in Petra with elaborately carved decoration. The side and rear walls have beautifully fluted half-columns carved into them, with niches in between, while the sandstone rock reveals beautiful swirling patterns and colours in its grain. It has been suggested that the complex dates originally from some time in the first century CE, implying that the carved statues were added after the Roman annexation of Petra in 106 CE.

Shortly after, on the right, is the **Renaissance Tomb**, so called for its unique, elegantly executed façade. Two tall pilasters support a low-pitched pediment topped by an urn, very much in traditional Nabataean style, but the central doorway is framed by pilasters supporting a beautifully proportioned arch, a feature unique to this tomb, although quite closely reflected in the façade of the Sextius Florentinus Tomb.

Finally, the path takes you past the **Broken Pediment Tomb**. This tomb is situated up on a ledge facing north and is easily missed as you must turn and look back the way you came in order to see it. The façade is compact and simple, but interesting in that the device of a broken pediment is used in isolation, without a central *tholos* rising between the two ends of the pediment, as found in the Treasury and Monastery, and without the mass of other architectural detail which at times threaten to clutter up the classical Nabataean façades. In addition, this façade has good examples of the swirling patterns and colours typical of Petra's sandstone rock.

Continuing on, the *wadi* opens out and the path forks; bear right to keep following the line of the cliffs in a northerly direction. There are numerous small tomb façades carved into the cliff side to your right, the best-preserved ones being higher up. Many of these display the distinctive Nabataean-style crow-step attic storey. If you keep following the line of the cliffs you end up back near the **theatre**. If you follow the track which branches off to the left you arrive in the vicinity of the **Qasr al-Bint**. Following the latter route takes you up onto the crest of a hillock and past a set of excavated ruins on the right just below the track, signposted 'Nabataean Chapel' but better known as the Az Zantur site. From here you can cut straight across to the solitary standing column of Zibb Pharon, or else follow the wide loop of the track, before continuing down to the Qasr al-Bint and central city ruins area.

Petra back roads

the side of Petra that few see

Petra is a hiker's delight and its vastness means there's always a trail to get away from the crowds if that's what you like.

To Zibb Pharon and Az Zantur ⓘ *Easy.*

The steep, rubble-strewn rise in the land to the south of the Qasr al-Bint has been described by Iain Browning as the "tip of an archaeological iceberg". The slope is not a natural one, but rather the accumulated debris of centuries, which once excavated will no doubt reveal a great deal more about the central city area. A path leads from behind the Qasr al-Bint in a southeasterly direction to a lone standing column known as **Zibb Pharon** (the Pharaoh's Phallus) which is thought to have marked the starting point for the trading route to Egypt. An identical column lies fallen on the ground nearby.

From the Zibb Pharon, one path heads southwest leading past **Umm al-Biyara** towards the Snake Monument and Jebel Haroun beyond. A second path heads southeast towards the Wadi Farasa and the **Jebel Madhbah High Place of Sacrifice** (see page 120). To the southeast of the Zibb Pharon, up on a small hillock, is an area of excavations known as **Az Zantur**. A sign by the excavation reads 'Nabataean Chapel', although the site is in fact a mixture of Nabataean and Roman domestic housing. Only the lower courses of the walls remain and the site is of little interest to the non-specialist.

Zibb Pharon to Umm al-Biyara ⓘ *Difficult, guide recommended.*

The sheer rocky massif of Umm al-Biyara towers to a height of 1178 m and dominates the whole Petra basin. Along the base of the cliffs of its eastern face there are numerous tomb façades carved into the rock displaying a wide variety of styles. These can be reached by heading southwest from the **Zibb Pharon** (arriving at the Zibb Pharon from the Qasr al-Bint, take the right-hand fork in the path). The route to the summit of Umm al-Biyara is not obvious, as well as being challenging in places, and a guide is strongly recommended. If you enjoy strenuous climbs, it's well worth the effort for the magnificent views from the top. The climb is best undertaken later in the day when the route is largely in shade. Allow at least three to four hours for the return trip and leave plenty of time to descend before darkness falls.

After an initial scramble up a loose scree slope, you join the original processional route, an unusually grandiose affair consisting of a smooth ramp chiselled deep into the rock to give smooth-sided vertical walls on either side. The ramp leads to a landing before doubling back to continue the ascent. Higher up it gives way to rock-cut stairs with precipitous drops on one side. The steps are now very badly worn and need to be negotiated with extreme care.

The large summit area is basically flat-topped, rising gently to its highest point in the northwest. Roughly in the centre are the excavated remains of an **Edomite settlement**. These excavations were carried out by the British archaeologist Crystal Bennett in the 1960s, an expedition of considerable logistical complexity which involved a team of archaeologists camping on the summit while all supplies were delivered by helicopter. The settlement has only been partially excavated, but has been dated with a fair degree of certainty to the sixth to seventh centuries BCE.

Turkmaniyeh Tomb Trail ⓘ *Easy.*

Across the bridge opposite the Qasr al-Bint, a wide, bare and exposed *wadi* ascends gently in a northeasterly direction with a good jeep track running along it. This is known variously as Wadi al-Turkmaniyeh or Wadi Abu Alleiqa, and leads up to the modern Bedouin village of Bdoul, on the road to Little Petra. In the cliffs to the left as you ascend the *wadi*, there are various façades carved into the rock. After approximately 1 km (around 15 minutes' walk), there is a temple façade on the left, close to the jeep track, known as the **Turkmaniyeh Tomb**. The lower half of this façade has been completely eroded away, most probably by flash floods. However, preserved between the two pilasters of the upper half is the longest Nabataean inscription to be found at Petra. The inscription is of great value in that it gives details of the additional features that originally complemented the tomb façades.

ON THE ROAD

The Bdoul: Petra's guardians

The local Bedouin who guided the European explorer Burckhardt into this lost city were from the Bdoul tribe, Petra's traditional custodians and inhabitants. The origins of the Bdoul are obscure and theories abound. Many (especially those that work with tourists at the site) claim to be the direct descendants of the Nabataeans, though there is no firm evidence to back up this claim. A more probable theory is that the Bdoul were a nomadic Bedouin tribe who, a few hundred years ago, came across the deserted caves of the Nabataean capital and gradually settled in the area.

Whichever theory is correct, the Bdoul are truly as much a part of Petra as the mighty Nabataean façades and pink-tinged patterned rock. Disparaged by most other Jordanian Bedouin tribes due to their insignificant number and impoverished living conditions, the Bdoul actually lived inside the archaeological site, utilizing the caves and tombs as their houses, up until the mid-1980s. When Petra was awarded UNESCO World Heritage Site status in 1985, the Jordanian government, in conjunction with USAID, launched a plan to relocate the Bdoul from their cave homes and build a new village on a ridge overlooking Petra.

The result was Umm Sayhoun village. Although the government promises of electricity and running water within their new homes didn't materialize straight away, the majority of the Bdoul moved here in 1985, spurred on by rumours that if they didn't occupy the still unfinished houses, that they would lose their right to one.

Although no longer living inside the site, most Bdoul still make their living there by selling souvenirs, working as guides or running tea shacks among the ruins, and as tourism has increased, so too have the Bdoul's prospects. Obviously the tribe still faces many difficulties and challenges for the future. Space for new buildings in Umm Sayhoun is quickly running out and a housing shortage is imminent; with modernization and the arrival of mass tourism (not to mention the introduction of satellite TV and the internet) many of the Bdoul traditions and customs are in danger of dying out with the passing of the older generation and being lost for good.

Despite these ongoing problems, the Bdoul are a resourceful and resilient people who have proved that they have been able to surmount significant difficulties in the past, and most remain cheerfully optimistic about their future as a tribe.

Wadi Siyyagh Trail ⓘ *Easy.*

If you feel in danger of overdosing on monuments Wadi Siyyagh makes for a pleasant, undemanding walk enjoyable mostly for the welcome contrast of lush green vegetation after so much bare rock. However the tranquillity of this *wadi* is slightly shattered by the noise of a generator that supplies the **Basin Restaurant** and Department of Antiquities offices with electricity.

At the bridge leading from the **Qasr al-Bint** across to the **Basin Restaurant**, follow the bed of the *wadi* around the base of Al-Habees mountain. Just a short walk into the *wadi* you'll come to a signpost on your right marking the **Painted Room**, and steps leading up to it. Scrambling up the stairs brings you to the remains of a cave house that contains an extremely rare and well-preserved example of Nabataean wall painting which was discovered in 1979. The room is barred-off so you cannot enter but the painted interior is easily viewed through the bars. Further along the *wadi* you pass an **ancient quarry**, at which point the *wadi* swings round to the left. From here on, the *wadi* becomes increasingly green and wooded, until you arrive at a **spring** complete with rock pools and even waterfalls when there are sufficient rains. Unfortunately, when we last visited the spring there was quite a bit of litter lying around, which destroys the pleasant atmosphere here somewhat. This was one of Petra's main water sources and irrigation channels would once have carried the water to the central city area.

On the way back, you have the option of bearing right after the quarry instead of left. This takes you along the bed of the **Wadi Kharroub** and brings you out at a point to the south of the Qasr al-Bint, along the route to the Snake Monument.

Snake Monument Trail ⓘ *Easy/medium.*

This is a longish walk, taking some 35-45 minutes from the Qasr al-Bint to the Snake Monument. Follow the path southeast from the Qasr al-Bint to the **Zibb Pharon**. Here the path forks; bear right to head southwest in the direction of Umm al-Biyara, descending to the Wadi Kharroub just before it forks.

Cross the *wadi* and continue southwest along a good 4WD track that follows the gentle slope of the hill edge until you arrive at a steep rise of solid sandstone rock speckled with rock-cut chambers and Djinn Blocks.

The **Snake Monument** is the square-based structure higher up and to the left on the sandstone escarpment, with what looks for all the world like a melting blob of ice cream on top, rather than a snake. If you wind your way up through the sandstone rock and onto the crest, above the Snake Monument, you'll get expansive views over the countryside and will also be able to see the tiny white tomb of Nabi Haroun on the summit of Jebel Haroun.

Jebel al-Khubtha Trail ⓘ *Easy/medium.*

By far our favourite Petra back road begins at the Royal Tombs, at the stairway between the **Palace Tomb** and the **Tomb of Sextius Florentinus**. Like the route to the Monastery it's up all the way (a steep 30-minute climb to the top), but the trail itself is easy to follow and the views on the way are magnificent. Simply follow the steps as they climb up the mountain; in places the stairway is newly built or restored, elsewhere it is rock-cut, weathered and ancient.

Towards the top there's a small ridge where you can look down on the theatre from above. At the end of the stairway you'll come to a huge plateau that is the **Jebel Umm al-Amr High Place of Sacrifice**. The remains here are not as well-preserved or extensive as at the Jebel Madhbah High Place of Sacrifice, but around the summit you can see traces of sacrificial areas cut into the fat rock, the heavy stonework of what was a dam built into a cleft, and the remains of various rock-cut water channels, caves and stairways. The views out over Petra are truly magnificent.

The stairway ends at a small cave house on the summit. Just to the left of the house there is a small set of steps cut into the rock. If you head down these and follow the narrow dirt trail across the rocky slope you'll eventually come (after about 15 minutes' walk) to a jagged ridge from where you get incredible views overlooking the **Treasury** (about 200 m below you); the perfect reward for that uphill climb.

Shrine of Nabi Haroun ⓘ *Difficult, guide recommended.*

The shrine of Nabi Haroun (the Prophet Aaron) is situated on the summit of Jebel Haroun, at 1396 m the highest mountain in the area. By foot this is a long and strenuous full-day's excursion, although you can go by camel or donkey as far as the base of Jebel Haroun. A guide is strongly recommended since the final ascent is by no means clear. The route is the same as for the Snake Monument, though from the point where the shrine comes into view, it's still a deceptively long way off. The shrine is kept locked; the key is held by the Bedouins living close to the foot of the mountain. Bear in mind that this is a sacred place of pilgrimage for Jews, Christians and Muslims – casual tourists wandering up there simply for the view are not particularly welcome. Unless the shrine is of special significance to you, it's far from noteworthy, and while the views are spectacular, there are plenty of equally impressive ones which are much nearer and more easily accessible.

The shrine is revered as the place where the prophet Aaron is buried, with Jebel Haroun being identified with biblical Mount Hor.

Wadi Muthlim Trail (an alternative entry to Petra) ⓘ *Medium. This trail should not be attempted after rainfall due to the risk of flash-flooding. If in any doubt at all, ask for advice at the visitor centre before beginning the trail.*

This is an excellent alternative trail from walking through the Siq into Petra, beginning just before the Siq and taking you through a narrow, snaking canyon before finishing at the Royal Tombs.

At the Siq entrance, veer off to the right from the bridge and enter the **Nabataean tunnel** that runs for 88 m along the bed of the *wadi*. At the end of the tunnel you'll find yourself in pretty **Wadi Muthlim** where you simply follow the path of the valley as it begins to narrow, eventually becoming only 1 m wide. This is where the fun begins as the path from here on is blocked in places by large rocks that you have to clamber over.

About 30 minutes into the walk (having successfully scrambled over the boulders) the trail splits into two. Look out for the painted arrow on the rock face on your left and follow the arrow marker as the *wadi* becomes even narrower until you finally emerge on the ridge at the back of the **Royal Tombs**. If you walk to your left from here you'll first come to the tomb of **Dorotheo's House**, then the **Tomb of Sextius Florentinus** before finally finding yourself staring down at the central city ruins from in front of the Royal Tombs.

Wadi Musa

Petra's service town, with all the tourist facilities

The scruffy town of Wadi Musa sprawls along the top of the hill that leads down to Petra. Even if you're sleeping down below beside the site entrance most travellers will end up here at some stage, even if it's only to use an ATM.

Ain Musa (Musa Spring)
Right at the top of the hill, roughly a 2-km walk from the centre of town.

The small domed whitewashed building here (on your left as you walk up the hill) marks the spot where the spring that still feeds Wadi Musa rises. According to local tradition (and hence the name) this is also the spot where Moses struck the rock and brought forth water.

Although in no way comparable to the grandness of Petra, Siq Al-Barid, once one of Petra's prosperous suburbs, has some interesting façades and cave houses scattered throughout its own mini-Siq. It's thought that Al-Barid acted as a transit area for the caravans on their way to Petra; a place where merchants and their camels could rest before their final march into the capital. Today it's a peaceful spot that sees only a handful of tourists. Nearby is the archaeological site of Al-Beidha which has heralded remains from Neolithic times. The sites are free to visit and open daily during daylight hours.

Little Petra (Siq Al-Barid)

From the car park the entrance to Siq Al-Barid (literally 'cold canyon' in Arabic) is straight ahead. You pass first a remarkably well-preserved temple façade on your right before passing through a mini-Siq. Once through this, you'll see a second well-preserved façade higher up in the cliff face on the left, with a set of rock-cut stairs climbing steeply up just before. This is the **biclinium**. If you climb up the stairs, into the chamber you can view one of the few examples of Nabataean wall-paintings that have survived. The fragments – depicting chubby cherubs amid floral decoration – were uncovered and restored by a British team in 2011. Following the narrow *wadi* bed you pass more rock-cut chambers (the majority badly weathered) as well as numerous rock-cut stairs leading to various

Wadi Musa

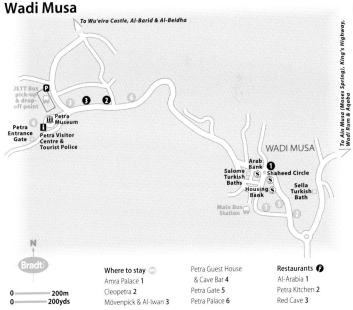

Where to stay
Amra Palace **1**
Cleopatra **2**
Mövenpick & Al-Iwan **3**

Petra Guest House
 & Cave Bar **4**
Petra Gate **5**
Petra Palace **6**

Restaurants
Al-Arabia **1**
Petra Kitchen **2**
Red Cave **3**

small High Places of Sacrifice. Further on the cliffs close-in sharply to leave just a narrow cleft, accentuating the bizarre weathered rock formations on either side.

A set of heavily worn steps climb up into the cleft and, if you can negotiate your way past the massive stone that blocks the way towards the top, you reach a ledge overlooking a larger *wadi* below. It is possible to scramble down into this *wadi* and explore further.

Tip...
You can get a taxi to Little Petra for about 10JD return including waiting time. If possible flag a taxi down on the road rather than picking one up at the taxi rank beside the Petra Visitor Centre as the drivers there tend to quote exorbitantly high figures for a ride anywhere.

Al-Beidha

Facing the entrance to Al-Barid, a rough track bears off to the left from the road-head leading to the excavated site of Al-Beidha, a 10- to 15-minute walk. Although to the untrained eye there's not a great deal to see here, in archaeological terms it's of major importance. The site was first discovered by the archaeologist D Kilbride in 1956, and although extensive work has been done on it over the years, the excavations are far from complete. The remains of the small settlement found here date back to the Pre-Pottery Neolithic period (7000-6500 BCE) when humans were making the transition from nomadic hunter-gathering to settled agriculture and animal husbandry. The majority of the tools found here are of flint and bone, while querns (stone mills for grinding grain) were found in abundance.

Little Petra to the Monastery Trail ⓘ *Medium, guide recommended.*

The beautiful Petra back road that leads from Little Petra to the Monastery is a wonderful chance to get away from the crowds and see some incredible mountain views. Although relatively easy, much of it is uphill, along a series of Nabataean stairways, so a decent level of fitness is required. The beginning of the trail is difficult to find and stay on, so a guide is recommended at least for the beginning of the trail from Little Petra to the stairway. From there the trail is straightforward. If you haven't already picked up a guide, ask at the Little Petra car park. The trail takes about 3½ hours in total.

Vertigo sufferers should be aware that for the last 20 minutes of the trail you are walking along an exposed ridge.

The track begins beside the Little Petra car park where a wide track (to the left) runs along a dried river bed leading past the Al-Beidha archaeological site. Not long after, this trail branches off into various directions and it's easy to wander off-track. Head left along a well-worn path where there are often a few Bedouin camps. After about 20 minutes the landscape really opens out and you find yourself amid a large area of small sand dunes. You really need a guide here for route-finding through the *wadi*.

After hiking through the sand dune area you will get to the crest of a hill with a small marker. Just below is the entry to the Nabataean stairway. This is the really beautiful portion of the walk as the stairs climb and wind around the red-rock mountain with stunning views over the mountain ranges to your right. For the last portion of the walk you traverse an exposed ridge before taking a set of rough, unrestored stairs into a gully. From down in the gully you can get your first glimpse of the Monastery, the top of the façade is just visible beyond the top of the small cliff. If you walk to your right along the gully there are several spots where it is a simple (and not overly steep) scramble up the cliff to the top of the plateau, from where there is a path heading left towards the Monastery itself.

Listings Petra and Wadi Musa *maps p110, p112, p115 and p127*

Tourist information

Petra

Petra Visitor Centre
Right at the end of the main road, after the Mövenpick Hotel, T03-215 6044, www.visitpetra.jo. Daily 0600-1630 winter, 0600-1800 summer.
At this large complex you'll find the ticket office, clean toilets and various souvenir shops and cafés. This is also where you can arrange a guide for the site and obtain tickets for the **Petra By Night** tour (see What to do, page 131).

Tourist Police
Based inside the visitor centre, T03-215 6487.

Where to stay

When choosing a place to stay it's important to consider location. The hotels down by the entrance gate have the obvious advantage of being within easy walking distance of Petra – though there are not many catering for those on a cheaper budget here. If you decide to stay up the hill in Wadi Musa town (see below) you will have an added 15- to 20-min walk uphill after your sightseeing in Petra is finished. See Wadi Musa map, page 127, for the location of hotels.

Petra

$$$$ Mövenpick
2 mins across the road from the visitor centre entrance, T03-215 7111, www.movenpick.com.
There may be no grand views, but this hotel is an elegant oasis far removed from the red dust of Petra. The grand and opulently arabesque atrium is the focal point of the hotel with its trickling fountains and in-laid furniture. All the 183 rooms and suites are suitably luxurious with a fresh modern look featuring gorgeous burnt-orange and white textiles. Breakfast included.

$$$ Petra Guest House Hotel
Beside the site entrance gate, T03-215 6266, www.petraguesthousehotel.com.
Right beside the entrance, and with its own Nabataean cave for a bar (see Entertainment, page 130), you don't get to sleep any closer to the site than this. The 41 light-filled rooms in the main building and 31 larger chalets set upon a sandstone hill have all been given a bright makeover and come with a/c, satellite TV, fridge and huge windows. Breakfast included and fantastic value for money.

$$$ Petra Palace
On the road to the site, T03-215 6723, www.petrapalace.com.
The 180 massive rooms here, overlooking the hotel's leafy garden, could really do with an update but the 2 swimming pools, bar and hamman manage to make up for it. You also can't argue with the location, just a short stroll from Petra's entrance gate. Wi-Fi (lobby only), breakfast included.

Wadi Musa

$$$ Amra Palace
T03-215 7070, www.amrapalacepetra.com.
The 72-room Amra Palace offers all the facilities of the luxury hotels but at a 3rd of the price. There's a swimming pool, large

terrace with bright Bedouin-style seating, off-street parking, restaurant and its own hammam. The nicely appointed rooms (a/c, satellite TV) come with comfortable beds, and the management are helpful and efficient. Excellent value, Wi-Fi, breakfast included. Recommended.

$$ Cleopetra
T03-215 709.
This well-run backpacker hangout has sparkling clean rooms and runs a complimentary shuttle service to Petra's entrance gate. Owner Mosleh works hard to create a homely atmosphere and regularly organizes delicious dinners for guests. Those on tight budgets can sleep on the roof in warmer months (7JD). Wi-Fi, breakfast included.

$ Petra Gate
T03-215 6908, www.hostelworld.com.
This little place is as basic as they come. Rooms (fan only) are clean and have decent-sized baths. The exceedingly friendly manager, Nasser, will drop you down to the site for free and entertains guests with regular music nights. Wi-Fi.

Restaurants

As you might expect for the nation's prime tourist attraction, food tends to be more expensive in Petra; even a bottle of water from the supermarket has a higher price tag here. Surprisingly, despite the flocks of tourists that descend upon the town, there isn't much choice for gourmets. For cheap eats head to Wadi Musa town.

Petra

$$$ Al-Iwan
Inside the Mövenpick hotel, T03-215 7111. Daily 1800-2230.
The place to come if you're celebrating something special. Al-Iwan serves slick Mediterranean-inspired dishes in elegant and intimate surroundings. Alcohol served.

$$$ Petra Kitchen
Below Made in Jordan, on the road to the site, T03-215 4444, T07-9177 7800, see Facebook. Daily 0630-2000.
More a culinary experience than simply just going for dinner. Petra Kitchen gives foodies the chance to learn how traditional Arabic dishes are made, and help make some of the dishes, before tucking into the food itself (35JD per person). It's an entertaining evening as well as a great meal. No alcohol is served but you may bring your own.

$$ Red Cave
On the road to the site, T07-9512 0869, see Facebook. Daily 0900-2200.
Set in a vaulted stone-walled building, Red Cave is a friendly and relaxed place with a large and varied menu of Jordanian and European dishes. The *mansaf* (a traditional meal of lamb and yoghurt) is particularly good.

Wadi Musa

Wadi Musa town has plenty of cheap diners churning out *shawarma*, falafel and chicken and chips on the main road.

$ Al-Arabia
Wadi Musa centre.
Head here for excellent falafel, which they start churning out in the morning and carry on throughout the day. There's also a good range of typical Arabic dishes on the menu and portions are huge so you won't leave hungry. It's a popular joint that's often packed. If it's hot, head upstairs to their a/c dining hall.

Entertainment

Petra

Cave Bar, *Petra Guest House, beside the site entrance. Daily 1500-late.* The perfect place to unwind with a beer after a full day in the site (if only because you can't walk any further). Set in a cave (as the name suggests), this is the vortex of Petra's night scene, which isn't saying much, as there's practically no competition. It's an atmospheric place though it can be a tad pricey, with an additional 5% service charge and 8% government tax added to your final bill.

What to do

Petra

Tours

Petra By Night, *tickets available from the visitor centre on the day or through your hotel; tours leave at 2030 on Mon, Wed, Thu (dependent on weather), 17JD, under 10s free.* Incredibly popular, this tour begins from the visitor centre and heads through a candlelit Siq before ending at the Treasury, where there's a short programme of Bedouin music and storytelling. The whole tour lasts 2 hrs, including the walk there and back through the Siq. Is it worth 17JD? Probably not, but it is your only chance of seeing the Siq and Treasury in a moonlit setting.

Wadi Musa

Hammams

There are a few places around town where you can get the red dust of Petra scrubbed off you.

Salome Turkish Bath, *central Wadi Musa, T03-215 7342. Daily 1500-2200.* A full sauna and scrub costs 24JD and they'll pick you up and drop you back at your hotel for free if you're feeling lazy.

Sella Turkish Bath, *across the road from the Sella Hotel, Ain Musa, T03-215 7170, www.sella hotel.com. Daily 1000-2400.* This modern hammam has separate areas for female and male bathers and a full list of massage options.

Transport

Wadi Musa

Bus and minibus The main bus station is a scruffy car park in Wadi Musa. Note that travellers are often charged more than locals on buses departing from Wadi Musa. All buses leave when they are full but below are some usual departure times. To **Amman** there are usually 3 buses daily 0500-0800, another at 1100, and one at 1300 (c4 hrs, 5-6JD). On Fri the only reliable Amman bus leaves around 0700. To **Aqaba** there are usually 4 buses daily at 0600, 0700, 0800 and 1500 (2½ hrs, 5JD depending on luggage). There are several buses daily to **Ma'an** (45 mins, 50 piastres), so if your bus to Amman or Aqaba looks like it's not going to leave for hours you can always hop on a minibus to Ma'an and change there.

Bus transport to **Wadi Rum** is a special bus service that's run by the hotels. The bus leaves at approximately 0600 daily and runs around the hotels picking up passengers before heading to Wadi Rum (1½-2 hrs, 7JD). Book the night before with your hotel.

The most comfortable way to head to **Amman** is with the JETT bus that leaves from the car park beside Petra Visitor Centre complex daily at 1700 in summer, 1600 in winter (4 hrs, 10JD). Tickets can be bought either through your hotel or about 30 mins before the bus is due to depart from a ticket seller in the car park.

Wadi Rum

There's a reason why the T E Lawrence description of Wadi Rum as "vast, echoing and godlike" has stood the test of time. This is one of the world's great landscapes. Amid its subtly hued sands, colossal rock formations reach for the sky, their strange and peculiar contours, with exteriors that seem to drip like icing running down a cake, envelop you in a desert-scape so enormous that, like Lawrence himself, you will feel humbled.

Long before Lawrence's escapades in the *Seven Pillars of Wisdom* brought Wadi Rum to the attention of the West, this area had been traversed by Bedouin tribes for millennia; the Thamudic tribes of Arabia and the Nabataeans both lived here, and have left their mark on the desert with rock inscriptions and ruins. Today the local Zelabieh tribe are the custodians of the Wadi Rum protected reserve; many making a living as guides and drivers in the tourism industry here.

Although you could, if pressed for time, see a selection of the main sites in the reserve on an afternoon 4WD excursion, this is a landscape that is worth savouring. To really appreciate it you need to spend at least one night here. The fantastic spectacle of the changing colours of light on rock and sand that comes with sunrise and sunset is an experience to be relished; as is sleeping outside in the desert sands at a Bedouin camp, under a blanket sky strewn with a million stars.

Essential Wadi Rum

Getting around

Public transport

The **JETT** buses (www.jett.com.jo) operate a daily direct service from Amman to Wadi Rum which departs the capital at 0730 (20JD) and leaves Wadi Rum for Amman at 1700. If you are only planning to visit Wadi Rum as a day trip from Amman a return ticket will cost 30JD.

From Aqaba there are (supposedly) three minibuses direct to Wadi Rum Visitor Centre daily, though these services are on-demand and quite often only one of them actually leaves (the 1130 service is the most reliable). The better and more reliable option would be to take the scheduled daily **JETT** bus service, which departs Aqaba at 0800 (15JD) and returns from Wadi Rum at 1830 (15JD).

If you've been dropped at the Wadi Rum turn-off at Rashidiyeh, it's usually easy to hitch a lift for the remaining 28 km to Wadi Rum Visitor Centre. There are normally also a couple of enterprising locals with minivans who wait beside the turn-off for passengers (the usual rate is 2-3JD).

Direct transport from Wadi Musa (Petra) is provided by a daily tourist bus that you can book through your hotel. It leaves at 0615 and picks up passengers from their hotels rather than the bus station. You need to book at least the night before. During quiet tourism periods, this bus doesn't always operate.

Within Wadi Rum

At Wadi Rum Visitor Centre you can hire camels or 4WDs and their drivers/guides to take you into the reserve on excursions of varying itineraries and lengths. You can bring your own 4WD vehicle into the reserve for 35JD, but unless you're an experienced desert specialist you shouldn't think of setting off by yourself.

Note that by using the 4WD and camel services from the visitor centre you are supporting the local economy of Wadi Rum's Zelabieh tribe and also helping provide funds for the continued conservation efforts within the protected area.

Site information

The official website is **www.wadirum.jo**. Entry to the reserve costs 5JD, under 12s free. Entry fees are paid at the Wadi Rum Visitor Centre (see page 140) on arrival. They can also organize excursions, such as walking, camel riding or 4WD and overnight stays in Bedouin camps.

When to go

Wadi Rum's desert blooms with a carpet of wild grasses and flowers during the months of March and April. October and November are also good times for visiting with pleasant temperatures. Between May and September prepare for extreme heat with temperatures regularly rocketing over 40°C. Winter can be just as brutal. From December to February, you'll need to wrap up well against the cold if you're planning to stay overnight.

Taking a tour

If you've booked a Wadi Rum overnight tour through a tour company in Amman, Aqaba or Wadi Musa you might want to check whether your Bedouin camp is actually inside the protected area. Many of the non-local tour companies use camps in nearby Disi which, though still in the desert, have none of the atmosphere or beautiful scenery of Wadi Rum. The Disi camps also tend to be huge affairs hosting massive groups of people (so a quiet commune with nature is generally out of the question), and as they're mostly owned and operated by outside tour companies you're not helping to contribute to the local economy (the camps inside the protected area can only be owned and run by local Bedouin).

Flora and fauna

Although on the surface Wadi Rum may appear inhospitable and barren, the desert here is in fact a complex ecosystem rich in life. Those fortunate enough to spend some time here and see the dramatic transformation that a little rain brings, carpeting the desert floor in flowers and wild grasses, can attest to this. Even during the dry months, a short walk into the Wadi S'Bach near Rum village reveals what a little water can do in this otherwise parched wilderness. Bushes such as tamarisk and artemesan form the bulk of the scrub vegetation. Near sources of spring water, these are complemented by numerous other bushes and plants, including wild watermelon, as well as palm trees. Higher up, juniper trees can also be found, although these are becoming increasingly rare. The desert is rich in herbs and medicinal plants, of which the local Bedouin have a detailed and extensive knowledge.

Tip...

Even a short time out in the dry desert heat, buffeted by the sandy wind, can cause heat exhaustion and sunburn, so come prepared. Wear a high-factor sunblock, hat and sunglasses. Lip balm to prevent chapped lips and wet wipes (for cleaning all that sand off you) are also particularly useful. There are a couple of basic stores in Rum village where you can stock up on water if you haven't brought enough. A torch is necessary if you're spending the night at a desert camp.

Unless you spend quite a bit of time here and seek out the more isolated spots, you are unlikely to come across much in the way of wildlife. Ibex, jackals and the Arabian sand cat can still be seen roaming around remote high mountain areas (though in ever decreasing numbers), as well as the more common hyrax. In 2002 a group of Arabian oryx (*Oryx leucoryx*) from the successful breeding project at **Shaumari Wildlife Reserve** were brought to Wadi Rum to be reintroduced, but the project was not successful. Since 2007 a new reintroduction project developed by **ASEZA** has been underway, with help from the RSCN.

Smaller mammals that inhabit Wadi Rum include gerbils, jirds and numerous other rodents. Reptiles are common and include geckos, agama and fringe fingered lizards, as well as Palestinian vipers, sand snakes and the horned cerastes snake, the latter being much feared by the Bedouin. Other nasty creatures include the camel spider, black widow and various scorpions, although the chances of coming face to face with any of these, let alone actually being bitten or stung by them, is very remote. Birds are numerous in the region; birds of prey include vultures, buzzards and eagles, while ravens, partridges, pigeons, sparrows, finches, larks and warblers are all common.

Sights

towering pinnacles, rippling orange-hued sands and star-strewn night skies

You really need to hire a camel or 4WD to explore Wadi Rum fully. Unless you have a specific plan or itinerary of your own, you can choose from many different itineraries advertised on the board at the visitor centre. If you prefer to walk, the trails around Rum Village make excellent desert hikes, but unless you are a desert-terrain expert you'd be a fool to set out by yourself. Knowledgeable walking guides can be hired from the visitor centre (see page 140).

There are a number of pleasant and interesting walks that can be undertaken in the immediate vicinity of Rum village. These take in what 'sights' there are here besides the natural landscape. There are also plenty of scrambles and climbs you can do near here. The narrow ridge that rises directly from **Wadi Rum Resthouse** camping area up to the

Wadi Rum

To Desert Highway

Freight Railway

Checkpost

To Disi

Jebel Umm
Hassa
(1044m)

Jebel
al-Liyha ▲
(1096m)

Jebel al-Sarabit ▲
(1254m)

Wadi Rum
Visitor Centre
Sunrise
Site

Jebel
al-Kafr ▲

Jebel
Rashrasheh ▲

Jebel
Umm Ishrin
(1753m)
▲

Jebel Sad ▲
(1400m)

Jebel
Mayeen ▲

Nabatean Temple
Rum
Village

Jebel
Barrah ▲

Siq Al Barrah

Jebel Rum ▲
(1754m)

Lawrence's
Spring

Jebel
Abu Judayda ▲

Abu Aineh

Jebel
Anfaishyya ▲

Jebel
Umm
Ulaydiyya ▲

Jebel
Umm
Kharg ▲

Jebel
Moharrag ▲

Jebel
Makheret ▲

Lawrence's
House

Desert route to Aqaba

Jebel
Qattar ▲

Jebel
Khazali ▲

Jebel
Qaber ▲
Amra

Burdah
Rock
Bridge

Jebel Burdah
(1560m) ▲

Umm Sabatah
Sunset Site

Umm Fruth
Rock Bridge

N

Bradt

0 —— 1km
0 —— 1 mile

Where to stay 🛏
Bedouin Whispers **1**
Mohammed Mutlak Camp **2**

Panorama Sunset **3**
Rum Stars **4**

Restaurants 🍴
Ali's Place **1**
Wadi Rum Resthouse **2**

Lawrence of Arabia

Archaeologist, adventurer, author and military strategist, Thomas Edward Lawrence remains one of the most enigmatic figures of the 20th century. Born on 16 August 1888 in Tremadoc, north Wales, Lawrence graduated from Oxford with first-class honours in history for his thesis on Crusader-era architecture. In 1911 he arrived at Carchemish in Syria to work as an archaeologist.

Following the outbreak of the First World War, Lawrence joined the army and was posted to the British intelligence unit in Cairo. Here Lawrence became involved with the Foreign Office campaign that would eventually culminate in the Arab Revolt. By creating an internal insurgency against the Ottomans, the British believed they could seriously undermine the Turkish military and prevent them from advancing on British-held Egypt. In return for Arab assistance, the British would offer them an independent Arabia. Lawrence was posted to Mecca to meet with Sherif Hussein and eventually became the British Liaison Officer for the incipient Arab Revolt, fighting alongside Emir Faisal in battle. Throughout 1917 Lawrence, Faisal and their Arab fighters embarked on a series of guerrilla-style raids attacking the Ottoman's strategically vital Hijaz railway line, which stretched from Damascus to Medina. The Ottomans' attempts to protect and repair the line prevented them from advancing troops into Palestine, rendering the Turkish troops in Medina impotent.

Following a camel trek through the harsh Al Houl desert, Lawrence and Emir Faisal, together with Arab fighters granted to them by Auda ibu Tayi of the Howeitat tribe, led a surprise attack on the Ottoman garrison at Aqaba, attacking from the desert while

peak of Jebel al-Mayeen to the north is a moderate scramble, but you'll need confidence and some prior experience of rock climbing to complete it. The first sections are the easiest and you can scramble up as far as you feel comfortable to get excellent views out across Wadi Rum before it starts to get more difficult. You can also descend into the Wadi S'Rach on the far (east) side of the ridge, where a spring waters palm trees and shrubs, and from there walk across to the Nabataean Temple and then up to Lawrence's Spring.

Nabataean Temple A short walk west from **Wadi Rum Resthouse** in Rum village, towards the east face of Jebel Rum brings you to the remains of a Nabataean temple dating from around the first century CE. Head towards the large water tank visible close to the base of Jebel Rum; the ruins are to the left of this. Only the basic outline of the square courtyard remains, along with the lower courses of the walls and some sections of columns. Alongside the great monuments of Petra these remains are very meagre, though they are important in that they confirm the existence of some sort of permanent Nabataean settlement here.

Tip...

There is no ATM or bank at Wadi Rum Visitor Centre or Rum village. Bring all the cash you need with you.

Abu Aineh Around 3 km to the south of Rum village is the spring and campsite of Abu Aineh. This can be reached easily by walking directly south from Rum village and then bearing off to the right to reach the British bombarded the town from the sea. The town fell easily and the Arab Revolt claimed its first victory on 6 July 1917. Lawrence then headed north, continuing to attack the Hijaz railway with daring guerrilla attacks. And it was at this point that he first encountered Wadi Rum, which would feature so poetically in his later writings.

In October 1918 Lawrence arrived with Faisal in newly British-liberated Damascus to learn of the British renege on the deal for Arab Independence. Following the war, Lawrence was active in attempting to set up an independent Arab state with Faisal as its king. He and Faisal attended the 1919 Paris Peace Conference but their hopes were shattered when it emerged that Britain and France had signed the secret Sykes–Picot Agreement, dividing up Arab lands between them. Totally deflated, he returned to England where he began work on his cathartic *Seven Pillars of Wisdom*, his account of the Arab Revolt, and became an advisor to Winston Churchill in the Colonial Office while continuing to try to advance the Arab cause. It was around this time that American journalist Lowell Thomas and his illustrated show 'With Allenby in Palestine, and Lawrence in Arabia', elevated Lawrence to celebrity status.

Shunning this sudden fame and riven with guilt at the British betrayal of the Arabs, in August 1922 Lawrence joined the RAF first as an airman under the name 'Ross' to avoid press attention, and then the Tank Corp under the name 'Shaw', and spent a year as a clerk at an RAF base in India. The *Seven Pillars of Wisdom* was published in 1926, with the abridged version, *Revolt in the Desert*, published the following year. Hugely successful, Lawrence donated the entirety of the books' royalties to an RAF charity, eschewing the opportunity to become wealthy.

Returning to England in 1929 Lawrence left the RAF in 1935 and on 19 May died as a result of a motorcycle accident in Dorset.

the sandy 'cove' at the foot of the mountains. Alternatively, from Wadi Shelaali you can scramble up over a small pass to the west of Jebel Ahmar and then skirt along the base of the cliffs before scrambling up to a second small pass and over into a small valley that leads down to Abu Aineh. This is an easy scramble, though the second pass is not that obvious and easily missed. There is usually a small Bedouin camp at Abu Aineh, close to the spring, where you may be offered tea.

Lawrence's Spring (Ain Shelaali) Continuing southwest from the Nabataean Temple, you enter the Wadi Shelaali. A good path zigzags up to Lawrence's Spring. The main source of the spring is now enclosed within a stone and concrete structure, making it impossible to bathe here as Lawrence did, but you can lean inside and take a drink. Various ancient rock drawings and inscriptions are dotted around, along with more recent additions, and there are long sections of a rock-cut water channel of Nabataean origin that once led down to the temple.

There is a semi-permanent Bedouin camp here where you can get a refreshing cup of Bedouin-style tea ('Bedouin whiskey' as the locals jokingly call it). It also has a small stall of locally made trinkets.

Khazali Canyon This picturesque *siq* is a firm favourite on the Wadi Rum tourist trail and for good reason. At its entrance sits multi-hued sand, washed down from the pink cliffs

BACKGROUND
Wadi Rum

The spectacular landscape of Wadi Rum (*wadi* means 'valley' in Arabic, *rum* means 'high places' in Aramaic, so literally 'the valley of the high places') was created by a slow process of erosion caused by wind and rain that carved out the canyons leaving huge pillars of sandstone rock between.

The first signs of human habitation in Wadi Rum date from the **Neolithic** period (6000-4500 BCE) with archaeological work at the Abu Nekheileh mound, inside the protected area, revealing Neolithic stone structures and flints; signs that people had actually been living settled lives inside Wadi Rum rather than just passing through.

In the **Iron Age** Wadi Rum became part of the vast trade routes that traversed Arabia through to modern day Lebanon and Syria. By the second century BCE the **Nabataeans** had moved into the area and began to control caravan trade in the region. Their contemporaries in Wadi Rum were **Thamudic** tribes, originally from southern Arabia, who left their mark on Wadi Rum with many rock inscriptions that can still be seen today. Most of the drawings depict animals and hunting scenes or stylized human figures and date from the third century BCE to the second century CE. Other inscriptions are in Greek or Minaean, the former reflecting the Greek influence on the region following **Alexander the Great**'s conquest in 332 BCE, while the latter were probably left by merchants from the southern Arabian state of Ma'in in Yemen, who controlled the incense trade before being supplanted by the Nabataeans. Aramaic inscriptions, left by the Nabataeans, can also be found, as well as much later Kufic inscriptions left by early pilgrims en route to or from Mecca and Medina.

There is plenty of evidence that early humans also worked to modify the environment to their advantage, most obviously by building dams, water channels and cisterns in order to collect and control the flow of water. Such remains, mostly of Nabataean origin, have been found scattered all over the region. Finally, although no

with their contours shaped like dripping candle wax. Inside the canyon you can walk along the rock to reach several good rock inscriptions carved into the walls on the left-hand side. The baby feet inscription is particularly clear.

Wadi Rum in the movies
Although still best known for being featured in David Lean's 1962 epic *Lawrence of Arabia*, Wadi Rum more recently received a starring role in another Hollywood blockbuster. Its majestic and otherworldly landscape was used as the backdrop for Mars in Ridley Scott's *The Martian* (2015), starring Matt Damon.

Lawrence's house Local legend has it that Lawrence lived here for a time during the Arab Revolt. The 'house' is built over the top of an old Nabataean ruin and not much of either building is left to see. The panoramic views over Wadi Rum from here are absolutely fantastic.

Rock bridges There are three main rock bridges that can be climbed without equipment by anyone with a decent fitness great centre of civilization existed here as at Petra, the remains have been found of what must have been a fairly substantial Nabataean temple close to Rum village. A number of other Nabataean temple or sanctuary remains have also been found elsewhere in the region, suggesting that there was some form of permanent settlement here during this period.

Roman rule came in 106 CE with the annexation of the Nabataean kingdom, when Wadi Rum, like the rest of modern-day Jordan, became part of the Provincia Arabia. The Nabataean caravan routes became part of the grand Via Nova Traiana that linked Aqaba with Damascus, though in Wadi Rum itself, there is little evidence of Roman settlement and it seems the protection of the route was left, mostly, to the local Bedouin.

Wadi Rum seems to recede from history during the Byzantine and later Islamic empires, probably used only by the local Bedouin on their nomadic circuits of the region. It next came to the attention of the West during the **Arab Revolt** against the Ottomans in the First World War when a group of Arab fighters, led by Emir Faisal and T E Lawrence, journeyed through here on their way to launch raids on the Hejaz railway to destroy the Ottoman supply lines to Mecca. Lawrence wrote poetically about the landscape of Wadi Rum in his now famous book the *Seven Pillars of Wisdom*, on which David Lean based his highly successful 1962 movie *Lawrence of Arabia*.

The first permanent building to be built in Wadi Rum was the Rum police station in the 1930s. The area around it has grown into Rum village as, over the past decades, many traditional Bedouin of the area have swapped their nomadic traditions for a more settled life. Rum village is mostly home to the Zelabieh tribe, while the outlying area of Disi (outside of the protected area) is home to the people of the Zuweida tribe.

In 1998 Wadi Rum was declared a protected reserve and tourism is now managed and developed within the area by the Aqaba Special Economic Zone Authority (ASEZA). Together with the Bedouin communities, they are endeavouring to provide a sustainable livelihood for the local people as well as cultivate a style of tourism that respects this unique and awe-inspiring environment.

level and a good head for heights. These fascinating formations were formed by soft rock being slowly eroded away leaving just the hard heart of the rock behind.

Burdah Rock Bridge is the largest and most difficult climb. To reach the rather terrifying 80 m summit it needs to be scaled from the western side. Slightly less scary is **Umm Fruth Rock Bridge**, which has a picture-perfect setting as well. It's only a short scramble up to the summit, but coming back down has been known to flummox even the most confident travellers. It's much easier to just come down slowly on your bottom if you don't think you can walk it. It can get busy with visitors here, especially in the afternoon when the light is at its best. An easier scramble is up **Little Rock Bridge**, which also boasts exceptional desert views from its summit.

Rock inscriptions The entire Wadi Rum area is dotted with ancient rock inscriptions made by the Nabataean and Thamudic people who once roamed through Wadi Rum. The **Anfashieh rock inscription** is a wonderful example, exceptionally detailed and huge in scale. It's thought to depict a camel caravan passing through the area. The **Alameleh inscriptions** near to the Disi district are also well-preserved examples of this ancient art.

Other sites There's a **sand dune area**, near Anfashieh rock inscription, where the active can hike up and then run down the dunes for a bit of fun, and there are plenty of designated **sunset sites** for watching the sun slowly dip below the horizon. There are also canyons such as **Burrah Canyon** to explore, which are slightly more off the main tourist trail. Wadi Rum contains numerous **cliffs** that are perfect for scrambling or climbing, but you need a qualified climbing guide to get you around to the sites and show you the way.

Rock climbing and trekking in Wadi Rum

For most it's enough simply to be amid the vast and spectacular desert scenery of Wadi Rum. However, for anyone with the merest trace of a predilection for clambering around over rocks, the mountains of Wadi Rum present an irresistible temptation.

In the early 1980s the Ministry of Tourism commissioned a British climber, Tony Howard, to explore the area and map the possibilities from a rock climber's point of view. He produced the book *Treks and Climbs in Wadi Rum* (4th edition, Cicerone Press, 2010), which gives detailed information on nearly 300 climbing routes in the Wadi Rum region, as well as background information on the area. Although now out of print, it may still be available on Amazon or via second-hand bookshops.

The sport is still very much in its youth in Jordan and you need to bring all your own equipment. There are now a few local Bedouins who are qualified to lead and guide Western-style ascents. As Tony Howard points out, the local Bedouin have been scaling the various mountains in the region while on hunting expeditions for generations; all that was needed was to get to grips with all the new-fangled accessories that Westerners brought with them. You should arrange a climbing guide before arriving at Wadi Rum.

If hanging precariously from vertiginous cliff faces isn't your cup of tea, there are plenty of non-technical walks and scrambles to enjoy. A booklet entitled *Walks and Scrambles in Wadi Rum*, published by Al Kutba (1993) and written by Tony Howard and Diana Taylor, gives good, detailed descriptions of these, complete with useful sketched maps. A newer book by the same team, *Jordan: Walks, Treks, Caves, Climbs and Canyons* (Cicerone Press, 2008), also includes a section on Wadi Rum, which covers a selection of walks and less strenuous climbs. Again, both these titles are now out of print but it may be possible to source them through Amazon or second-hand bookshops.

Listings Wadi Rum *map p135*

Tourist information

Wadi Rum Visitor Centre

7 km north from Rum village, T03-209 0600, www.wadirum.jo. Daily 0800-sunset.
This is the first port of call for visitors to the reserve and the hub of all tourism-related activities within Wadi Rum. This is where you pay your reserve entrance fee (5JD, under 12s free), arrange camel and 4WD safaris, overnight camping excursions and hire experienced walking guides. Within the centre there are well-maintained toilets, a couple of excellent souvenir shops managed by local women's cooperatives, a restaurant and an interpretation hall where you can watch a short (15-min) film about Wadi Rum. Outside the visitor centre, climb up the steps to the viewing platform for a brilliant view of the 'Seven Pillars of Wisdom' (the mountain named after TE Lawrence's famous book).

Tourist Police

Based at the visitor centre, T03-201 8215. Or dial the unified emergency number 911 for ambulance, fire and police.

Where to stay

All the camps below are inside Wadi Rum protected reserve and are run by the local Bedouin. Usual camp rates are a package deal including a Wadi Rum tour, dinner – which is often a Bedouin *zarb* (traditional BBQ cooked underground) – breakfast the next morning and transport back to Rum village. Mattresses and duvets/blankets are provided at all the camps, so you don't need to bring a sleeping bag.

If you haven't made a booking before coming to Wadi Rum, the visitor centre can help organize an overnight stay for you.

$$ Bedouin Whispers
T07-7562 7501, see Facebook.
Pushed right up against a massive rock face, this lovely peaceful place is well sheltered from the wind. Aodeh is a gracious host and a mine of information on the area. He runs a good selection of tours and Wadi Rum itineraries, as well as longer treks throughout the region. Booking essential.

$$ Mohammed Mutlak Camp
T07-7633 4814,
www.mohammedmutlakcamp.com.
Based in a picturesque spot, this simple camp is the perfect escape from the real world. They have an excellent range of camel, 4WD and climbing tours available. Booking essential.

$$ Panorama Sunset
T07-9557 7026, www.panorama.
wadirum.8m.net.
A stone's throw away from the perfect cliff to take in the sunset, this little gem of a camp is run by the affable and entertaining

Zayid al-Jwean. Zayid can arrange all manner of camel and 4WD tours in the area and also longer treks through the desert to Wadi Musa. Call 2 days beforehand to book.

$$ Rum Stars
T07-9512 7025, www.rumstars.com.
This well-organized camp run by Ahmed is far away from any others so you're guaranteed one of the most silent nights of your life here. They also run a wide variety of camel and 4WD tours. Booking essential.

Rum village

$ Wadi Rum Resthouse
Rum village, T07-7934 7883,
www.wadirumresthouse.com.
The only accommodation in Rum village is the campground in the sandy yard behind the resthouse. You can use one of their rather ratty-looking 2-man tents, which include mattress and bedding (25JD per person, including breakfast and lunch), pitch your own (free) or park your campervan here (free). There's a communal bathroom that's kept pretty clean. It's very basic, but it's cheap.

Restaurants

There are 3 small grocery stores on the main road through Rum village, **Seven Pillars of Wisdom**, **Lawrence of Arabia** and **Radwan**. All are good for stocking up on last-minute supplies but they are rather basic.

$$ Rum Gate
Wadi Rum Visitor Centre, T03-201 5995.
Daily 0900-1600.
This pleasant stone building, tucked into a corner of the visitor centre complex, is a nice shady place for lunch. They have a daily lunch buffet featuring 12 salads, 5 hot dishes and dessert (12JD) or you can just grab a sandwich (4.5JD). No alcohol.

$$ Wadi Rum Resthouse

Rum village, T07-7934 7883. Daily 0600-2400.
The restaurant here is nearly always packed
with tour groups enjoying the large lunch
and dinner buffets (5-10JD). If you're not
that hungry, you can just grab a tea or
beer and drink it on the outside terrace
with a prime seat for viewing the daily life
of the village. They also do simple Arabic
breakfasts.

$ Ali's Place

Rum village.
For a cheap and simple meal of *fuul*, falafel
and hummus look no further. This tiny place
is a good pit-stop for the hungry traveller.

What to do

4WD tours

There's a huge variety of 4WD tours available
from the visitor centre with costs ranging
from 25JD for a quick 1-hr tour to 80JD
for a whole day. As well as the displayed
tour itineraries (which the visitor centre
has organized under 2 separate headings:
'Operator 1' and 'Operator 2', see below),
you can make up your own tour and hire
the driver and car for the day (80JD). All the
drivers are local Bedouin and know the area
well, though don't be surprised if your 4WD
turns out to be a beaten-up old jalopy; these
vehicles have seen some serious desert
action over the years.

Operator 1

1 Nabataean Temple and Lawrence's
Spring, 2 hrs, 25JD.
2 Nabataean Temple, Lawrence's Spring
and Khazali Canyon, 2 hrs, 35JD.
3 All of the above and a sunset site,
2½ hrs, 44JD.
4 Nabataean Temple, Lawrence's Spring,
Khazali Canyon and sand dunes, 3½ hrs, 51JD.
5 Nabataean Temple, Lawrence's Spring,
Khazali Canyon and Little Rock Bridge,
3 hrs, 44JD.

6 Same as 5 but also including Lawrence's
house, sand dunes and Anfashieh rock
inscription, 3½ hrs, 59JD.
7 Same as 6 but also including Umm Froth
Rock Bridge, 4 hrs, 67JD.
8 Same as 7 but also including Burdah Rock
Bridge and sunset site, 5 hrs, 75JD.
9 Nabataean Temple, Lawrence's Spring,
Khazali Canyon, sand dunes, Little Rock
Bridge, Umm Froth Rock Bridge, Burdah
Rock Bridge, Burrah Canyon and sunset site,
8 hrs, 80JD.

Operator 2

1 Alameleh rock inscriptions, 1 hr, 25JD.
2 Alameleh rock inscriptions, sand dunes,
Lawrence's *siq*, 2 hrs, 35JD.
3 All of the above and a sunset site,
2½ hrs, 44JD.
4 Alameleh rock inscriptions, Lawrence's
house, Lawrence's *siq* and Burrah Canyon,
3 hrs, 51JD.
5 Alameleh rock inscriptions, sand dunes,
Umm Ishrin, Lawrence's house, Um Froth
Rock Bridge and Burdah Rock Bridge, 4 hrs,
67JD.
6 Same as 5 but also including Burrah
Canyon and Lawrence's *siq*, 8 hrs, 80JD.

Camel tours

You're obviously going to see fewer sites
on a camel than on a 4WD tour but, by
travelling slowly and open to the elements,
you get to experience Wadi Rum from a
whole different angle.

Itineraries

1 Nabataean Temple 30 mins, 4JD.
2 Lawrence's Spring, 1½ hrs, 10JD.
3 Sand dunes, 5 hrs, 20JD.
4 Al-Mogher sunset site, 3 hrs, 18JD.
5 Lawrence's Spring and Khazali Canyon,
4 hrs, 20JD.
6 Umm Sabata sunset site, 5 hrs, 25JD.
7 Sand dunes and Little Rock Bridge,
5 hrs, 25JD.
8 Full-day camel ride, 8 hrs, 30JD.

9 Overnight camel trip to Burdah Rock Bridge via Lawrence's Spring and Khazali Canyon, overnight, 60JD.
10 Day hire for luggage camel, 8 hrs, 30JD.

Climbing

Bedouin Roads, *Rum village, T07-9589 9723, www.bedouinroads.com*. A good local company offering climbing and scrambling tours around Wadi Rum as well as more classic 4WD, camel and trekking trips.

Wadi Rum Bedouin Guides, *Rum village, T07-7735 9856, www.wadirumbedouinguide. com*. Excellent option for a wide range of tours run by Feras, who was born and bred in Rum and offers hiking and scrambling, camel rides and sand boarding, as well as the usual 4WD trips and also hot air balloon trips (see below).

Horse riding

Jordan Tracks, *Rum village, T07-9648 2801, www.jordantracks.com*. This local company offers a high standard of service and a great variety of riding trips within Wadi Rum and further afield. Guides speak English, French and Dutch. Not suitable for beginners.

Hot air ballooning

Petra Balloon, *T07-9800 1088, www. petraballoon.com. Daily sunrise-2100*. Opened in July 2023, this tethered hot air balloon ride takes a maximum of 30 visitors at a time up to 300 m above Petra, affording unrivalled aerial views of the site. The flight takes 20 mins and the balloon can accommodate wheelchairs and baby prams. Note that the Jordan Pass is *only* valid for Jordanian nationals and residents for this attraction.

Royal Aero Sports Club of Jordan, *T03-205 8050, see Facebook*. A truly magical experience and a chance to see this incredible landscape from a completely different angle. Phone for details.

Wadi Rum Bedouin Guides, *T30-697 796 9683, www.wadirumbedouinguide.com*. Starting early from the visitor centre at around 0430, this company offer an hour-long hot air balloon flight over the Rum landscape soaring to a height of 900 m. Not the cheapest trip option, but gives an unrivalled view of the stunning desert landscape below (165JD pp, children 7-11 120JD pp, children under 7 not permitted).

Local guides

If you want a walking guide or would like a guide to accompany you on your 4WD or camel trip, you can hire them through the visitor centre. Local guides here work on a rota system, which means that everyone has equal employment opportunities.

Transport

Bus and minibus

Always check the day before what time your bus is scheduled to leave (if you're at a camp in Wadi Rum your hosts can phone for you). Be sure to be ready in plenty of time as the buses sometimes leave early if they are already full, but be prepared also to wait around for an hour or so. Buses leave from the car park beside **Wadi Rum Resthouse**. There's 1 bus daily (except Fri) to **Aqaba**, usually leaving around 0700 (1 hr, 3JD) and a bus to **Wadi Musa** (**Petra**) daily (except Fri) at 0830 (2 hrs, 7JD). Note that the Wadi Musa bus sometimes doesn't run in low season so check beforehand. If you miss these, or you want to head to **Amman**, the **JETT** bus company (www.jett. com.jo) runs a daily service to the capital departing at 1700 (3–3½ hrs, 20JD).

Aqaba

Situated at the northern tip of the Gulf of Aqaba and the northernmost port on the Red Sea, Aqaba is Jordan's quintessential aquatic year-round playground, where average annual temperatures seldom dip below 20°C in winter and can soar to over 40°C during the summer months. With such year-round dry and sunny weather, this relaxed, family-friendly town is a popular retreat for Jordanians, as well as for neighbouring Saudis and a growing number of other international visitors, complete with all the trappings of a seaside holiday resort and accommodation options to suit most budgets. The principal offering to visitors is, of course, the sea, full of stunningly beautiful and varied marine life that's accessible from shore as well as by boat. Scuba diving and snorkelling are the main activities here, but Aqaba also has a few notable cultural and historic sites, which help to complete the Jordanian historical jigsaw. With a flight time from Amman of under an hour and Petra and Wadi Rum less than two hours away, this sun-kissed city can make for a very pleasant seaside detour from desert ramblings.

Essential Aqaba

Getting around

Public transport

National carrier **Royal Jordanian** (www. rj.com) currently operates two **flights** daily between Amman and Aqaba (55 mins); the one-way fare was a little under 45JD at the time of writing.

Although there are plenty of daily bus services from Amman to Aqaba, by far the best and most efficient option is provided by **JETT**, who operate high-quality, comfortable services on a/c buses; departure times differ depending on which bus station you use. There are also daily JETT services to Aqaba from Petra and Wadi Rum.

Self-drive and taxi

A taxi from Amman to Aqaba will cost around 100JD (4 hrs) for the one-way trip and around 150JD for the return to Amman if you are visiting just for the day. The highly recommended **Jordan Taxi Tours** (T07-8706 5083) operate 24/7. If you are on a self-drive visit, Aqaba is easily reached from Amman by driving south along either the King's Highway (5 hrs) or the (less scenic) Desert Highway (4 hrs).

Within Aqaba

All the main sites in Aqaba are fairly accessible by foot, but there is no shortage of taxis in the town; most trips cost no more than 2JD, though expect to pay around 10JD to Tala Bay and environs. **City Sightseeing Aqaba** (T07-9720 7771, www. citysightseeingaqaba.weebly.com) operate a number of good-value, red double decker hop-on hop-off bus tours of Aqaba, which take in the main sites and areas of interest and could be a good way to combine a leisurely excursion with a walking tour. See the website for details of their tour offerings, prices and departure times.

When to go

Spring (March-May) and autumn (September-November) are the standout seasons to visit Aqaba, avoiding the intense and stifling heat of summer (June-August) when the mercury can soar past 40°C. Winter (December-February) can also be a pleasant time to visit with mild temperatures hovering around 20°C, guaranteed winter sun and negligible rainfall.

Time required

On a day trip you could comfortably take a dip in the Red Sea and see a few of the town's land-based sites, but a two- to three-night stay would allow for more extensive sightseeing and time to sample the laid-back ambience and local cuisine. Keen divers and snorkellers could spend a week or more here exploring the bountiful depths of the marine ecosystem.

Sights

Although the main draw of Aqaba is its attractive seaside location, kaleidoscopic marine life, coral reefs and associated activities, the town still has a number of engaging sights which provide further insights into Jordan's history and its natural world. For active visitors, it's also possible to tour the city by bicycle or quad bike, or play volleyball and golf, which many hotels here can help organize.

BACKGROUND

Aqaba

With its coastal location and access to underwater springs, Aqaba has been settled for millennia. Archaeological excavations at Tell al Khalifa, just a few kilometres west of Aqaba, have unearthed evidence of a major copper production industry in the biblical city of Ezion-Geber. Since then, the town has hosted numerous civilizations on its shores. The Nabataeans occupied Aqaba and prospered from numerous ports and trade in perfume and spices from around the third century BCE. During Roman rule, the city was occupied by a garrison and called Aqabat Ayla, or Pass of Ayla, and, following construction of a highway around 111–14 CE by the Roman Emperor Trajan (ruled 98–117 CE), became the most southerly point of a trade route from the Nabataean capital at Bosra in southern Syria. During the Byzantine or late Roman Empire, Aqaba became the seat of a bishopric, then around 636 CE, Muslim armies occupied Aqaba on their northward expansion out of Arabia. The town prospered during the Islamic era and became an important transit point for pilgrims to and from Mecca.

During the Middle Ages, King Baldwin I of Jerusalem met little resistance when he took Aqaba in 1116 as part of his Crusader territorial ambitions. The occupation was fairly short-lived, however, as Ayyubid sultan Saladin captured the city in 1170 and, despite later attempts by crusader prince Reynold of Châtillon to reclaim Aqaba in 1182-1183, the town would never again be in Crusader hands. By around 1260 the Mamluks had ousted the Crusader presence and in the 16th century Aqaba came under the banner of the Ottoman Empire, after which point the town's fortunes declined.

Aqaba Bird Observatory
Wadi Araba border, T03-205 8825, www.facebook.com/aqababirds, Sun-Thu 0800-1500, 7JD.

Established in 2004, this RSCN-managed artificial bird habitat and wetland covers an area of just 0.5 sq km but is an annual stop-off point for some half a million birds each year on their migratory routes between Africa, Asia and Europe. Some 271 different species have been sighted here, accounting for over 60% of Jordan's recorded bird species, including osprey, booted eagle, flamingo, Arabian bee-eater, sandpipers, purple heron and ringed plover. A birdwatcher's paradise, the observatory also boasts a 2 km walking trail which winds its way around the many lakes and forested areas.

Aqaba Aquarium
Near port, T03-201 5144, Sun-Thu 0800-1600, Fri-Sat and public holidays 0800-1700, 7JD.

If you'd prefer to get up close and personal with Aqaba's variety of aquatic life through a pane of glass rather than face to face, this aquarium could be the answer. Forming part of the Aqaba Marine Science Station, a research institute operated by Jordan University and Yarmouk University to study the Red Sea ecosystem and assist with its environmental management, the various tanks show you the wealth of underwater life in the Gulf of Aqaba, from the various corals to lionfish, parrotfish, moray eels, turtles and the (deadly) stonefish.

By the outbreak of the First World War in 1914, Aqaba remained a small fishing village with a population numbering perhaps 1000 souls with small residential properties peppering the coastline. The token Ottoman garrison occupying the town, whose defences were orientated towards the sea, were totally surprised and overwhelmed by the land attack by the forces of the Arab Revolt and T E Lawrence, who took Aqaba with ease on 6 July 1917 (a victory spectacularly portrayed in David Lean's 1962 film *Lawrence of Arabia*). Subsequently, the British forces used Aqaba as a supply route from Egypt for the Arab army.

Aqaba's fortunes would gradually begin to change in the following decades. In 1965 the boundary between Transjordan and Saudi Arabia was finally agreed upon, with King Hussein granting Saudi Arabia 6000 sq km of Jordan's desert territory in exchange for Jordan being given a 12 km extension of coastline. This greatly enhanced Aqaba's economic prospects, which saw new and improved port facilities constructed – Aqaba port is today the main outlet for Jordan's main export, phosphates, as well as other goods.

Historically speaking, Aqaba was never a major trading port or commercial hub, but since 2000 the town and its environs has been administered by the Aqaba Special Economic Zone Authority (ASEZA) which has transformed Aqaba into a low-tax, duty-free city, attracting plenty of investment and growth and placing the town firmly on the map as a major tourism destination. Together with Petra and Wadi Rum, Aqaba is now part of Jordan's so-called 'golden triangle of tourism', with the town receiving some 1.9 million visitors in 2023. One particularly notable investment is the Ayla Oasis, a multi-billion-dollar luxury resort project consisting of luxury hotels, restaurants, beach club, aquatic adventures, tennis courts and an 18-hole golf course designed by former Australian golfer Greg Norman.

Aqaba Castle (Mamluk Fort)
Near King Hussein St, Fri-Sat 1000-1700, Sun-Thu 0800-1700 summer, Fri-Sat 1000-1600, Sun-Thu 0800-1600 winter, 3JD.

Well worth a visit, this fort, measuring approximately 50 m by 50 m, has had a colourful history since construction. Its origins date to around 1510-1517, during the rule of the penultimate Mamluk sultan Qanswah al-Ghawri, as depicted in the inscription just inside the castle's entrance. Its eastern room bears a further inscription suggesting that the fort underwent renovation by the Ottomans in 1587 and again in 1628. The castle was in use throughout the succeeding Ottoman era and likely functioned as a *khan* or *caravanserai* (travellers' inn) for pilgrims en route to Mecca. During the First World War, British warships inflicted heavy damage on the fort; shortly after the victory of the Arab Revolt against the Ottomans in 1917, the Hashemite coat of arms was raised above the castle's entrance.

Aqaba Archaeological Museum
King Hussein St, Fri-Sat 1000-1700, Sun-Thu 0800-1700 summer, Fri-Sat 1000-1600, Sun-Thu 0800-1600 winter, free.

Occupying the building that was once the former home of Sharif Hussein Bin Ali, great-great-grandfather of present king Abdullah II, Aqaba Archaeological Museum is well worth the visit to see its collection of coins and pottery from the early Islamic eras.

Aqaba

To 5 — Amman, Airport, Wadi Araba Crossing

Al Istiqlal St

Al Ghazale St

Al Rashid St

Royal Jordanian Airlines

King Hussein St

JETT Buses

Al Nahda St

Dawud Sulieman Mosque

Al-Sa'ada St

Princess Haya Circle

Al-Hammamat Al Tunisyya St

Al Tabri St

Petra St

Souk by the Sea

Sinbad

Aqaba Gateway

City Sightseeing Aqaba

Ayla Circle

Tourist Information Centre

Al Yarmouk St

King Talal St

Marina

Zahran St

Sharif Al Hussein Bin Ali Mosque

Bus station (for Wadi Musa (Petra) & Wadi Rum)

Raghadan St

Al Razi St

Al Jam St

Kuwait St

Beirut St

Al-Humayma St

Buses to Kerak

Al Malek Abdullah ben Al Hussein St

Gulf of Aqaba

King Hussein St (Corniche)

Prince Mohammad St

Aqaba Archaeological Museum

Aqaba Castle (Mamluk Fort)

Great Arab Revolt Flagpole and Plaza

N

To 1 — South Beach, Neptune Submarine Vision, Aquarium, Bird Observatory, dive centres, Saudi Arabian border

Bradt

0 — 100m
0 — 100yds

Where to stay
Aqaba Adventure Divers 1
Captain's Hotel & Restaurant 2
InterContinental 3
Kempinski 4
Oryx 5

Restaurants
Al Fardous Café 1
Ali Barber 2
Al-Mohandes Café 3
Rovers Return 4
Royal Yacht Club 5

Islamic Hospital & Aqaba Modern Hospital

Great Arab Revolt Flagpole and Plaza
Open 24/7, free.

At some 137 m high and measuring 20 m by 40 m, the flag here is one of the tallest in the world and celebrates the 1917 capture of Aqaba by T E Lawrence and the Arabs in their revolt against the Ottoman Empire's rule over the Middle East. The flag you see is actually the banner of the Great Arab Revolt, not the Jordanian national flag, and was designed by former British diplomat Sir Mark Sykes, co-architect (along with his French counterpart François Georges-Picot) of the 1916 Sykes–Picot Agreement between Britain and France, which carved up Arab lands.

Sharif Al Hussein Bin Ali Mosque
King Hussein St, open 24/7, free.

Named after the great-great-grandfather of current king Abdullah II, who was the Emir of Mecca and initiator of the Great Arab Revolt against the Ottomans, this exquisite white mosque with its stunning minarets and glass windows is a fine example of Islamic architecture and the principal place of worship for Aqaba's residents.

Listings Aqaba *map p148*

Tourist information

Tourist Information Centre
Al-Hammamat Al-Tunisyya St, T03-203 5360, www.aqaba.jo, daily 0900-1700, 1000-1500 during Ramadan.
This friendly office can furnish you with lots of information and brochures about all things Aqaba and its environs.

Where to stay

Aqaba has an extensive and varied range of accommodation; many of the luxury hotels can provide or arrange a host of watersports activities as well as offering spas, jacuzzi, massage, beauty treatments, fitness and health club facilities.

$$$$ InterContinental Hotel
King Hussein St, T03-209 2222, www.ihg.com.
The height of style and luxury, the grand InterContinental comes complete with spa, gym, outdoor pool and beautifully manicured gardens, and the entire hotel is wheelchair friendly.

$$$$ Kempinski Hotel
King Hussein St, T03-209 0888, www. kempinski.com.
Tastefully decorated, ultra-bright and comfy

rooms in this luxury hotel backed up by superb service, a variety of restaurants, 24/7 gym, swimming pool and luxury spa spread over 2 floors. Highly recommended for those with deep pockets.

$$$$ Oryx Hotel
Al Sharif Shakir Bin Zayd St, T03-205 1111, www.oryx-hotel.com.
Nicely located in the heart of the city, this 7-storey luxury hotel has wonderfully spacious rooms with warm, classical décor and ultra-comfy beds with city, pool and sea view options. Their excellent facilities include a couple of restaurants serving international cuisine, pool bar, tea room, gym, spa, well-equipped business centre and heated rooftop pool.

$$$ Captain's Hotel
Al Nahda St, T03-206 0710, www.captains.jo.
Aqaba's boutique hotel offering boasts warm, cosy rooms, lovely en-suite bedrooms and a range of facilities including business centre, health club, jacuzzi, swimming pool and an excellent seafood restaurant (page 150). Breakfast is an extra 7JD; free Wi-Fi.

$$ Aqaba Adventure Divers
South beach, T03-201 9060, T07-9694 7185, T07-9907 8450 (24/7), www.aqaba-diving.com.

A good option if you are undertaking one of their PADI diving courses, or even for non-divers seeking some seaside R&R in a cordial environment. Simple, clean, though unexciting accommodation with nice sea views; en-suite double rooms 35JD per night, including breakfast and free Wi-Fi. Recommended.

Restaurants

Aqaba's numerous culinary options cater to most budgets, with local Jordanian and international options available. Many of the top-end hotels also have excellent restaurants and, of course, Burger King, KFC, McDonalds etc are available for those wanting a fast-food fix.

$$$ Ali Barber Restaurant
Raghadan St, T03-201 3901, T07-9510 4141. Daily 1200-2400.
A popular place with indoor and outdoor dining and a good-value menu of mainly local dishes, including *mansaf*, *sayyadiya*, soups, salads, stews and seafood. A good range of beers, local and international wines, cocktails, spirits and *arak* are also available. A full English food menu is also available consisting of seafood, steaks and a variety of grills. Recommended.

$$$ Captain's Restaurant
Al Nahda St, T03-201 6905, T07-9923 3111, www.captains.jo. Daily 1200-2320.
A very popular restaurant with locals and visitors alike, serving a mouth-watering selection of Jordanian and international cuisine and a variety of seafood options, including the delicious *sayyadiya* (fish served on a bed of rice). Recommended.

$$$ Royal Yacht Club (Romero)
Royal Yacht Club, T03-202 2404, T07-7844 1444, www.romerogroup.jo. Daily 1200-2300.
Nicely located with lovely views over the marina, this excellent restaurant is ideal for a delicious romantic sunset meal. Specialising in mainly Italian cuisine, they also serve *mezze*, the local favourite *sayyadiya*, sushi, seafood salads and a good range of alcoholic beverages. Highly recommended but note that 7% VAT and a 10% service charge is added to the final bill.

$$ Rovers Return
Aqaba Gateway, T03-203 2030, T07-7500 0033. Daily 1200-0030.
This lively venue and environs may lack the iconic cobbled streets, terraced housing and Mancunian ambience of *Coronation Street*, but fans of the long-running soap are sure to enjoy their good value Betty's Hot Pot (beef stew with white/brown bread, 10.75JD). The menu also includes seafood, salads, sandwiches, platters and desserts. A good range of local and English beers are served and there is a pleasant outdoor dining/drinking area.

$ Al-Mohandes Café
At-Tabari St, T03-201 3454. Open 0700-2400.
What Al-Mohandes lacks in style and character is more than compensated for by its excellent, cheap-as-chips Jordanian food. Popular with locals, it's a great venue to gorge yourself on tasty hummus, falafel and shawarma.

$ Al Fardous Café
Zahran St, nr Ali Baba Restaurant, T07-9698 5634. Daily 0700-0300.
A decent, welcoming café with a nice authentic local vibe and outdoor seating to enjoy a coffee, tea, soft drink, puff on a *nargileh* or *sheesha* and watch the locals playing backgammon and chess.

Shopping

The central area of Aqaba has a good range of shopping outlets selling all the essential day-to-day items, from food and clothes to medicines. They also offer the usual tourist souvenirs, but for something a little different try the following option.

Souk by the Sea, *Al Nahda St. Fri 1800-2300*. This year-round weekly Friday evening market takes place close to the Captain's Hotel and sells a range of locally produced handicraft items. It is a particularly good choice for families as there is food and entertainment on offer, with all proceeds benefitting the local Aqaba community.

What to do

Diving, snorkelling and boat trips

With the sea and its underwater treasures the undoubted highlight of a visit to Aqaba, there are, unsurprisingly, plenty of opportunities for scuba divers and snorkelling enthusiasts of all levels to sample the aquatic wonders around the Gulf of Aqaba. There are more than 20 dive sites and a large number of companies offering snorkelling, scuba diving, PADI and underwater photography courses. The following represents just a selection of the numerous options available.

Ahlan Aqaba Scuba Diving Center, *www.diveinaqaba.com*. Offers a good range of boat excursions on its 21-m *Sea Breeze* vessel. Dive packages include Aqaba's popular wreck dive site, the *Cedar Pride*, a Lebanese freighter which lies around 200m offshore between two reefs. Following a fire in 1982 that caused extensive damage, the ship was deliberately sunk at the request of King Abdullah II, himself a keen scuba diver, and it has since been colonized by a range of hard and soft corals and is now home to several species of fish and other sea critters. Lying at a depth varying between 10 m and 27 m, the ship can be accessed from shore as well as by boat, and is thus suitable for both seasoned and less experienced divers.

Aqaba Adventure Divers, *South Beach, T03-201 9060, T07-9694 7185, T07-9907 8450 (24/7), www.aqaba-diving.com*. As well as offering an excellent range of PADI dive courses from beginner to advance level, and dives from shore and boat, they have decent, clean, though unexciting accommodation for divers and non-divers (page 149).

Aqaba Diving Academy, *South Beach, T07-9264 5333, www.aqabadive.com*. Excellent range of scuba-diving courses from beginner to advanced level.

Deep Blue Dive Center, *Tala Bay, T03-203 5006, www.deepbluedivecenter.com*. A highly regarded company who offer a wide range of PADI-certified courses from beginner to advanced levels, and dives from shore and boat including Aqaba's popular *Cedar Pride* wreck and underwater military museum.

Dive Aqaba, *T07-9072 0320, www.diveaqaba.com*. Long-established and respected professional dive outfit offering an excellent range of PADI courses for all levels and an extensive range of dive sites.

Red Sea Dive Center, *South Beach, T03-201 8969, www.aqabascubadiving.com*. A highly recommended PADI scuba training and dive centre which also has its own on-site hotel with 13 en-suite rooms providing clean, comfortable, simple accommodation (double 40JD including breakfast).

Royal Diving Club, *South Beach, T07-7800 0416, www.royaldivingclub.com*. In addition to its range of diving, snorkelling, boat trips and PADI courses, the Club offers the Royal Sea Trek (40JD) for those who prefer not to don aqualung or snorkel – a 25-min walk along the seabed to view the underwater world in a special air-supplied helmet 3 m below the surface of the water.

Neptune Submarine Vision, *Tala Bay, T07-7943 0969, www.neptuneglassboat.com*. For those who prefer to stay dry while ogling the Red Sea's underwater wonders, a 90-min *Neptune* glass-bottomed boat tour, offering superb panoramic views from its fully submerged glass hull, could be the answer. Between 4 and 6 tours take place daily; 20JD, children 4-10 years 15JD, under 3s free.

Sindbad *T03-205 0077, T79-963 6363, T79-889 9004, www.sindbadjo.com.* This excellent company offer a number of yacht and boat trips around the Gulf of Aqaba. One highlight is their Discovery Glass Bottom Boat with Snorkelling excursion: a 2-hr tour around the Gulf of Aqaba which includes 1 hr snorkelling and 1 hr coral reef viewing through the boat's glass hull. Snorkelling equipment and non-alcoholic drinks included, as is a day pass to the Berenice Beach Club (daily 1300-1500, 23JD, children 13JD). They also offer a range of water sport activities, including kayaking, paddleboarding, kite surfing, water skiing, jet skiing.

Bus

From **Amman**, the departure times for the **JETT** bus (4 hrs, 10JD one-way) vary depending on which station you leave from. From Abdali station, there are 6 daily departures to Aqaba between 0700 and 2100 every 2-4 hrs; Tabardour station also has 6 daily departures, leaving between 0730 and 1830 at roughly 1-2 hr intervals. JETT also offer a twice daily (0830 and 1630) VIP service to Aqaba from their Amman headquarters on 7th Circle, which offers an enhanced level of comfort with complimentary snacks included (adults 20JD, children 14.20JD).

From **Petra**, JETT operate a daily service to Aqaba departing Petra at 1700 (15JD) and a daily return service from Aqaba to Petra leaving at 0800 (15JD).

From **Wadi Rum**, JETT run a daily service to Aqaba that leaves Wadi Rum at 1830 (15JD) with a daily return bus to Wadi Rum departing Aqaba at 0800 (15JD).

Background

History

Although Jordan only came into existence as a nation-state during the 20th century, the land it occupies boasts a history dating right back to the earliest dawn of civilization, and beyond.

To describe Jordan as standing at the 'crossroads of history and civilization' may sound like the clichéd hyperbole of tourist brochures, but geographically it has indeed acted as a causeway linking movement between North Africa and Eurasia. For most of its history, the land that comprises modern-day Jordan has acted as a battleground for the invading armies of more powerful neighbours, being periodically incorporated into their empires and, to a greater or lesser extent, influenced by their cultures.

Jordan's modern history has been equally influenced by international events. Sharing borders with Israel, Syria, Iraq and Saudi Arabia, it has been obliged to maintain a delicate and often highly pragmatic balancing act in order to ensure its own survival. Although lacking in wealth and natural resources, and with its facilities and economy under intense strain due to the current refugee crisis, high unemployment and acute water shortages, Jordan continues to be (both socially and politically) relatively stable. Against all the odds, it has achieved a remarkable level of cohesion, and even the seeds of a democratic process. Perhaps most importantly, however, in the context of a region dogged by deep-rooted conflicts and tensions, it has also earned itself international respect as the voice of moderation.

The prehistoric era

The **Palaeolithic** period stretches back to around 1,500,000 years ago in the Middle East. The oldest clear evidence of human activity in Jordan, found at the site of Ubeidiyeh in the northern Jordan Valley, dates back to around 700,000 BCE (during the Lower Palaeolithic period).

Early settlement

All around the peripheries of the Middle East, the Fertile Crescent provided the ideal conditions for the development of settled agriculture. This occurred towards the end of the Epipaleolithic (Mesolithic) period and during the early stages of the **Pre-Pottery Neolithic** period (8500-6000 BCE). In the Jordan Valley, wheat and barley appear to have been first cultivated around 10,000 years ago.

The first cities and empires

By the **Early Bronze Age** (3300-2250 BCE), settled agricultural communities could be found across the Middle East. Gradually these grew in size and complexity, giving rise to the first city-states (urban centres supported by an agricultural hinterland).

The city-states which evolved in Jordan – at sites such as Bab adh-Dhraa in Wadi Araba, Zeiraqoun and Jawa – developed trade links as far afield as Egypt, Cyprus and Greece. All, however, were influenced by the upheavals of the **Middle Bronze Age** (2250-1550 BCE) when first the **Amorites**, a Semitic people, emerged from the deserts to the south and east, and then (by around 1900 BCE) the city-states of the southern Levant came under the influence of the Middle Kingdom pharaohs of Egypt.

Ancient 'superpower' rivalries

The region which today comprises Jordan was to remain for the most part under Egyptian domination until the end of the Late Bronze Age. It was also probably towards the very end of the Late Bronze Age that the famous **Exodus** took place, when Moses led the **Israelites** out of slavery in Egypt and back to the 'Promised Land', with his successor Joshua leading the 12 tribes across the Jordan River into Palestine.

Iron Age (1200-539 BCE)

The start of the Iron Age saw the departure of the Egyptians, which in effect left a power vacuum. This was filled by a series of small competing territorial states. The most important of these, running north to south roughly between Amman and Aqaba, were the **Ammonite**, **Moabite** and **Edomite** kingdoms.

Rabbath Ammon (modern-day Amman) flourished as the capital of the Ammonite kingdom. This was also the period when King Mesha, the ruler of Moab from around 853-830 BCE, recorded his military victories over the Israelites on the famous **Mesha Stele** (also known as the Moabite Stone), thus providing for the first time an alternative literary source for this period other than the Old Testament.

Persian period (539-333 BCE)

Neo-Babylonian dominance of the region was short-lived, with the **Achaemenid Persians**, led by Cyrus the Great, capturing their capital Babylon in 539 BCE, taking over control of their empire and extending it to include all of the Middle East, Egypt and Asia Minor. The eastern kingdoms appear to have fared well under the Persians, with trade flourishing.

Hellenistic period (333-64 BCE)

Although the Persians were at first successful in their battles with the Greeks, ultimately it was the latter who triumphed, with Alexander the Great of Macedon defeating the forces of Darius III at the Battle of Issus in 333 BCE.

After his death, Alexander's empire was partitioned between his generals. Ptolemy I Soter gained control of Egypt and the southern Levant, founding what became known as the **Ptolemid** empire. Seleucus I Nicator meanwhile gained control of Mesopotamia, Asia Minor and northern Syria, establishing what became known as the **Seleucid** empire.

Over the next century, the Seleucids extended their control southwards, driving the Ptolemids back into Egypt, though at the same time they lost Asia Minor to the Romans and Mesopotamia to the Parthians (who arose from the ashes of the Persian empire). Thus present-day Jordan came to be controlled by the Seleucids.

The Seleucids continued the process, begun under Alexander, of Hellenization. Cities such as Philadelphia (present-day Amman), Gerasa (Jerash), Pella and Gadara (Umm Qais), all flourished. By the second century BCE though, the Seleucid empire was beginning to crumble. At the same time, the **Nabataeans**, who had already established themselves as a powerful, semi-independent trading state in Petra, began to push northwards.

Roman period (64 BCE-395 CE)

The final fall of the Seleucid empire came with the conquest of Antioch and the creation of the province of Syria by the Roman general Pompey in 64 BCE. Roman rule brought with it peace and an orderly, efficient administration – the so-called *Pax Romana* – which allowed the region to flourish economically. The loose federation known as the **Decapolis**, or 'Ten Cities' emerged, straddling the borders of present-day southern Syria and northern Jordan, with cities such as Jerash in particular benefitting from the north–south trade between Damascus and the Red Sea.

Throughout Jordan, it is the monuments of the Roman era that have survived; the ubiquitous building projects of the Romans having overlain those of the Greeks whom they replaced. Socially and culturally, however, the region's Hellenistic influences continued to be felt long afterwards.

In 106 CE, during the reign of Trajan, the empire was substantially reorganized. The **Nabataean** kingdom of Petra was incorporated into the empire and a new province of Arabia created alongside that of Syria.

Byzantine period (395-636 CE)

In 312 CE Constantine had himself converted to Christianity, which was already spreading throughout the empire. A year later, the Edict of Milan officially gave Christians the right to practise their religion, and by 380 CE Christianity had been adopted as the official religion of the Roman Empire.

Many of the former pagan temples of the Romans were converted into great churches during the Byzantine era, for example at Jerash and Petra. It was during Emperor Justinian's rule that Byzantine culture and architecture truly flourished and cities such as Madaba became important religious centres.

In 602 CE, under the leadership of Chosroes II, the Sassanids launched a massive invasion into the Byzantine lands and by 616 CE the Byzantine empire was on its knees, and in no position to resist the onslaught of the new power emerging from the deserts of Arabia, that of the Muslim Arabs.

The beginning of the Islamic era (632-661 CE)

After the death in 632 CE of the founder of Islam, the Prophet Muhammad, the Arab tribes which he had welded together into such a formidable force set about conquering the fertile lands to the north and west. Led by the military commander **Khalid ibn al-Walid**, the Muslim Arab army captured Amman and Damascus in 635 CE and then withdrew to defeat forces of Byzantium at the Battle of Yarmouk in 636 CE, effectively marking the end of Byzantine rule in the region. They again occupied Damascus the same year, and then proceeded to sweep through the lands of present-day Jordan, Syria and Lebanon, meeting little resistance from the local peoples.

The Umayyads (661-750 CE)

When Damascus was declared the seat of the caliphate and capital of the Umayyad empire by Mu'awiya (the first Umayyad caliph), it heralded the start of one of the most glorious periods of the region as a whole. Jordan in particular benefitted, both from its proximity to the political heart of the empire, and from the annual passage of pilgrimage caravans through its territory en route between Damascus and the holy cities of Mecca and Medina.

The Abbasids (750-1258 CE)

As successive Umayyad caliphs fell into incompetency, the Abbasids were waiting in the wings to claim the caliphate title. They abandoned the blending of Eastern and Western influences which characterized Umayyad rule and brought to the empire a distinctively Mesopotamian and Persian emphasis, moving the capital first to Kufa and then Baghdad. Jordan, no longer close to the political heart of the empire, became a relatively insignificant backwater.

Initially the Abbasids managed successfully to administer an empire which encompassed all the former Umayyad lands (except Spain and Morocco). However, by the mid-ninth century their power was beginning to fragment with numerous local dynasties appearing, including the Fatimids who went on to make Cairo their capital in 973 CE and later extended their power into Syria.

The First Crusade (1096-1099)

During the first part of the 11th century, the Fatimid caliph Al Hakim had ordered the destruction of 30,000 churches in Egypt, Palestine, Jordan and Syria. This prompted Pope Urban II to call for a crusade to restore the Holy Lands to Christian control.

Thus the First Crusade set off from Europe, arriving in Syria in 1097. To their surprise, instead of a formidable enemy, what they found was a region deeply divided and fragmented into numerous petty principalities. After an eight-month siege they took Antioch then continued southwards along the Mediterranean coast to Jerusalem which fell to the Crusaders on 15 July 1099.

The Crusaders quickly realized the importance of establishing some 'strategic depth' to their narrow strip of coastal territory. The highlands to the east of the Dead Sea and Jordan River were of particular significance in that whoever controlled them also controlled movement along the inland route between Syria and Egypt. Thus King Baldwin I crossed into present-day Jordan and established a castle at Shobak in 1115 (see page 102). This was followed by castles at Wu'eira (in the vicinity of Petra), Al-Habees (inside Petra) and Tafila (on the King's Highway between Shobak and Kerak). The construction of Kerak castle came later, sometime around 1140, by which time the administrative district of **Oultre Jourdain** had been established (forming part of the Seigneury of Montreal, itself part of the Kingdom of Jerusalem).

Zengids and Ayyubids (1128-1260)

A concerted response to the Crusaders came from the **Zengids**, nominally subservient to the Seljuks. In 1169 Nur ud-Din sent a huge force against the Fatimids in Egypt. Led by Salah ud-Din (better known in the West as Saladin), the Zengid forces overthrew the Fatimids in 1171, restoring the authority of the Abbasid caliph.

After Nur ud-Din's death, Salah ud-Din returned to Syria and by 1186 had succeeded in uniting all the Muslim lands from Cairo to Baghdad under the **Ayyubid** dynasty (named after his father Ayyub). In 1187, having defeated the Crusaders at the Battle of Hattin, he recaptured Jerusalem and also regained Acre, Sidon, Beirut and Byblos. The following year he conducted a whirlwind campaign which saw no fewer than 50 Crusader positions fall (including Kerak, Wu'eira and Shobak).

The fall of Jerusalem prompted the **Third Crusade** (1187-1192) which ended in a peace treaty in 1192. After Salah ud-Din's death the following year, his successors failed to capitalize on the gains he had made and the Crusaders were able to recapture much of their former territory along the coast.

The Mamluks (1260-1516)

The Ayyubid line in Damascus was brought to an abrupt end in 1260 by the invasion of the **Mongols**, who swept across Syria and the southern Levant leaving a trail of destruction in their wake. Already in Cairo, the Mamluks had risen to power in a coup in 1250 and they were able to decisively defeat the Mongols at the Battle of Ayn Jalut in Palestine on 3 September 1260. One of the Mamluk generals at this battle was a man named Baibars, who subsequently made himself sultan and took over from the vanquished Ayyubids.

Baibars (ruled 1260-1277) proved himself to be a formidable adversary, unleashing the full force of his military genius on the Crusaders. In Jordan, commercial and pilgrimage traffic moved freely along the King's Highway once again. Agriculture also flourished, with intensive irrigation schemes bringing large areas of the Jordan Valley under cultivation. However, towards the end of the 14th century the Mamluks were suffering from internal power struggles which left their empire increasingly vulnerable to renewed attacks by the Mongols. The most devastating of these, led by Tamerlane, came in 1400, leaving a trail of destruction in its wake. Under the sultan Qait Bey (1468-1495), the Mamluks recovered somewhat, but they never achieved their former greatness, and in the first quarter of the 16th century they were overthrown by the Ottomans.

Ottomans (1516-1918)

The Ottoman Turks, who had already established themselves in Asia Minor during the middle of the 15th century and made Constantinople their capital, met little resistance when they swept into Syria, Jordan and Palestine in 1516, led by the sultan Selim I (ruled 1512-1520). Jordan, however, appears to have fallen into relative decline. Though the Ottomans maintained the caravan and pilgrimage routes, other aspects of the social and economic infrastructure were clearly neglected. In many areas, intensive agriculture gave way to semi-nomadic pastoralism, while towns and cities appear to have shrunk in size.

The First World War and the Arab Revolt

The modern political geography of the Middle East was largely shaped during the decade from 1914 to 1924. The onset of the First World War was of enormous significance to the region, which suddenly became a focus of international concern. The decision of the **Ottoman Turks** to ally themselves with the **Central Powers** (Germany and Austria-Hungary) placed them in direct opposition to the **Allies**. The harsh indifference of the Turks to local Arab populations, along with a breakdown of civic administration as the Turks focused their attentions on the war, brought widespread famine and epidemics. Arab feelings against the Turks increased, culminating in the **Arab Revolt**, with the Sharif of Mecca, Hussein Ibn Ali, the figurehead.

End of the First World War and broken promises

The triumphant entry of the Allies and the Arab nationalist forces into Damascus on 1 October 1918 signalled the final collapse of the Ottoman Empire and defeat of the Central Powers. Sharif Hussein's third son, **Feisal**, was established in Damascus as the head of an Arab government but although the British commander General Allenby recognized Feisal's government, he described it as "purely provisional".

Feisal attended the Paris Peace Conference of 1919 and secured the promise of an International Commission of Inquiry to look into the question of Syrian unity. The **King-Crane Commission**, as it became known, recommended that "the unity of Syria be preserved, in accordance with the earnest petition of the great majority of the Syrian people". However, at the **San Remo Conference** in April 1920 Britain and France formally divided historic Syria between them, putting into effect the 1916 Sykes–Picot Agreement in which the two nations had secretly agreed to carve up the region between them. The French Mandate covered present-day Syria and Lebanon, while the British Mandate covered Palestine and Transjordan, and on 24 July 1920 Feisal was forced out of Damascus by the French.

The status of the area known as **Transjordan** was rather muddy at this point. Ostensibly it was part of Britain's Palestine Mandate, administered from Jerusalem, though in reality the British recognized three separate governments in the area, with each having a special British adviser assigned from Jerusalem. In practice, the separate regions proved impossible to govern and when **Abdullah**, brother to Feisal and second son of Sharif Hussein, arrived at Ma'an on 11 November 1920 and declared his intention of redeeming the 'Arab Kingdom of Syria', the British greeted him with relief and allowed him to set up a central administration in Amman.

Emir Abdullah and the Emirate of Transjordan

Thus on 15 May 1923, the **Emirate of Transjordan** was formally declared an independent constitutional state. Many of the provisions of the British Mandate still applied, however, with the new emirate being prepared for full independence under the tutelage of the British high commissioner in Jerusalem. Abdullah was to rule as emir with the aid of a constitutional government and British advisers.

In 1928 a treaty was signed giving Transjordan a further degree of independence. A constitution for the new emirate was written up and a legislative council established. Britain, however, still retained control over foreign affairs, the armed forces, communications and state finances.

The Second World War and independence

Abdullah's Arab Legion served on the Allied side with distinction during the Second World War. At the conclusion of the war Abdullah was 'rewarded' by the British for his loyalty, though his reward was not quite the prize he desired.

On 22 March 1946 the **Treaty of London** was signed between Abdullah and the British, which provided for independence for Transjordan (subject to some provisions, such as British military facilities on its territory in exchange for subsidizing the Arab Legion), and on 25 May 1946 the Transjordanian cabinet voted to change Abdullah's title from emir to king (and the country's name from Transjordan to the **Hashemite Kingdom of Jordan**). This was a significant step, though still a far cry from the ambition that Abdullah had cherished ever since arriving in Ma'an in November 1920, namely to reclaim the Arab nation of Greater Syria.

State of Israel and the 1947-1949 war

Jordan's newly found independence was not graciously accepted by the rest of the world. Pressure from the Jewish lobby in the United States delayed recognition from that quarter (on the grounds that Transjordan was part of the land that had been earmarked as a 'national home for the Jews'), while the Soviet Union went as far as blocking Jordan's admission to the UN (regarding Abdullah as the latest puppet of Western imperialism).

Nevertheless, the status of Transjordan was not the main regional concern at this point; the future of Palestine continued to occupy the thoughts of the key policy makers. King Abdullah joined the rest of the Arab League in condemning the call for partition in the 1946 Anglo-American Committee of Inquiry's report (even though it had been hinted at that the Arab parts of Palestine would go to Jordan). Abdullah also stood firm with the Arab League in rejecting the United Nations Special Committee on Palestine's partition recommendation in 1947, after Britain had unilaterally handed over the perceived poison chalice of Palestine to the UN.

The UN vote on the partition of Palestine was grudgingly accepted by the Zionists (on the grounds that it provided a starting point for future expansion), but was resoundingly rejected by the Arab world. However, Jordan was perhaps the only Arab country that was really prepared for the inevitable consequence of this vote: war. During the 1947-1949 war that followed, the only Arab army that was really a match for the Jewish forces in terms of training and equipment was Jordan's Arab Legion, which succeeded in gaining control of the West Bank, as well as the Old City and eastern districts of Jerusalem.

End of the 1947-1949 war

A series of armistices finally ended the war in 1949, with Jordan concluding its ceasefire agreement with Israel on 3 April 1949. The terms of the ceasefire agreement meant that Jordan (now formally recognized by the USA) stood in possession of East Jerusalem and the **West Bank**, representing a significant portion of the Arab state that had been envisaged in the UN partition plan. Spring 1950 saw new elections to the Jordanian parliament, with Palestinians being invited to both vote and stand for office. The result was a motion to 'unite' the two banks of the Jordan River, and following a constitutional amendment, the 'West Bank' became part of the Hashemite Kingdom of Jordan.

The implications of this action were enormous. The population of the 'united' Jordan was now swollen to some 1.5 million, though less than a half of this figure were 'native Transjordanians'. This population also included a significant number of Palestinian refugees, as many as 500,000 of whom were living in camps.

Jordan from 1951 to 1967

On 20 July 1951 King Abdullah was assassinated by Mustafa Ashu, a 21-year-old apprentice tailor and Palestinian nationalist, as he entered the al-Aqsa mosque in Jerusalem's Old City for Friday prayers. He was succeeded by Talal, his eldest son. Talal, however, suffered from schizophrenia, which worsened after taking over as king. Within a year the situation was so bad that parliament voted that he should step down in favour of his son Hussein.

On 2 May 1953, at the age of just 18, **King Hussein** assumed the throne, a position which he held until his death on 7 February 1999. The early years of his reign were, however, turbulent ones. In 1954 the rise of Egypt's Gamal Abdul Nasser and his doctrine of pan-Arab unity spread unrest and tensions within Jordan and the country found itself isolated from its neighbouring Arab nations.

In April 1957 the pro-Nasserist government was forced by the king to resign. In the following weeks popular demonstrations spread throughout the country and there was an attempted coup. Finding himself in such a precarious position, King Hussein declared a state of emergency and imposed martial law.

King Hussein, however, was an adept politician and born survivor. In 1960 he offered full Jordanian citizenship to all Palestinians within the country and gradually Jordan managed to end its isolation in the Arab world.

1967 Six-Day War

Escalating tensions between Israel and its Arab neighbours had been simmering in the years following the Suez Crisis of 1956. Jordan's attendance at an Arab League summit in Cairo in 1964 saw the founding of the Palestine Liberation Organisation (PLO) and a consequent increase in *fedayeen* (Palestinian fighters) attacks on Israel. Tensions were further increased when Egypt ordered the c4500 international military personnel of the

United Nations Emergency Force (UNEF) – installed in the wake of the 1956 Suez Crisis to help maintain peace between Egypt and Israel – to withdraw from the Sinai Peninsula, Gaza Strip and the Strait of Tiran on 18 May, thus removing a buffer zone which had existed between the two countries. Less than a week later, on 22 May, Egypt closed the Strait of Tiran to Israeli shipping, including any oil tankers destined for Israel's port of Eilat, a vital maritime closure which the Jewish state deemed a justification for war.

At 0745 local time on 5 June 1967 Israel launched Operation Focus, a pre-emptive air strike against Egypt, an attack of surprise that owed at least part of its success to Egypt's failure to act on warnings received from Jordan's Ajlun early-warning radar station. In under three hours the Israeli air force had destroyed all of Egypt's bomber aircraft and 85% of its fighter aircraft and rendered its radar systems and runways inoperable, giving Israel total air supremacy over Egypt. Turning their attention to Jordan and Syria, the Israeli air force destroyed the totality of the former's much smaller air force around midday and during the course of the same afternoon had devastated two-thirds of Syria's air force. Having secured air superiority Israel engaged in a series of fierce artillery, infantry and tank battles with the armies of Egypt, Jordan and Syria and by the time a UN ceasefire came into effect on 10 June, the Israelis had achieved a devastating and total military defeat of the combined Arab forces. Moreover, the Arab military debacle had also come at huge territorial cost, with Israel now occupying the entire Sinai Peninsula, the Gaza Strip, the West Bank (including East Jerusalem) and the Golan Heights (Al-Jawlān).

Aftermath of the Six-Day War

The repercussions of the Six-Day War for Jordan were particularly disastrous. In addition to losing the entirety of the West Bank and the hallowed city of Jerusalem it resulted in a further influx of c300,000 Palestinian refugees, thus exacerbating the strain on an economy already devastated by the losses of war. On 22 November 1967 the UN Security Council passed Resolution 242 calling for the withdrawal of Israeli forces from the occupied territories and for all Middle Eastern nations to "live in peace within secure and recognised boundaries"; a land for peace initiative which to this day remains the bedrock of the Arab-Israeli conflict. The resolution was supported by Egypt and Jordan but rejected by the PLO, Syria and Iraq as it implied recognition of the State of Israel and a perceived end of the quest for an independent Palestinian state.

Rising militancy by Palestinian factions was the hallmark of the immediate post-1967-war era, which witnessed a series of airliner hijackings by the Popular Front for the Liberation of Palestine (PFLP) and Yasser Arafat's Fatah movements' commando operations against the Israelis. This certainly raised the global profile of the Palestinian cause, but placed the Palestinians and Jordanians on a collision course, with the former critical of King Hussein's Western-leaning ideology while the latter were alarmed at the impunity with which the Palestinians operated from Jordanian soil and the perceived threat to the monarch's rule. Armed conflict was inevitable and over the course of 10 days beginning on 17 September 1970, fighting between Jordanian forces and the Palestinians devastated the capital Amman and destroyed Palestinian camps, as well as costing some 3000 Palestinians and hundreds of Jordanians their lives. This drive to oust the Palestinians from Jordan, known as **Black September**, culminated in a ceasefire with the Palestinians and Yasser Arafat expelled to nearby Lebanon where he set up new headquarters.

Jordan from 1973 to 1991

Shortly after 1400 on Saturday 6 October 1973, Egypt and Syria unleashed a coordinated attack against Israel. Timed to take place during Yom Kippur, the most sacred day of the Jewish calendar to maximize the element of surprise, it became widely known in Israel as the **Yom Kippur War** and to Arabs as the **October** or **Ramadan War**. The early stages of battle saw Egyptian and Syrian forces inflict significant losses on Israel's air and ground forces in the Sinai and Golan Heights. Although Jordan remained officially neutral it did despatch a small token force of infantry and armoured units to assist Syria in its defence of the Golan Heights as Israeli forces counter attacked. The war officially ended on 26 October, which was militarily inconclusive but politically advantageous for the Arabs.

On 31 July 1988, having once again dissolved parliament and put an end to West Bank representation in the legislature, King Hussein formally renounced Jordan's claim to the West Bank. The PLO in turn made the 'Algiers Declaration' on 15 November of that year, declaring Palestinian 'statehood'. In November 1989, after riots over increases in taxes and food prices, Jordanians were allowed to vote in the first general election since 1967, though these were still non-party elections. By 1992, however, the ban on political parties had been lifted and martial law, also in force since 1967, revoked. In 1993 a one-person-one-vote system was put in place and the first multi-party elections for 34 years took place.

Peace process

Between 30 October and 1 November 1991 Jordan participated in the Madrid Conference on Arab–Israeli peace, co-sponsored by the USA and Soviet Union, and attended by a Palestinian delegation in order to circumvent the Israeli refusal to negotiate directly with the PLO. The talks themselves produced no major breakthrough but on 13 September 1993, following secret negotiations in Oslo (Norway), much to everyone's surprise Israeli premier Yitzak Rabin and PLO chairman Yasser Arafat signed the Declaration of Principles (DOP, widely known as the **Oslo Accords**) on the White House lawn. It set out the basis of a peace agreement that would give Palestinians control of the Gaza Strip and the West Bank town of Jericho, which Arafat saw as "the beginning of the Palestinian state". It was an agreement which King Hussein quickly realized could be used to Jordan's advantage in both the economic and political arenas.

On 25 July 1994 King Hussein and Israeli prime minister Yitzak Rabin signed the **Washington Declaration** at the White House, which ended the decades-long state of war between the two countries in order to achieve "a just, lasting and comprehensive peace between Arab states and the Palestinians, with Israel". This was followed, on 26 October of the same year, by a formal peace treaty between Jordan and Israel, the ceremony taking place in a tent straddling the border near the Wadi Araba crossing.

The death of King Hussein

On 19 January 1999 King Hussein returned to Jordan after a six-month absence during which he had been undergoing treatment for lymphatic cancer in the USA. On the night of 26 January, exactly a week after his return, King Hussein was on his way back to the USA and few doubted that his cancer was active again. Abdullah, his son by his English second wife Antoinette (Toni) Gardiner, was made crown prince.

On 5 February 1999 King Hussein once again flew back to Jordan from the USA. This time he was on his deathbed. At 1143 on 7 February 1999, he died aged 63. Spanning some 46 years, King Hussein's rule had been the longest lasting in the Middle East.

King Abdullah II and Jordan today

Following the death of King Hussein after nearly 47 years on the throne and amid fears of a power struggle mounted by his brother Hassan – who had surprisingly been cut off as his successor less than two weeks prior to his death in favour of his eldest son Abdullah – the transition of power was a remarkably smooth event. This was despite Abdullah being a relatively young 37 years, and with a military career to date that had done little to prepare him for the demands of becoming a ruling monarch.

Since his succession King Abdullah II has faced enormous domestic and regional challenges. As a Western-leaning modernizer, Abdullah forged ahead with economic and social reforms and established close economic ties with the USA in order to generate additional financial aid for the country. On the regional and wider international stage, Abdullah has attempted to emulate his father as a peacemaker and to maintain Jordan as an example of stability in an otherwise unstable neighbourhood.

The new king inherited a country with a crippling rate of unemployment and high levels of poverty. With the assistance of foreign aid and by creating opportunities for foreign investment Jordan has achieved some economic growth. However, a high unemployment rate and nation-wide water shortages (Jordan is one of the world's water-poorest nations) remain ongoing problems which have yet to be tackled effectively.

Despite choosing the path of modernization and progress, and with Jordan often upheld in the West as the region's white elephant of stability, King Abdullah himself has been oft-criticized for stalling on furthering Jordan's democratic processes and for permitting corruption to thrive within his inner circle.

The stimulus for Jordanians to stress the growing problems in their own country – rampant inflation, soaring food prices, high unemployment and lack of political reform – was provided by the Egyptian uprising in early 2011. Throughout February 2011 thousands of Jordanians took to the streets of the capital to protest at the government's mismanagement of the country. Unlike in other more despotic Middle Eastern countries, however, the protests were (and remain) relatively peaceful and untainted by government troops using excessive force against demonstrators.

The years since 2011 have seen Jordan confront numerous domestic, international and regional challenges. The Arab Spring uprisings and the resulting war in Syria, as well as the continuing conflict in Iraq, now sees some 1.3 million Syrian refugees (around 12% of the population) and around 33,951 Iraqi refugees residing in the country, which serves to put additional strains on essential services such as education, healthcare and housing. The Covid-19 pandemic (which has claimed over 14,000 Jordanian lives to date) and the effects of the war in Ukraine (which supplies 10% of Jordan's grain) also proved difficult. The current regional crisis of concern to Jordan stems from the Operation Al-Aqsa Flood attack by the Palestinian group Hamas (Islamic Resistance Movement) against Israel on 7 October 2023, infiltrating southern Israel from the Gaza Strip, killing some 1139 Israelis and taking over 240 hostages. Jordan's response to the intense and wide-ranging Israeli reprisals has been decidedly frosty towards its neighbour, who it accuses of 'war crimes' against the Palestinians. Reiterating its long-term stance of a two-state solution as the only way to end the violence between the Palestinians and Israel and Jordan's long-standing solidarity with the Palestinian cause (indeed Queen Rania herself is of Palestinian parentage), Jordan nonetheless remains opposed to accepting additional refugees. Despite the country's damning rhetoric, the peace treaty with Israel seems safe for now in the absence of a mass displacement of refugees or a wider conflagration that could, in the words of current Jordanian prime minister Bisher al Khasawaneh, pose an "existential threat" to the 1994 peace treaty between the two countries.

Aside from regional issues impacting Jordan, the country's continuing stability is likely to depend on how King Abdullah and his government navigate their way through pressing domestic, economic and social matters. With national elections scheduled for November 2024 the focus will likely be on easing high unemployment, declining living standards and food shortages.

Practicalities

Getting there

Jordan's principal international airport is **Queen Alia International Airport** (www.qaiairport.com, see page 43 for further airport details), located 35 km south of Amman. Jordan's other two airports are **Amman Civil Airport** (aka **Marka Airport**, www.jac.jo) around 3 km northeast of Downtown Amman which handles mainly charter and VIP flights and **King Hussein International Airport** (www.khiaops.com) in Aqaba which handles mainly internal and charter flights.

Flights from the UK From London Heathrow **British Airways** (www.britishairways.com) and the national carrier **Royal Jordanian Airlines** (www.rj.com) fly regularly to Amman. Royal Jordanian also operate non-stop flights from London Stansted to Amman three times a week, and from Manchester airport twice weekly. From London Luton budget airline **Wizz Air** (www.wizzair.com) offers return flights to Amman for under £400. If you don't mind a stopover, you can save money by flying indirect with airlines such as **Turkish Airlines** (www.turkishairlines.com) who fly to Amman and Aqaba via its hub at Istanbul, or **Egypt Air** (www.egyptair.com).

Alternatively, if having evidence of a visit to Israel in your passport isn't a problem (Iran and Lebanon *will* refuse you entry) and you want to save money, you could fly into Israel and enter Jordan overland. Budget carrier **Easyjet** (www.easyjet.com) has one-way fares from London Gatwick, London Luton and Manchester airports to Tel Aviv (Ben Gurion) from around £150. Turkish budget airline **Pegasus** (www.flypgs.com) operates flights from London Stansted to Tel Aviv via Istanbul (Sabiha Gokçen International Airport) with one-way fares from around £130.

Flights from the rest of Europe Royal Jordanian operates direct flights from cities including Amsterdam, Barcelona, Brussels, Dusseldorf, Frankfurt, Geneva, Madrid, Milan, Paris, Rome, Stockholm and Zurich. Other airlines which fly direct include **Air France** (www.airfrance.fr), **Lufthansa** (www.lufthansa.com) and **Austrian Airlines** (www.austrian.com). As with the UK (see above), it could be worth saving money by considering indirect flights.

Flights from North America From the USA, **American Airlines** (from Chicago and Detroit, www.aa.com) and **United Airlines** (from Washington DC, www.united.com) now fly direct to Amman. Royal Jordanian flies direct from Chicago, Detroit, Montreal, New York and Toronto. Savings can often be made by flying indirect with **Air France**, **Emirates** (www.emirates.com), **Egypt Air** and **Turkish Airlines**, all flying from New York (John F Kennedy) to Amman via their respective hubs.

Flights from Australia and New Zealand Emirates, **Qantas** (www.qantas.com.au) and **Etihad** (www.etihadairways.com) fly from Australia to Amman via their hubs in the Gulf, costing from about AUS$1900 return. From New Zealand the price is higher with return flights priced at around NZ$2200. Alternatively you can fly from Australia with oneworld partners **Qantas** and **Malaysia Airlines** (www.malaysiaairlines.com), connecting to **Royal Jordanian** at Bangkok and Kuala Lumpur.

Flights from the Middle East **Royal Jordanian** flies to Amman from all the main Middle Eastern cities such as Beirut, Cairo, Dubai, Abu Dhabi and Kuwait. Using regional budget airlines **Flydubai** (www.flydubai.com) and **Air Arabia** (www.airarabia.com) you can pick up one-way flights to Amman from Dubai and Sharjah in the UAE from about US$150. **Air Arabia** also flies direct to Amman from Alexandria and Sharm el-Sheikh in Egypt with one-way prices beginning at US$160. **Egypt Air** and **Royal Jordanian**, flying out of Cairo, tend to be more expensive. From Israel, flights operated by **Royal Jordanian** are pricey for such a short hop, averaging about US$250. Both **MEA** (www.mea.com.lb) and **Royal Jordanian** fly between Beirut (Lebanon) and Amman with one-way fares beginning at around US$112.

Road

Jordan has land borders with **Syria**, **Israel**, **Iraq** and **Saudi Arabia**. Due to ongoing conflicts in Syria and Iraq, the only viable land borders for travellers to use are with Israel and Saudi Arabia. You cannot cross directly by land from Egypt but you can cross overland from Egypt's Taba border in the Sinai, via Eilat in Israel and enter Jordan through the Yitzhak Rabin/Wadi Araba border.

From Israel

Border crossings with Israel **King Hussein Bridge (Jordan)–Allenby Bridge (Israel)** ⓘ *Sun-Thu 0800-1730, Fri-Sat 0800-1530, closed for the 1st day of Eid al-Adha and Yom Kippur, departure tax Jordan 10JD, departure tax Israel 175NIS. Facilities: banks, money exchange, restaurant*. The most direct route between Jerusalem and Amman. If you're in Jerusalem you can get a *sherut* (service taxi) from Damascus Gate to the border (40NIS), and on the Jordanian side pick up a service taxi (8JD) or private taxi (25-35JD) to Amman. Note that Jordanian visas are not issued at this border. You must have purchased one beforehand or use either of the other borders.

Entering Israel from Jordan on this border, it is possible to do a side trip to Israel without having a Jordanian multiple-entry visa, as long as your single-entry visa is still valid upon your return to Jordan.

Prince Hussein Bridge (Jordan)–Jordan River (Israel) ⓘ *Sun-Thu 0630-2100, Fri-Sat 0800-2000, closed for Eid al-Hijara (Islamic New Year) and Yom Kippur, departure tax Jordan 10JD, departure tax Israel 101NIS. Facilities: banks, money exchange, duty free, restaurant*. In the north of Israel, the easiest border to use is the Prince Hussein Bridge/Jordan River crossing. Hop in a private taxi to the border from Beit Shean. Jordanian visas are issued on arrival. Once on the Jordanian side, service taxis (2JD) and private taxis (about 20JD) head to Irbid, from where you can pick up buses to Amman.

Wadi Araba (Jordan)–Yitzhak Rabin (Israel) ⓘ *Sun-Thu 0630-2000, Fri-Sat 0800-2000, closed Eid al-Hijara (Islamic New Year) and Yom Kippur, no departure tax from Jordan, departure tax Israel 101NIS, US$ also accepted. Facilities: banks, money exchange*. By far the easiest crossing between Jordan and Israel, the Wadi Araba border is much quieter and quicker than the Jordan Valley border points. From Eilat, there are plenty of private taxis and *sheruts* plying the short route from town to the border. At the time of writing you can't obtain a Jordanian visa at this crossing and you must have obtained a visa in advance. On the Jordanian side, private taxis (10-15JD) wait for fares to take you into Aqaba.

From Saudi Arabia

The Kingdom of Saudi Arabia (KSA) has opened its borders to non-Muslim visitors in recent years, and citizens from over 60 countries, including North American and UK nationals, can enter Jordan from any of the KSA's air and three land border crossings with Jordan. To apply for a Saudi entry visa your passport must be valid for six months from your date of entry into the KSA and must not contain evidence of a visit to Israel. The cost of the visa varies from country to country and visas are valid for one year, permitting multiple entries for a total stay of up to 90 days. For more information visit www.visitsaudi.com.

The following border crossings between Saudi Arabia and Jordan are open 24/7 and you can enter Jordan from any of these provided you hold a Jordanian visa:
• Umari border crossing, south of Azraq and around 155 km from Amman
• Mudawara border crossing, 322 km from Amman
• Durra border crossing, south of Aqaba and 349 km from Amman

Sea

From Egypt (Nuweiba)

The **Arab Bridge (AB) Maritime Company** (T03-209 2000 Aqaba office, T06-585 9554 Amman office, www.abmaritime.com.jo) operates a couple of ferry services that connect Egypt with Jordan. At the time of writing the Nuweiba ferry crossing from Egypt to Aqaba departs daily at 1200, arriving in Aqaba at 1700 (EGP2950, children under 2 EGP800, US$ also accepted). The Aqaba to Nuweiba service departs daily at 2200, arriving in Nuweiba at 0100 (US$80, children under 2 US$15). Cars cost US$200 and motorbikes US$75.

From Egypt (Taba)

AB Maritime also run a much faster (1 hr) catamaran service from the Egyptian port of Taba to Aqaba. At the time of writing this service departs Taba at 1330 on Sunday, Tuesday and Thursday-Saturday, arriving in Aqaba at 1430 (US$65, children 1-6 US$55, children under 1 US$15). From Aqaba to Taba the service departs on Tuesday, Thursday and Friday at 1000, arriving in Taba at 01.00 (US$70, children 1-6 US$50, children under 1 US$15).

For EU, UK and US nationals travelling to Nuweiba or Taba in Egypt, upon arrival you will be issued with a free entry stamp valid for 15 days but you *must* obtain a full Egyptian visa (30-day single entry £25) if you intend to stay longer or travel beyond these areas such as to Cairo. A full Egyptian visa can be purchased at Nuweiba or Taba port or at Egypt's Sharm el Sheikh airport.

Getting around

Air

Jordan is so small there is really no need to fly. The only internal air connection is between Amman and Aqaba with **Royal Jordanian** (www.rj.com) operating two to three flights daily between the two cities.

Road *See also Road safety, page 176.*

Bicycle

Cycling is increasingly popular in Jordan, although the hilly terrain and heat make this a particularly strenuous and demanding way of getting around. The King's Highway is perhaps the most appealing route for cyclists in terms of the limited traffic and spectacular scenery, although it involves a number of very long and steep descents/ascents as you cross the *wadis* that drain into the Dead Sea.

In Amman, contact **Bike Rush** (Al-Jafn St, 7th Circle, T07-9945 4586, see Facebook) who rent bikes for 10-20JD per day and can also organize a range of guided rides around the country. If you are bringing your own two wheels they also sell spare parts and can undertake repairs. For experienced riders it could be worth considering riding all or part of the **Jordan Bike Trail** (www.jordanbiketrail.com), an undulating 730 km route the length of the country from Umm Qais in the north to Aqaba in the south.

Bus, minibus and service taxi

The most comfortable and efficient way to get around is on the air-conditioned **coaches** run by JETT (www.jett.com.jo). This company operates services between Amman and Petra, the King Hussein border crossing, Aqaba and many destinations in between.

All other public transport in Jordan is a motley collection of banged up old **buses** and **minibuses** that run to no set schedule, simply departing when full. If you're unlucky, you could be waiting up to an hour at the bus station to depart. The bonus is that you get to meet ordinary Jordanians and the fare costs are minimal, although on some minibus routes you may have to pay extra for a large backpack. Unlike JETT buses you can hop on or hop off anywhere along the route. If you know where you want the bus to stop, simply tap on your window to let the driver know to pull over, or let the driver know beforehand. Most Jordanian minibus drivers will go out of their way to help foreign visitors.

Service taxis operate on popular routes and are more expensive than bus or minibus but generally get you to your destination faster. You still have to wait for them to fill up before you leave but since there are only four seats to fill your waiting time is usually minimal. Unfortunately there are certain sections of Jordan where bus and minibus transport is seriously irregular or virtually non-existent. Parts of the King's Highway and the Dead Sea Highway are particularly bad and hiring a car/driver for these is worthwhile.

Car

Hiring a car Hiring a car within Jordan can save you a lot of time and makes life much easier for certain trips (notably the King's Highway and Dead Sea Highway). Amman is

TRAVEL TIP
Road rules and driving conditions

Vehicles drive on the right. The speed limit in built-up areas is 40 kph, outside of urban areas 80 kph, and on the highways 120 kph. On-the-spot fines of 15-150JD are issued by police if you are caught exceeding these legal speed limits. It is compulsory for the driver and front-seat passenger to wear a seatbelt.

The road system in Jordan is generally very good. Main highways are well-maintained good quality fast roads. On minor roads though, you need to watch out for potholes and well-concealed speed bumps in villages. Amman is a hectic place to drive; as well as getting to grips with the complicated interchanges at major junctions, you have to cope with the legions of taxi drivers who merrily cut up anything in sight.

In the majority of cases, routes are clearly signposted in English as well as Arabic with tourist sites indicated by brown signs with white writing. The one thing you will have to watch out for are misspelt signs. There is no official phonetic transliteration of Arabic into English and so English place names on signs can be written in a variety of different ways.

the main place for car hire, with a range of international firms and literally hundreds of local companies scattered all over the city. Car hire rates start from around 40-50JD per day. Most companies have a minimum rental period of two days, and have unlimited mileage as standard. Drop-off fees apply if you return the car to a different office than the one you hired from.

Car hire insurance You should pay very careful attention to the insurance arrangements and general terms and conditions. All companies require that you leave a deposit (generally 300-500JD, either in cash or in the form of a credit card imprint), which you lose if you crash the car. The better firms offer the option of taking out additional Crash Damage Waiver (CDW) insurance (usually in the region of 10-15JD per day), which protects you from additional charges in the event of an accident (though even then, some still charge for an initial 'excess', so check carefully).

Negotiating rides/hitchhiking

Hitchhiking in the Western sense (ie: for free) is not a widely accepted concept in Jordan. However, in rural areas, where there is no regular public transport, it's quite common to flag a ride down and offer payment at the end of it. Hitchhiking anywhere carries inherent risks and no one (especially females) should ever hitchhike alone.

Taxis

Jordan's towns all have plentiful yellow private taxis. Metered fares are the norm for trips within Amman but outside of the capital, meters are rarely used and you'll usually have to negotiate the fare. Private taxis can be hired for a day for a negotiated fee and make a good option for travelling the King's Highway and Dead Sea where public transport is sparse.

Essentials A-Z

Accident and emergency

Jordan's centralized emergency line, with English-speaking operators, T911, can be used for ambulance, fire and police services.

Children

Jordanians love children. Children are positively welcomed in restaurants, most hotels will go out of their way to accommodate them and you will constantly find yourself receiving offers of help and hospitality.

Disposable nappies are difficult to find outside of Amman, so stock up before leaving the capital. Car seats are also a rarity so if you're planning on hiring a car/driver bring your own.

Due to the heat, parents should be extra vigilant with sun protection. Beat the noon heat and plan outdoor activities in either early-morning or late-afternoon hours and keep an eagle-eye on children's liquid intake to prevent dehydration and heat exhaustion.

Customs and duty free

The standard duty free allowance is 200 cigarettes/200 g tobacco/25 cigars and 1 litre of alcohol. Perfume (1 or 2 bottles for personal use only) is allowed to be brought in, as are gifts up to an equivalent value of US$150.

Discounts

Introduced in 2015, the **Jordan Pass** (www.jordanpass.jo) offers a substantial discount for travellers. The pass allows entry to over 40 tourist sites, including the major attractions of Petra, Jerash, Amman Citadel, Kerak Castle and Wadi Rum and, if bought before travelling, also waives the tourist visa fee (for those staying a minimum of 3 nights in the country). There are 3 different pass options: 70JD (with 1-day Petra entry); 75JD (2-day Petra entry), and 80JD (3-day Petra entry). All passes are valid for 2 weeks from 1st use.

Electricity

220 volts, 50 AC. European round 2-pin plugs are the norm.

Embassies and consulates

For embassies and consulates overseas, see www.embassypages.com/jordan.

Health

See your GP or travel clinic at least 6 weeks before departure for general advice on travel risks and vaccinations. Make sure you have sufficient medical travel insurance, get a dental check, know your own blood group and if you suffer from a long-term condition such as diabetes or epilepsy, obtain a Medic Alert bracelet/necklace (www.medicalert.org.uk). If you wear glasses, take a copy of your prescription.

On the whole, standards of hygiene are good, and the health risks are generally very low. As a rule, the worst you can expect is an upset stomach, though more serious food poisoning or gastric infections are not unknown.

The standards of medical facilities are high in Jordan. There are plenty of international-standard hospitals in Amman and even the smaller clinics are usually excellent.

Vaccinations

No vaccinations are mandatory, but it is wise to be up to date with polio, diphtheria, tetanus, typhoid, hepatitis A and hepatitis B shots. You may be asked for a yellow fever certificate if you have been travelling in an endemic country immediately before travelling to Jordan.

Health risks

Insect bites Malaria is not a concern, but mosquitoes, ticks and sandflies may transmit other infections during the day and night. Cover up and apply a repellent (containing DEET or icaridin) to exposed skin.

Rabies This fatal disease is spread through the saliva of infected dogs, bats and other mammals. Wash any wound thoroughly with soap and water and seek medical advice immediately if bitten or scratched by any mammal. Vaccination before travel simplifies the treatment and is worth considering if at increased risk, eg: if travelling remotely or working with animals.

Diarrhoea Stomach upsets are common. They're mainly caused by the change in diet (Middle Eastern food is heavy on oil, which can be hard to digest for people unused to this diet). More serious diarrhoea can be caused by eating contaminated food or drinking tap water. To avoid this, stick to boiled, filtered or bottled water and avoid ice cubes. Raw fruit and vegetables are a potential hazard unless you have washed or peeled them yourself.

Any kind of diarrhoea, whether or not accompanied by vomiting, responds well to the replacement of water and salts with a rehydration solution – take frequent small sips. Seek medical treatment if the diarrhoea continues for more than 3 days or if you have severe abdominal pain or notice blood in the diarrhoea.

Heat illness In the summer months, heat exhaustion and heatstroke are common. They are prevented by drinking enough fluids throughout the day (your urine will be pale if you are drinking enough). Symptoms of heat exhaustion include dizziness, tiredness, nausea and headache. Use rehydration salts mixed with water to replenish fluids and salts and find somewhere cool and shady to recover.

Some may progress to heatstroke, a more severe breakdown of temperature control. It can lead to reduced or absent sweating, flushed skin and disorientation leading to unconsciousness. Cool the body down quickly (cold showers are particularly effective) and seek urgent medical treatment.

If you get sick

Good-quality healthcare is available in larger cities. Private hospital treatment can be expensive, especially hospitalization. Adequate insurance is vital.

Recommended hospitals

Amman Hospital, Zahran St, Jebel Amman, Amman, T06-464 1261, www. ammanhospital.com; recommended by many major hotels and foreign embassies. **Italian Hospital**, Mayden St, Kerak, T03-235 1045.
Queen Rania Hospital, Petra, T03-215 0635, 5 km out of town on the road to Taybet.

Useful websites

www.travelhealthpro.org.uk A-Z of vaccine/health advice for each country.
www.cdc.gov/travel US government site with travel health advice.
www.gov.uk/foreign-travel-advice/ jordan The UK Foreign, Commonwealth & Development Office (FCDO) travel site has useful and up-to-date information on each country, including health advice.

Insurance

Always take out comprehensive insurance before you travel, including full medical cover and extra cover for any activities (hiking, riding, etc) that you may undertake. Check exactly what's included, the maximum cover for each element and also the excess you will have to pay in the case of a claim. Keep details of your policy and the insurance company's telephone number with you at all times. Get a police report for any lost or stolen items.

Language

Arabic is the national language, although English is also widely spoken. The Arabic spoken in Jordan is known as Levantine Arabic, as opposed to Egyptian Arabic, although with Egypt being so close by, there is some blending of the 2. Learning a few basic phrases of Arabic before you go really isn't that difficult and goes down very well once you are there. Learning to recognize and pronounce the numerals is also easy and of considerable practical use. See Useful Arabic words and phrases, page 17.

LGBTQIA+ travellers

Although homosexuality was decriminalized in 1951 (with 16 years being the age of consent), it remains very much a taboo subject. A gay scene does exist in Amman, but it is extremely hidden. LGBTQIA+ travellers are therefore advised to be discreet about their sexuality.

Further information on Jordan's gay scene can be found at www.globalgayz.com and www.nomadicboys.com

Local customs

Jordanians are generally very open and welcoming and will often go out of their way to help foreigners.

Dress

Jordanians place a lot of importance on smartness and cleanliness and making the effort to be presentable in public will earn you greater respect. While very liberal dress codes can be found in the affluent areas of Amman, as soon as you get out of the capital, far more conservative attitudes prevail. The key to remember is shoulders and knees (and everything in-between) should be covered at all times. This rule applies to men as well as women.

Visiting mosques

Non-Muslims are often not allowed to enter mosques in Jordan, or else are only allowed into the outer courtyard and not the prayer hall itself. Always seek permission before entering a mosque, and be prepared to give way if you are refused entry. If you are allowed in, remember that shoes must be removed before entering the prayer hall. Both men and women should make sure their arms and legs are entirely covered. Women should also wear a headscarf.

Tips…

- Do not take pictures of women without their consent, or more importantly that of their male escort.
- Except among more cosmopolitan people it is not usual for a man and woman to shake hands when meeting. Instead, place your right hand across your heart, which can also be used as a sign of thank you as well.
- Displays of affection between couples are not generally acceptable in public and can cause great offence. Conversely, it is completely normal for friends of the same sex (male and female) to hold hands and link arms in public.
- Always tuck your feet in towards you when sitting down. Feet are considered unclean and it's considered rude to point them at someone.

Money

£1 = 0.92JD, US$1 = 0.71JD, €1 = 0.78JD (Sep 2024)

The unit of currency is the Jordanian Dinar (JOD), popularly referred to as the 'JD' (pronounced jaydee). Notes come in denominations of 1, 5, 10, 20 and 50. The dinar is divided into 100 piastres (or qirsh) and come in denominations of 5, 10, 25 and 50 piastres.

The system is made somewhat more complicated by the fact that many Jordanians use the older system of dividing the dinar into 1000 fils with many shop tills and some taxi meters still working on this system. If you just remember to lop the last zero off you'll generally be OK.

ATMs
ATMs are numerous and for many travellers in Jordan, this is the predominant form of obtaining cash. Most bank ATMs accept foreign cards though some only accept cards from certain networks. In general Visa is the more widely accepted card.

Cash
The major foreign currencies of US dollars, euro and UK pounds can be changed without problem and there should be no fees or commission for cash. You can also easily change leftover currency from neighbouring Israel and Egypt in Amman and in Aqaba. On the whole, banks offer marginally better rates than money changers.

You can change JD back into hard currencies without any problem before you leave the country, although, officially, you must show exchange receipts for the value you wish to reconvert.

Credit cards
You can use your credit card to pay the bill at all luxury hotels and many mid-range ones. Many upmarket restaurants and shops (and tourism-related services such as travel agents and car hire firms) also accept cards. Check what the commission fee is beforehand as sometimes it is very high. You can also use your credit card at most banks to obtain a cash advance.

Transferring money
Western Union Money Transfer (www. westernunion.com) is represented in Jordan by the Cairo Amman Bank (www. cab.jo), which has a number of branches in Amman and around the country. The fees charged are very high but this can be a good option in an emergency.

Opening hours

Banks, government offices and post offices Sun-Thu 0830-1500.
Shops Daily 0900-2000, some close or keep shorter hours on Fri.
Tourist sites Daily 0800-1800, many stay open longer during summer and some keep shorter opening hours on Fri. Many smaller museums and sights close on Tue.

Photography

Avoid taking pictures of military installations or anything that might be construed as 'sensitive', particularly if you are close to the Israeli border.

Public holidays

Note that the following are fixed public holidays – many of the major Muslim and Christian holidays are also public holidays, although their precise dates vary from year to year. In most cases public holidays mean that banks and government offices will be closed for the day, but restaurants and many shops remain open. See also Festivals, page 12.

Fixed-date holidays
1 Jan New Year's Day
1 May Labour Day
25 May Independence Day

10 Jun Army Day and anniversary of the Great Arab Revolt (banks and government offices generally stay open on this day)
25 Dec Christmas Day

Islamic holidays

Islamic holiday dates are calculated according to the lunar calendar and therefore fall on different days each year, moving back around 10-11 days annually.

Ras as-Sana (Islamic New Year) 1st Muharram. The first 10 days of the year are regarded as holy, especially the 10th.

Ashoura 9th and 10th Muharram. Anniversary of the killing of Hussein, commemorated by Shi'ite Muslims (Shi'ites are a small minority in Jordan, so this event is not widely celebrated). Ashoura also celebrates the meeting of Adam and Eve after leaving Paradise, and the end of the Flood.

Moulid an-Nabi The Prophet Muhammad's birthday. 12th Rabi al-Awwal.

Leilat al-Meiraj Ascension of Muhammad from Haram al-Sharif (Temple Mount) in Jerusalem. 27th Rajab.

Ramadan The Islamic month of fasting. The most important event in the Islamic calendar. 21st Ramadan is the *Shab-e-Qadr* or 'Night of Prayer'.

Eid al-Fitr Literally 'the small feast'. 3 days of celebration, beginning 1st Shawwal, to mark the end of Ramadan.

Eid al-Adha Literally 'the great feast'. Begins on 10th Zilhaj and lasts for 4 days. Commemorates Ibrahim's (Abraham's) near sacrifice of his son Ismail (though in Christian and Judaic tradition it is Isaac who is nearly sacrificed), and coincides with the Hajj, or pilgrimage to Mecca. Marked by the sacrifice of a sheep, feasting and donations to the poor.

Christian holidays

In addition to Christmas, **Good Friday** and **Easter Sunday** are both public as well as religious holidays.

The majority of Jordan's Christian population is Orthodox, meaning that Christian holidays are celebrated according to the Julian (as opposed to our own Gregorian) calendar. **Christmas**, however, is still generally celebrated on 25 Dec (Orthodox Christmas falls on 7 Jan). **Easter** is celebrated according to the Julian calendar and the date varies between 2 weeks before and after the Western Easter. For the Orthodox Church it is also the most important Christian festival, far outweighing Christmas in significance.

Safety

Theft and violent crime are extremely rare in Jordan and even in large cities like the capital Amman it is possible to wander around freely and safely by day or night. Petty crime such as stealing from hotel rooms (use the hotel security boxes if available), car theft, pick-pocketing and bag snatching are rare but not unheard of events. See also Women travellers, page 179.

Road safety

Probably the biggest danger that tourists face is on the roads. Although the road system is extremely good, Jordanians love to drive fast and use of indicators when turning is erratic, to say the least. Especially in Amman, you need to keep a close eye on traffic when using the roads.

When crossing a busy road as a pedestrian, use your right hand to make the hand signal for 'ustena' ('wait' in Arabic); bring the tip of your thumb to meet in the middle of the tips of your fingers and show this hand gesture to oncoming traffic. Surprisingly, this is actually extremely effective at stopping traffic.

If you've hired a driver never be afraid

to tell them to slow down or stop if you're not comfortable. The best advice if you're driving on Jordanian roads is to practise defensive driving and always be aware of what might be coming around the corner.

Political instability and terrorism

Despite regional insecurity in the aftermath of the Arab Spring uprisings in 2011, ongoing conflicts in neighbouring Syria and Iraq and more recently the war between Hamas and Israel in the Gaza Strip and other areas of the Occupied Palestinian Territories, Jordan remains an essentially safe and stable country. Visitors are advised, however, to avoid the border area with Iraq and all travel to within 3 km of the border with Syria and to remain vigilant in areas where intermittent (though usually peaceful) political demonstrations are taking place, especially in Amman. The Israeli and US embassies in the capital have recently been the focus for protests against the conflict in Gaza (see page 164), and there have been protests on a Friday on the Jordanian–Israeli border, so you should remain vigilant in the vicinity of these areas in view of the increase in anti-Western feeling.

Security is a top priority for the Jordanian government. After the 2005 Amman terrorist attack, when suicide bombers targeted 3 luxury hotels, resulting in 60 deaths, security in-country was visibly stepped up and there is a high police and military presence in public spaces, including at tourist sites.

Tax

Airport departure tax

The airport departure tax (currently 40JD) and airport terminal usage fee (currently 12JD) is usually included in the price of your airline ticket so there are no additional costs when you leave the country by air.

Land/sea departure tax

Land/sea departure tax is 10JD.

Other taxes

Luxury hotels add a government tax of 16% onto the bill and sometimes a service tax of 10%. Many upmarket restaurants also add the 10% service tax to your bill and some also charge the government tax as well.

Telephone *Country code +962.*

To call Jordan from overseas, dial your country's international access code, followed by Jordan's country code **962** and then the area/town code (dropping the 0).

Mobile phones

Due to the relatively cheap cost of local mobile phone calls in-country, the most convenient method of making calls is by purchasing a Jordanian SIM card for your mobile phone when you arrive. Pay-as-you-go SIM cards are available from phone shops, mobile phone provider offices and many grocery stores all over the country.

The 3 main mobile service providers in Jordan are **Orange** (www.orange.jo), **Zain** (www.jo.zain.com) and **Umniah** (www.umniah.com) and they have offices in all main towns. If you plan on staying for more than a month you need to register your SIM card (either over the phone or at a phone shop) or your account will be cancelled.

Mobile numbers in Jordan begin with '07'.

Phone cards

You can buy international phone cards (which give cheap rates on overseas phone calls from a private phone) from most grocery stores.

Time

2 hrs ahead of GMT/UTC Oct-Mar, and 3 hrs ahead Apr-Sep during Daylight Saving Time; Eastern Standard Time (EST) +8.

Tipping

Tipping is very much a way of life in Jordan. In more expensive restaurants and hotels a service charge is added directly to your bill. Any person who provides a service (driver, guide, hotel porter) will most likely expect a tip and what you give them is really down to your own discretion. 10% is a good guideline for restaurant tipping.

Tourist information

The **Jordan Tourism Board** has offices in North America, the UK and in various cities in Europe. The website (see right) is an excellent introduction to Jordan and the sights of the country. All main towns and tourist centres in Jordan have a visitor centre where you can pick up free maps and pamphlets though staff, on the whole, aren't much help with actual information.

Travelling with a disability

Although Jordan is making great strides in catering for the needs of travellers with disabilities, it is still currently the case that some of the country's visitor attractions present challenging conditions. A very informative and useful country specific website for travellers with disabilities is www.accessiblejordan.com. The UK Foreign, Commonwealth & Development Office also has general information about travelling for people with disabilities at www.gov.uk/guidance/foreign-travel-for-disabled-people.

Useful websites

www.gov.uk/foreign-travel-advice/Jordan The UK Foreign, Commonwealth & Development Office (FCDO) website has useful and up-to-date information on each country such as entry requirements, health, people, money, safety and a list of UK embassies and consulates.

www.calendar.jo An excellent website detailing artistic, cultural, business, entertainment, sport and other events happening all over Jordan.

www.jordantimes.com Jordan's English-language daily newspaper with excellent coverage of local and international current affairs .

www.rscn.org.jo The official site of Jordan's Royal Society for the Conservation of Nature with information on all the hikes/activities/accommodation found in the RSCN's nature reserves. Also allows you to book reserve trips online.

www.visitjordan.com The official site of the Jordan Tourism Board has a vast array of information on the country, including practical considerations for tourists, Jordan's history and culture, and a rundown of all the activities and sites.

Visas and immigration

A full passport valid for at least 6 months from your time of arrival is required to visit Jordan.

All foreign nationals (except those from Egypt, Syria and the Gulf States) require a visa to enter Jordan. Most nationalities can obtain Jordanian visas (40JD, valid for 1 month) upon arrival at Jordan's land, sea and air points of entry, except the King Hussein Bridge/Allenby Bridge crossing from Israel (see page 168) which doesn't issue Jordanian visas upon arrival.

Only single-entry visas are issued at point of entry. If you want a multiple-entry visa, you can apply at the Jordanian embassy in your own country. Visas obtained abroad must be used within 3 months of the date of issue.

Note As long as your Jordanian single-entry visa will still be valid when you return to Jordan, you can go to Israel as a side trip on the single-entry visa if using the

King Hussein Bridge/Allenby Bridge border crossing for both exit and re-entry.

ASEZA visas

If your point of entry into Jordan was Aqaba (either through Aqaba Port, King Hussein International Airport or the Wadi Araba border crossing) the visa you receive is free of charge and granted by the **Aqaba Special Economic Zone Authority** (ASEZA; www.aseza.jo). It is valid for 1 month and the only condition is that if you want to extend your stay after that it has to be done at the **ASEZA** office in Aqaba.

Visa extensions

Although in theory you can apply for a visa extension at the police headquarters of any governorate (administration district), the only place where this really works is Amman.

Visa extensions in Jordan are relatively easy. The police station will usually require your hotel (or other accommodation) to provide confirmation that you're staying there, a couple of forms need to be filled in and (sometimes) you'll be asked to provide proof that you are HIV free. If this is asked for, blood tests (20JD) in Amman can be carried out at the **Ministry of Health Laboratory** (beside the Arab Collage, Washi Altal St, Shmeisani). It will take 1-2 days for your results to come back.

Once the process is completed you'll be issued with a free 3-month visa extension. Tourist visa extensions can only be extended once, up to a total of 6 months. After that you will have to exit the country and re-enter. It's worth noting that if you're only planning to overstay your visa by a couple of days it's less hassle to simply pay the penalty fee on departure. The penalty is 2JD per day overstayed.

The police station you apply for your extension at in Amman is **Al-Madinah Police Station** (opposite Arab Bank, King Faisal St, T06-465 7788) where you pick up

forms and lodge your extension request. When the paperwork is finished head to **Muhajireen Police Station** (Al-Ameera Basma bin Talal St, T06-464 6101) where you'll get your final stamp.

Getting visas for bordering countries

For many nationalities, obtaining a visa upon arrival is no problem for Lebanon, Egypt, Turkey or Israel. And you can now also obtain a tourist visa for Saudi Arabia upon arrival at one of the country's international airports or land borders or by applying apply in advance online for an E-visa (see page 169 for further details).

Weights and measures

Metric.

Women travellers

Jordan is one of the most relaxed Middle Eastern countries for women travellers. Harassment is much less of an issue than in neighbouring Egypt and although solo female travel can be more demanding, in the vast majority of situations women travellers are treated with respect. Seasoned female travellers in Jordan argue that they get the best of both worlds. As a foreigner they are generally accorded the status of 'honorary males' in public, while in private they have access to female society, from which men are excluded.

Dress

Women travellers should make an effort to dress modestly. The main reason for this is to show respect for Jordan's traditional values and not cause offence. Dressing conservatively (shoulders and knees covered) also helps you interact with local women, many of whom wouldn't approach a foreign female wearing hot pants and a strappy top.

Sexual harassment

Cases of violent sexual assault are extremely rare but minor harassment (particularly in and around Petra) does occur. This is fuelled in part by a widely held perception of Western women as having 'loose' sexual morals based on the images in international magazines, films and satellite TV, and by the number of female travellers deciding to have holiday flings with hotel staff and tour guides which has reaffirmed this image.

For the most part, harassment in Jordan consists of constant offers of marriage and, despite this being wearying, can be easily ignored. A firm, unambiguous response will deal with most situations. For more serious incidents, don't be afraid to cause a scene. The phrase 'haraam aleik!'(shame on you!) is extremely useful for stopping any harassers in their tracks.

Feedback request

At Bradt Guides we're aware that guidebooks start to go out of date on the day they're published – and that you, our readers, are out there in the field doing research of your own. You'll find out before us when a fine new family-run hotel opens or a favourite restaurant changes hands and goes downhill. So why not tell us about your experiences? Contact us on T01753 893444 or info@bradtguides.com. We will forward emails to the author who may post updates on the Bradt website at www.bradtguides.com/updates. Alternatively, you can add a review of the book to Amazon, or share your adventures with us on Facebook, Twitter or Instagram (@BradtGuides).

Index

*Entries in **bold** refer to maps*

About the author

Photographer and travel writer Paul Doyle has specialized in and travelled extensively around the Middle East since the 1990s, with Jordan's people, history and architecture representing some of the main highlights of his travels around the region. Paul is also the author of Bradt's *Lebanon* guide.

Acknowledgements

A special mention must go to Jordan's friendly and hospitable people who help make the country what it is; an endearing and pleasurable place in which to travel. A big thank you also to the friendly team at Bradt and, in particular, my Project Manager Elspeth Beidas, whose sharp eye and meticulous attention to detail was a pleasure to work with.

Credits

Second edition published October 2024
Originally published by Footprint Handbooks
Bradt Travel Guides Ltd
31a High Street, Chesham, Buckinghamshire, HP5 1BW, England
www.bradtguides.com
Print edition published in the USA by The Globe Pequot Press Inc,
PO Box 480, Guilford, Connecticut 06437-0480

Text copyright © Bradt Travel Guides Ltd, 2024
Maps copyright © Bradt Travel Guides Ltd, 2024; includes map data © OpenStreetMap contributors
Photographs copyright © Individual photographers, 2024 (see below)
Project Manager: Elspeth Beidas
Cover research: Pepi Bluck, Perfect Picture

ISBN: 9781804692257

British Library Cataloguing in Publication Data
A catalogue record for this book is available from the British Library

Photographs All photographs © individual photographers credited below; those from picture libraries are credited as follows: Dreamstime.com (D); Shutterstock.com (S)
Front cover Wadi Rum (Reinhard Schmid/4Corners Images)
Back cover, clockwise from top left Petra (Fcastello/D); Dead Sea (NickolayV/S); Byzantine mosaic, Madaba (FrentaN/S); Bedouin man making tea (Siempreverde22/D)
Inside front cover Jerash (top; E.J.Melian/S); Amman Market (middle; Curioso.Photography/S); underwater life in the Red Sea, Aqaba (bottom left; Marketa Novakova/D); Bethany Beyond the Jordan (bottom right; Jiri Vlach/S)
Title page, clockwise from top left Boats on the Red Sea, Aqaba (Mariusz Prusaczyk/D); King Abdullah I Mosque, Amman (Hamdan Yoshida/S); Mujib Biosphere Reserve (Ondrej Prosicky/S); baklava (Fotokon/D)
Page 2 Wadi Rum (Lubo Ivanko/S)
Page 4 Amman (leshiy985/S)
Page 5 Jerash (Hamdan Yoshida/S); Dead Sea (Pawel Uchorczak/S); King's Highway (vvoe/S); Madaba (FrentaN/S)
Page 6 Dana Biosphere Reserve (iwciagr/S)
Page 7 Petra (sabo SA/S); Wadi Rum (rontav/S); Aqaba (marketa1982/S)
Page 22 Jerash (volkova natalia/S)
Page 62 King's Highway (Simone Matteo Giuseppe Manzoni/D)
Page 104 Petra (tenkl/S)
Page 153 Aqaba (Nancy Pauwels/S)

Maps David McCutcheon FBCart.S. FRGS

Typeset by Ian Spick, Bradt Guides
Production managed by Zenith Media; printed in the UK
Digital conversion by www.dataworks.co.in

Paper used for this product comes from sustainably managed forests, and recycled and controlled sources.

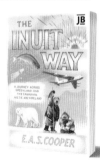